CORBA® For Dummies®

Cheat Sheet

Y0-ABG-852

Describing CORBA Objects

1. Think about the problem to discover the server's name, data, and behavior.

2. Use the CORBA Interface Definition Language (IDL) to define the server.

3. Compile the IDL file.

The "Abilities" of CORBA

- **Interoperability** is the ability of a component to be invoked across networks, languages, operating systems, and tools. For CORBA, interoperability means the ability of objects and applications to exchange requests via ORBs — in other words, the ability to make requests and respond to requests on the same machine or across a network that uses the CORBA standard.

- **Reusability** is the ability of a system to grow in functionality through the extension of existing components and the ability to combine existing components in heretofore unforeseen ways in order to create new components.

- **Portability** is the ability to transfer a program from one hardware or software environment to another.

What Exactly Is an ORB?

- Responsible for the communication between distributed heterogeneous applications
- Something that sits between servers and clients and lets them talk

Flavors of ORBs

- **Client and Implementation resident ORB:** ORB resides in the client application and the object implementation application.

- **Server-based ORB:** ORB exists as a separate process, which acts as a server that routes communications between clients and object implementations.

- **System-based ORB:** ORB is like the Server-based flavor except that the ORB is actually part of the operating system, an arrangement that enhances security.

- **Library-based ORB:** ORB is like the Client and Implementation resident flavor except that it's implemented using shared libraries.

...For Dummies: Bestselling Book Series for Beginners

CORBA® For Dummies®

Cheat Sheet

Making requests out of method calls

1. The client obtains an object reference for the server.

2. The client packages this reference along with the method's name, its parameters, and the type of return value.

3. The client executes the server's method by calling the corresponding method in the client stub.

4. Inside the client stub, the call is turned into a request.

5. Because ORBs deal in requests, an ORB Interface operation is called to pass the newly created request to the ORB.

IDL Keywords

any	float	short
attribute	in	string
boolean	inout	struct
case	interface	switch
char	long	TRUE
const	module	typedef
context	Object	unsigned
default	octet	union
double	oneway	void
enum	out	wchar
exception	raises	wstring
FALSE	readonly	
fixed	sequence	

...For Dummies: Bestselling Book Series for Beginners

CORBA® FOR DUMMIES®

by John Schettino and Liz O'Hara

IDG Books Worldwide, Inc.
An International Data Group Company

Foster City, CA ♦ Chicago, IL ♦ Indianapolis, IN ♦ New York, NY

CORBA® For Dummies®

Published by
IDG Books Worldwide, Inc.
An International Data Group Company
919 E. Hillsdale Blvd.
Suite 400
Foster City, CA 94404
www.idgbooks.com (IDG Books Worldwide Web site)
www.dummies.com (Dummies Press Web site)

Library of Congress Catalog Card No.: 98-87905

ISBN: 0-7645-0308-1

Printed in the United States of America

10 9 8 7 6 5 4 3 2 1

1B/QW/RQ/ZY/IN

Distributed in the United States by IDG Books Worldwide, Inc.

Distributed by Macmillan Canada for Canada; by Transworld Publishers Limited in the United Kingdom; by IDG Norge Books for Norway; by IDG Sweden Books for Sweden; by Woodslane Pty. Ltd. for Australia; by Woodslane (NZ) Ltd. for New Zealand; by Addison Wesley Longman Singapore Pte Ltd. for Singapore, Malaysia, Thailand, Indonesia and Korea; by Norma Comunicaciones S.A. for Colombia; by Intersoft for South Africa; by International Thomson Publishing for Germany, Austria and Switzerland; by Toppan Company Ltd. for Japan; by Distribuidora Cuspide for Argentina; by Livraria Cultura for Brazil; by Ediciencia S.A. for Ecuador; by Ediciones ZETA S.C.R. Ltda. for Peru; by WS Computer Publishing Corporation, Inc., for the Philippines; by Unalis Corporation for Taiwan; by Contemporanea de Ediciones for Venezuela; by Computer Book & Magazine Store for Puerto Rico; by Express Computer Distributors for the Caribbean and West Indies. Authorized Sales Agent: Anthony Rudkin Associates for the Middle East and North Africa.

For general information on IDG Books Worldwide's books in the U.S., please call our Consumer Customer Service department at 800-762-2974. For reseller information, including discounts and premium sales, please call our Reseller Customer Service department at 800-434-3422.

For information on where to purchase IDG Books Worldwide's books outside the U.S., please contact our International Sales department at 650-655-3200 or fax 650-655-3297.

For information on foreign language translations, please contact our Foreign & Subsidiary Rights department at 650-655-3021 or fax 650-655-3281.

For sales inquiries and special prices for bulk quantities, please contact our Sales department at 650-655-3200 or write to the address above.

For information on using IDG Books Worldwide's books in the classroom or for ordering examination copies, please contact our Educational Sales department at 800-434-2086 or fax 317-596-5499.

For press review copies, author interviews, or other publicity information, please contact our Public Relations department at 650-655-3000 or fax 650-655-3299.

For authorization to photocopy items for corporate, personal, or educational use, please contact Copyright Clearance Center, 222 Rosewood Drive, Danvers, MA 01923, or fax 978-750-4470.

 is a trademark under exclusive license to IDG Books Worldwide, Inc., from International Data Group, Inc.

IDG BOOKS WORLDWIDE

About the Authors

John Charles Schettino, Jr. Yes, that's really his full name. John has been involved with computers almost as long as Bill Gates. Sadly, he didn't think up MS-DOS, but he has had several bright ideas in the past 20 or so years. Many of them even involved computers. John's nonwriting job is as a Principal Member of The Technical Staff at GTE Laboratories, Incorporated, in Waltham, Massachusetts. That's where he gets to learn about the latest advances in computer science and telephones.

Liz O'Hara. Actually, Elizabeth Anne O'Hara-Schettino is her full name, but it just doesn't fit on the spine of the book, and it's too hard to pronounce. Liz has spent a good part of her adult life attaining very advanced degrees in information technology. Oh, let's just come out and say it — she has a PhD. However, she's also learned quite a bit about how to teach people difficult concepts without putting them to sleep!

Liz has done it all in the computer field. She's worked on commercial software, done research (really cool stuff with NASA satellites), and taught at several universities. She coauthored two fabulous books with John. These days she spends her nonwriting hours as a domestic engineer and as a mom to Kiera.

ABOUT IDG BOOKS WORLDWIDE

Welcome to the world of IDG Books Worldwide.

IDG Books Worldwide, Inc., is a subsidiary of International Data Group, the world's largest publisher of computer-related information and the leading global provider of information services on information technology. IDG was founded more than 25 years ago and now employs more than 8,500 people worldwide. IDG publishes more than 275 computer publications in over 75 countries (see listing below). More than 90 million people read one or more IDG publications each month.

Launched in 1990, IDG Books Worldwide is today the #1 publisher of best-selling computer books in the United States. We are proud to have received eight awards from the Computer Press Association in recognition of editorial excellence and three from *Computer Currents'* First Annual Readers' Choice Awards. Our best-selling *...For Dummies*® series has more than 50 million copies in print with translations in 38 languages. IDG Books Worldwide, through a joint venture with IDG's Hi-Tech Beijing, became the first U.S. publisher to publish a computer book in the People's Republic of China. In record time, IDG Books Worldwide has become the first choice for millions of readers around the world who want to learn how to better manage their businesses.

Our mission is simple: Every one of our books is designed to bring extra value and skill-building instructions to the reader. Our books are written by experts who understand and care about our readers. The knowledge base of our editorial staff comes from years of experience in publishing, education, and journalism — experience we use to produce books for the '90s. In short, we care about books, so we attract the best people. We devote special attention to details such as audience, interior design, use of icons, and illustrations. And because we use an efficient process of authoring, editing, and desktop publishing our books electronically, we can spend more time ensuring superior content and spend less time on the technicalities of making books.

You can count on our commitment to deliver high-quality books at competitive prices on topics you want to read about. At IDG Books Worldwide, we continue in the IDG tradition of delivering quality for more than 25 years. You'll find no better book on a subject than one from IDG Books Worldwide.

John Kilcullen
CEO
IDG Books Worldwide, Inc.

Steven Berkowitz
President and Publisher
IDG Books Worldwide, Inc.

Eighth Annual Computer Press Awards ≥1992

Ninth Annual Computer Press Awards ≥1993

Tenth Annual Computer Press Awards ≥1994

Eleventh Annual Computer Press Awards ≥1995

IDG Books Worldwide, Inc., is a subsidiary of International Data Group, the world's largest publisher of computer-related information and the leading global provider of information services on information technology. International Data Group publishes over 275 computer publications in over 75 countries. More than 90 million people read one or more International Data Group's publications each month. International Data Group's publications include: **ARGENTINA:** Buyer's Guide, Computerworld Argentina, PC World Argentina; **AUSTRALIA:** Australian Macworld, Australian PC World, Australian Reseller News, Computerworld, IT Casebook, Network World, Publish, Webmaster; **AUSTRIA:** Computerwelt Österreich, Networks Austria, PC Tip Austria; **BANGLADESH:** PC World Bangladesh; **BELARUS:** PC World Belarus; **BELGIUM:** Data News; **BRAZIL:** Annuário de Informática, Computerworld, Connections, Macworld, PC Player, PC World, Publish, Reseller News, Supergamepower; **BULGARIA:** Computerworld Bulgaria, Network World Bulgaria, PC & MacWorld Bulgaria; **CANADA:** CIO Canada, Client/Server World, ComputerWorld Canada, InfoWorld Canada, NetworkWorld Canada, WebWorld; **CHILE:** Computerworld Chile, PC World Chile; **COLOMBIA:** Computerworld Colombia, PC World Colombia; **COSTA RICA:** PC World Centro America; **THE CZECH AND SLOVAK REPUBLICS:** Computerworld Czechoslovakia, Macworld Czech Republic, PC World Czechoslovakia; **DENMARK:** Communications World Danmark, Computerworld Danmark, Macworld Danmark, PC World Danmark, Techworld Denmark; **DOMINICAN REPUBLIC:** PC World Republica Dominicana; **ECUADOR:** PC World Ecuador; **EGYPT:** Computerworld Middle East, PC World Middle East; **EL SALVADOR:** PC World Centro America; **FINLAND:** MikroPC, Tietoverkko, Tietoviikko; **FRANCE:** Distributique, Hebdo, Info PC, Le Monde Informatique, Macworld, Reseaux & Telecoms, WebMaster France; **GERMANY:** Computer Partner, Computerwoche, Computerwoche Extra, Computerwoche FOCUS, Global Online, Macwelt, PC Welt; **GREECE:** Amiga Computing, GamePro Greece, Multimedia World; **GUATEMALA:** PC World Centro America; **HONDURAS:** PC World Centro America; **HONG KONG:** Computerworld Hong Kong, PC World Hong Kong, Publish in Asia; **HUNGARY:** ABCD CD-ROM, Computerworld Szamitastechnika, Interneto online Magazine, PC World Hungary, PC-X Magazin Hungary; **ICELAND:** Tolvuheimur PC World Island; **INDIA:** Information Communications World, Information Systems Computerworld, PC World India, Publish in Asia; **INDONESIA:** InfoKomputer PC World, Komputek Computerworld, Publish in Asia; **IRELAND:** ComputerScope, PC Live!; **ISRAEL:** Macworld Israel, People & Computers/Computerworld; **ITALY:** Computerworld Italia, Macworld Italia, Networking Italia, PC World Italia; **JAPAN:** DTP World, Macworld Japan, Nikkei Personal Computing, OS/2 World Japan, SunWorld Japan, Windows NT World, Windows World Japan; **KENYA:** PC World East African; **KOREA:** Hi-Tech Information, Macworld Korea, PC World Korea; **MACEDONIA:** PC World Macedonia; **MALAYSIA:** Computerworld Malaysia, PC World Malaysia, Publish in Asia; **MALTA:** PC World Malta; **MEXICO:** Computerworld Mexico, PC World Mexico; **MYANMAR:** PC World Myanmar; **NETHERLANDS:** Computer! Totaal, LAN Internetworking Magazine, LAN World Buyers Guide, Macworld Netherlands, Net, WebWereld; **NEW ZEALAND:** Absolute Beginners Guide and Plain & Simple Series, Computer Buyer, Computer Industry Directory, Computerworld New Zealand, MTB, Network World, PC World New Zealand; **NICARAGUA:** PC World Centro America; **NORWAY:** Computerworld Norge, CW Rapport, Datamagasinet, Financial Rapport, Kursguide Norge, Macworld Norge, Multimediaworld Norge, PC World Ekspress Norge, PC World Nettverk, PC World Norge, PC World ProduktGuide Norge; **PAKISTAN:** Computerworld Pakistan; **PANAMA:** PC World Panama; **PEOPLE'S REPUBLIC OF CHINA:** China Computer Users, China Computerworld, China InfoWorld, China Telecom World Weekly, Computer & Communication, Electronic Design China, Electronics Today, Electronics Weekly, Game Software, PC World China, Popular Computer Week, Software Weekly, Software World, Telecom World; **PERU:** Computerworld Peru, PC World Profesional Peru, PC World SoHo Peru; **PHILIPPINES:** Click!, Computerworld Philippines, PC World Philippines, Publish in Asia; **POLAND:** Computerworld Poland, Computerworld Special Report Poland, Cyber, Macworld Poland, Networld Poland, PC World Komputer; **PORTUGAL:** Cerebro/PC World, Computerworld/Correio Informático, Dealer World Portugal, Mac*In/PC*In Portugal, Multimedia World; **PUERTO RICO:** PC World Puerto Rico; **ROMANIA:** Computerworld Romania, PC World Romania, Telecom Romania; **RUSSIA:** Computerworld Russia, Mir PK, Publish, Seti; **SINGAPORE:** Computerworld Singapore, PC World Singapore, Publish in Asia; **SLOVENIA:** Monitor; **SOUTH AFRICA:** Computing SA, Network World SA, Software World SA; **SPAIN:** Communicaciones World España, Computerworld España, Dealer World España, Macworld España, PC World España; **SRI LANKA:** Infolink PC World; **SWEDEN:** CAP&Design, Computer Sweden, Corporate Computing Sweden, Internetworld Sweden, it.branschen, Macworld Sweden, MaxiData Sweden, MikroDatorn, Natverk & Kommunikation, PC World Sweden, PCaktiv, Windows World Sweden; **SWITZERLAND:** Computerworld Schweiz, Macworld Schweiz, PCtip; **TAIWAN:** Computerworld Taiwan, Macworld Taiwan, NEW ViSiON/Publish, PC World Taiwan, Windows World Taiwan; **THAILAND:** Publish in Asia, Thai Computerworld; **TURKEY:** Computerworld Turkiye, Macworld Turkiye, Network World Turkiye, PC World Turkiye; **UKRAINE:** Computerworld Kiev, Multimedia World Ukraine, PC World Ukraine; **UNITED KINGDOM:** Acorn User UK, Amiga Action UK, Amiga Computing UK, Apple Talk UK, Computing, Macworld, Parents and Computers UK, PC Advisor, PC Home, PSX Pro, The WEB; **UNITED STATES:** Cable in the Classroom, CIO Magazine, Computerworld, DOS World, Federal Computer Week, GamePro Magazine, InfoWorld, I-Way, Macworld, Network World, PC Games, PC World, Publish, Video Event, THE WEB Magazine, and WebMaster; online webzines: JavaWorld, NetscapeWorld, and SunWorld Online; **URUGUAY:** InfoWorld Uruguay; **VENEZUELA:** Computerworld Venezuela, PC World Venezuela; and **VIETNAM:** PC World Vietnam. 5/7/98

Dedication

To the memory of Rose Annette O'Hara, whose love will never be forgotten. We miss you, Mom.

Author's Acknowledgments

Thanks go to several people at IDG Books Worldwide. First, to Jill Pisoni, our acquisitions editor. That's the technical term for being the person who gave us the opportunity to write this book. Next, to Pat O'Brien, our ever-diligent and understanding project editor. We're learning, Pat! We'd also like to thank Christy Beck, who had the ill fortune to have to copyedit every single word you're about to read. Finally, there are many other people at IDG Books, without whom this book would have never reached your hands. You know who you are, and we do appreciate the effort.

Thanks also to IONA Technologies PLC and Inprise Corporation, who supplied evaluation ORBs for the CD-ROM and provided plenty of technical support during the writing of the example chapters.

Thanks to Kiera, who gave Mommy and Daddy the time to write this book when we could have been playing with her. We're all done now!

Thanks to a unique concentration of sunspots, loads of candy bars, and endless bags of sunflower seeds that made all the jokes possible.

Publisher's Acknowledgments

We're proud of this book; please register your comments through our IDG Books Worldwide Online Registration Form located at http://my2cents.dummies.com.

Some of the people who helped bring this book to market include the following:

*Acquisitions, Editorial, and
Media Development*

Project Editor: Pat O'Brien

Acquisitions Editor: Jill Pisoni

Copy Editor: Christine Meloy Beck

Technical Editor: Chris Harper

Media Development Technical Editor:
Joell Smith

Associate Permissions Editor:
Carmen Krikorian

Editorial Manager: Mary C. Corder

Media Development Manager:
Heather Heath Dismore

Editorial Assistant: Darren Meiss

Production

Project Coordinator: Karen York

Layout and Graphics: Lou Boudreau,
Maridee V. Ennis, Angela F. Hunckler,
Jane E. Martin, Brent Savage, Janet Seib,
Michael A. Sullivan

Proofreaders: Kelli Botta, Rachel Garvey,
Rebecca Senninger, Ethel M. Winslow

Indexer: Steve Rath

General and Administrative

IDG Books Worldwide, Inc.: John Kilcullen, CEO; Steven Berkowitz, President and Publisher

IDG Books Technology Publishing: Brenda McLaughlin, Senior Vice President and
Group Publisher

Dummies Technology Press and Dummies Editorial: Diane Graves Steele, Vice President and
Associate Publisher; Mary Bednarek, Director of Acquisitions and Product Development;
Kristin A. Cocks, Editorial Director

Dummies Trade Press: Kathleen A. Welton, Vice President and Publisher; Kevin Thornton,
Acquisitions Manager

IDG Books Production for Dummies Press: Michael R. Britton, Vice President of Production
and Creative Services; Cindy L. Phipps, Manager of Project Coordination, Production
Proofreading, and Indexing; Kathie S. Schutte, Supervisor of Page Layout; Shelley Lea,
Supervisor of Graphics and Design; Debbie J. Gates, Production Systems Specialist;
Robert Springer, Supervisor of Proofreading; Debbie Stailey, Special Projects Coordinator;
Tony Augsburger, Supervisor of Reprints and Bluelines

Dummies Packaging and Book Design: Robin Seaman, Creative Director; Kavish + Kavish,
Cover Design

◆

The publisher would like to give special thanks to Patrick J. McGovern,
without whom this book would not have been possible.

◆

Contents at a Glance

Cartoons at a Glance

By Rich Tennant

page 355

page 287

page 179

page 341

page 41

page 7

Fax: 978-546-7747 • E-mail: the5wave@tiac.net

Table of Contents

Introduction

. . . .

You can find some really good reasons to use CORBA stuck to the bumpers of cars. We're not talking about those "My other car is a Mercedes" stickers. Instead, we're talking about the ones that say things like "Think Globally, Act Locally," "Celebrate Diversity," and "Recycle." These catchphrases of the '90s have much more to do with CORBA than you may expect.

The idea of thinking globally while acting locally means that you keep a wider view of your actions in mind. You focus on the changes you can make in your daily actions to bring about larger change. CORBA is like that, in a way. You think about what local actions you're already doing that may be helpful to the larger community. That's one way you identify what parts of your problem need to be local and what parts need to be shared. CORBA makes the sharing part easy.

In this book, we show you just how easy it is to create applications that are CORBA-compliant. Not only can you use CORBA to create powerful, distributed, cross-platform applications that contain reusable pieces, you can also slap some really cool bumper stickers on your workstation. When people ask you about them, you can explain what they mean in CORBA terms.

What's All This Hoopla about CORBA?

CORBA is an acronym for Common Object Request Broker Architecture. Pretty scary-sounding, isn't it? Just the name puts most people off. The name is just a fancy way of saying that a bunch of people got together and decided to standardize the ways to represent information in and passed between programs — no matter what the actual operating systems, programming languages, or hardware devices involved.

Why Should You Consider CORBA?

CORBA isn't for everyone. If your applications are never going to leave your machine, forget it. We could spend several pages listing reasons why you should use CORBA, but we decided against it. Instead, we came up with what we consider the top five reasons:

1. **You're a cross-platform kind of person.**

2. **You've got a tough nut to crack.**

3. **You're into open standards.**

4. **You think it looks good on your resumé.**

5. **You think it looks good on your progress report.**

What This Book Can Do for You

Although we can't foresee the future, we can make an educated guess about what you'll be able to do after reading this book:

- ✔ You'll create applications that are social butterflies — they don't really care where they run or who they talk to.

- ✔ You'll read pages and pages of code and not care in the least bit what it says.

- ✔ You'll create servers, clients, and applications that do really cool stuff.

Variations on a Theme

CORBA is a specification that is updated continuously. Through a standardized (what else?) review process, new additions are made. These changes are collected to create a new version. When a version is adopted, it is given a new, higher number than the previous version.

CORBA 1.0 came out in 1991. The latest version, and the one that this book focuses on, is CORBA 2.2.

We also talk a bit about future versions of CORBA. CORBA 3.0, or possibly 2.3, is the next revision of the CORBA specification. Even after the specification is accepted, vendor products are unlikely to be available for about half a year.

How This Book Is Organized

Each chapter in this book covers a complete topic and stands alone. If you have some experience with or already know a bit about CORBA, you can simply find and read those chapters that explain what you want to know.

We have arranged the chapters so that you can also read the book from beginning to end. If you have no experience with creating distributed heterogeneous object-oriented applications, consider reading the book this way.

Part I: Beating CORBA Performance Anxiety

We use a step-by-step approach in Chapter 1 to build a client, a server, and an application that uses them. This plan of action serves two purposes. First, you're given the instant gratification of building a CORBA application in your first sitting. Second, you're introduced to some of the terms and concepts that are important to CORBA.

We end this part with a chapter on CORBA basics so that you know what CORBA is all about. We talk about CORBA's architecture, its definition language, and the steps involved in creating a simple CORBA application.

Part II: Who Put the ORB in CORBA?

The ORB (Object Request Broker) is the heart of CORBA. It facilitates the communication between clients and servers. This part gives an overview of how an ORB works.

After this part, you can say that you are CORBA-compliant.

Part III: The Great Communicators

CORBA is more than just clients and servers. It's about creating applications out of distributed and diverse components in a cohesive way.

Part IV: Services and Facilities Are Always Welcome

If CORBA were just an ORB, it would be quite a lot. However, it's more than that. It also includes CORBAservices. CORBAservices are handy services that you often need when developing distributed applications in CORBA.

Part V: The Part of Tens

The part of tens is our favorite part of the book. If you only have ten minutes to read some part of this book, flip there right now. You get key information on what to consider both before and after choosing CORBA, things to avoid when using CORBA, and places to go on the Web to get more information.

Stuff You Must Know and Have

This book makes certain assumptions about what you already know, as well as assumptions about the tools that you have.

An object-oriented point of view

CORBA is based on the object-oriented way of software development — you know, objects, classes, and inheritance.

Target languages and their tools

In creating CORBA applications, you're going to use a target language such as C++ or Java. In this book, we provide examples in both languages, so it makes sense that you know at least one of them. We also assume that you have access to and know how to use a development environment for your target language. You need to be able to create files to compile, link, and run.

Operating system(s) and hardware

You don't create software in a vacuum — you don't get very far and you just annoy the vacuum. Instead, you need to know the operating system and hardware for the target application. Much of the time, the OS and the hardware is the same as what you use for development.

An Object Request Broker product

The one thing that's truly new for you is the ORB (Object Request Broker). The ORB is the thing that you use to easily create runable CORBA-compliant applications.

ORBs are specific to the target languages and operating systems they support, so you need to find an ORB that matches your needs. The CD-ROM that accompanies this book has several demonstration versions of ORBs from which you can choose. If you don't like any of those, you have to purchase or download one before you can try the examples. Even if you do like one of the ORBs on the CD-ROM, you will need to purchase it when the demonstration period (60 days) runs out. If you're strapped for cash or looking for a different ORB than those provided on the CD-ROM, check out Chapter 26 for Web links to free ORBs you can download.

You need a CORBA 2.0- (or later) compliant ORB. In addition, you may want to purchase some CORBAservices to make your life easier. We talk about these goodies in Part IV of the book, so you may want to check it out before buying a lot of stuff.

Neat CD — What's on It?

Golly, the CD-ROM is chock-full of really rad stuff. We always wanted to put such a smarmy sentence in a book. Hey . . . we also wanted to use the word *smarmy* in a sentence — it's a bonus day, dude!

Use the CD-ROM to get what you need. That's why we stuck it to the inside back cover of this book (and we can still taste the adhesive!). We included everything we could to help you become a CORBA-compliant kind of person.

Take a look at what you'll find on the CD. We provide

- Evaluation ORBs so that you can try out CORBA development for yourself.
- Example programs from the book.
- Miscellaneous files that add something to the discussion of CORBA but were just too much to include in the book itself.

A Picture Is Worth a Thousand Words

Throughout the book, you see little round pictures in the margins of the pages. These pictures are called *icons* and are used to bring your attention to specific pieces of information.

A Technical Stuff icon paragraph provides a more in-depth look at a subject. This information can be skipped the first time around or altogether. Pocket protector is optional.

A Tip icon marks an action you can take to make life a bit easier.

An idea or concept that is important enough to put a cute icon next to it gets a Remember icon.

Be cautious when taking an action described in a paragraph attached to a Warning icon, or simply don't do it.

A step-by-step description of what you should do when performing a task follows a Blow by Blow icon.

A paragraph alongside a Definition icon provides the meaning of one or more terms.

An On the CD icon means that you can find the item described on the CD-ROM, in addition to your fingerprints.

Beginning Your CORBA Adventure

You now know what you need, why you need it, and what you've been given to get it. Prepare yourself for an enjoyable and educational trip through the world of distributed heterogeneous object-oriented computing.

Part I
Beating CORBA
Performance
Anxiety

The 5th Wave — By Rich Tennant

KYLE AND TODD'S
SOFTWARE Co.

"That's right, Daddy will double your allowance if you make him more CORBA applications."

In this part . . .

Part I is where you discover how to relax and love CORBA. It's just not *that* hard to use or even to understand. You build a simple but complete CORBA server object, server application, and client application in C++, right off the bat. You get an overview of how CORBA works and how the Object Management Group (OMG) decides what is and isn't CORBA. We also introduce you to the Interface Definition Language, which CORBA uses to describe server objects.

After you read this part, much of the mystery surrounding CORBA is dispelled. You see what CORBA is, how it works, and what an application using it looks like.

Chapter 1
Instant CORBA Application

· ·

In This Chapter

▶ Beginning your CORBA adventure

▶ Defining a CORBA server

▶ Implementing a CORBA server and client in C++

▶ Building and running the application

· ·

*W*elcome to the world of *distributed heterogeneous object-oriented computing.* Now that all the buzzwords are out of the way, relax. That first sentence is the most complex thing you'll read in this chapter. It's the job of the Common Object Request Broker Architecture, or CORBA for short, to make it easier than ever to create software that runs as clients and servers. These clients and servers can run on different machines connected via a network or the Internet. They don't have to be the same kind of machines, either. In CORBA, servers are described as if they were objects. If you put all that together, you get distributed heterogeneous object-oriented computing. Here's a couple more buzzwords to get out of the way — you may have heard client/server systems referred to as two-tier or even n-tier systems. It all really means the same thing, that there is more than one application involved in a system.

What CORBA is all about:

- ✔ **Distributed:** A distributed application is one whose parts (objects, components, and so on) are dispersed across processes. These processes may exist on the same machine or may be located across machines on a network.

- ✔ **Heterogeneous:** A heterogeneous application is one whose parts are located on machines that vary by hardware or by operating system (UNIX versus Windows, for example) or by programming language.

- ✔ **Object-oriented computing:** The use of objects and all the stuff that goes with them as the approach of choice when developing applications.

Distributed heterogeneous object-oriented computing also looks very impressive on a status report. "Today, I added support for distributed heterogeneous object-oriented computing to the accounting system." Sounds like you should get a raise!

You use CORBA to build distributed heterogeneous object-oriented applications. Fortunately, CORBA does most of the work automatically. Making an application that uses CORBA is actually pretty easy. Obviously, if you have a really complex problem to solve, even the CORBA solution will be complex. Even when you find yourself facing these complex problems, you can take advantage of some of the more advanced features of CORBA to ease your burden.

We get you up and running in just this one chapter. As you go through it, you'll see

✔ How to build an entire CORBA application in C++

✔ Most of the tools you use to build applications that use CORBA

What you won't see in this chapter are a bunch of detailed explanations. If something doesn't make a whole lot of sense right now, just skip over it.

The example code for this chapter is on the CD-ROM in the `Examples\Chapter1` directory.

Getting Ready to Rumble

Before you get your hands dirty, you should know what you're sticking them into. You need to have the proper tools to create CORBA applications on your computer.

This is where we start doing a great deal of throat-clearing and hand-waving. You see, CORBA runs on many different operating systems and is implemented by many vendors. C++ adds to the complexity because various vendors have implemented it across operating systems, too. This means there are billions and billions of combinations of operating systems and C++ compilers out there, all of which support CORBA just fine.

We have no way of knowing which operating system, development environment, or CORBA implementation you're using. So what's an author to do? The answer is simple: We tell you throughout the book what we use, and then we leave it up to you to get your own stuff ready. A bit harsh, but, lucky for both you and us, most of what you see in this book applies to many systems and environments.

Standard wishy-washy disclaimer

If you're going to try the examples in this book, you need to do a little legwork first. You need to install the following on your computer:

- ✔ A C++ or Java (or maybe even both) development environment
- ✔ A CORBA ORB (Object Request Broker)

What's an ORB? For most people, it's something that Zelda the Mysterious gazes into when she's telling their fortune. However, for CORBA techies, it's the *Object Request Broker.* The ORB is the cornerstone of CORBA. It provides platform- and language-independent treatment of data. Its purpose is to manage the communication between clients and servers.

On the CD-ROM are evaluation versions of several ORBs for Windows 95 and Windows NT that you can use to work the examples. You need to install an ORB onto your system — each one has a Windows installation program that does all the hard work for you.

You're probably better off installing just one ORB for a particular language at a time. Each ORB wants to modify your system's environment variables so that its tools can run correctly, its link libraries are accessible, and so on. If you install several ORBs, it's possible that they won't operate as expected, since the environment variables may not be set correctly. If you're a wizard at this sort of thing, install away! If not, just install at most one C++ and one Java ORB at a time.

We assume that you know how to perform the standard software development tasks, such as compiling source files, eating pizza, linking object files and libraries to create executables, and eating more pizza.

The stuff we use to get the job done

We use Windows NT along with the Microsoft Visual C++ 5.0 Professional development environment and Sun's Java 1.1.5. Lucky us. All the figures, examples, and explanations in this book pertain to this operating system/ development environment combination, but the concepts apply to any combination. If you're using Windows 95/98 along with Visual C++ 5.0 or later, or any Java compatible with Java 1.1, everything will work just fine as well. We've made every effort to create the examples such that they will work on all those other billions and billions of combinations of operating systems and compilers.

When compiling source files and linking object files and libraries to create executables, we use *Makefiles* (which are included in the Example directories on the CD-ROM). These Makefiles are designed to work with Visual C++

and the Orbix ORB for Windows 95/98/NT. We know you know what a Makefile is, but just in case, here's a definition: A Makefile is a text file containing the dependecies between source code and compiled objects, along with rules for creating the latter from the former. Put more simply, the Makefile runs the right compiler tools at the right time to turn source code into executable files.

If you're using a different ORB or a different operating system, you need to make your own Makefiles. You can use ours as a guide, or you can check the documentation included with your ORB.

You're on your own here. We can't really help you set up your development environment; CORBA works with so many different development environments, and we don't know which one you're using. We can't even give you specific directions for compiling or linking, because those instructions also vary, depending on your development tools, operating system, and ORB.

If you haven't yet spent the time to get everything ready, do it now. We'll wait.

Describing a CORBA Object in IDL

In this chapter, we create a simple but useful CORBA application. It doesn't take all day to create, either. When you're done with this example, CORBA will seem more real and more simple than it may have before. Before we get started, we need to tell you what IDL means. The Interface Definition Language (IDL) is used in CORBA to describe the interfaces of objects. Everything you need to know about IDL is in Chapter 4, but for now just trust us.

This example solves a simple problem that actually comes up in the real world from time to time. We're going to make an application that dispenses sequential numbers on demand, like when you take a number to wait for service in a shop. If you'd like to, you can follow along and make the application too!

This CORBA application is handy for transaction processing or for when you need unique numbers to identify invoices. Since we use CORBA, the "application" is really made up of a server and a client.

Exactly what are servers and clients? They are the participants in the great dance that is CORBA:

- ✔ **Servers** accept requests and deliver (or do) something. In other words, a server *serves the needs* of client objects or applications.

- ✔ **Clients** request and receive something. In other words, a client *uses the services* of server objects.

Beware the IDL of March

The Interface Definition Language (IDL) is used in CORBA to describe the interfaces of objects. Yes, it's yet another language to learn. No, it's not hard to learn. It looks like C++ and Java. Chapter 4 is the place to go to get the full details of IDL.

Specifically, IDL defines the modules, interfaces, and operations for applications. It is a declarative language only. In other words, IDL isn't used to implement applications — that's done by your *target language* — C++, Java, C, COBOL, or whatever you're using to actually write the server and client applications.

Like most politicians, objects and applications can have multiple personalities. They can be both clients and servers, meaning that they can both use and provide services. To create our application, we need to figure out what the server does. Then we describe the server object using IDL. Then we write some C++ code! When describing server objects in IDL, you must identify which are

- ✔ Servers
- ✔ Clients
- ✔ Both clients and servers
- ✔ Clueless

To begin describing the object, follow these steps:

1. **Think about the problem to discover the server's name, data, and behavior.**

   Caffeine, a Ouija board, a Magic 8 ball, or some other formal software engineering method usually helps here.

2. **Use the CORBA Interface Definition Language (IDL) to define the server.**

3. **Compile the IDL file.**

These three steps are described in greater, more humorous detail in the following sections.

I dream of servers

To create any CORBA application, we need to figure out what the server is supposed to do. Then we can describe the server object using IDL. The first step to writing the IDL is to think about the problem to discover the server's *name, data,* and *behavior.* You can do this any way you wish. There are many ways to do this, ranging from the informal to the academic. What you're trying to come up with is a clear idea of what to call the server, what information it holds, and what operations it performs.

Close your eyes and take a deep, cleansing breath. Now open them so that you can read the rest of this paragraph. Imagine a pink elephant wearing a party hat and a green pants suit. We mean it — really try to "see" this elephant. Well, if you have any luck at all, you have enough imagination to figure out what we should call our server, what data it deals with, and what behavior it exhibits. Give it a try.

We want to give the server a meaningful *name,* so we'll call it `Counter`, because its main purpose in life is to maintain a count. The *data* that it deals with can easily be called `CounterValue`.

The *behavior* that the server exhibits is a bit trickier to figure out. We want the server to keep generating the next higher number, so we need some way of getting the next higher value for the counter. We call it the `GetNextValue()` method.

We use the term *method* here because we are implementing this example in C++. The IDL equivalent of a method is an *operation.* An operation is an action that an object performs. It is one of the standard elements of CORBA's IDL, and it's discussed in detail in Chapter 4.

IDL-speak

After deciding on the server's *name, data,* and *behavior*, the next step is to use the CORBA Interface Definition Language (IDL) to describe the `Counter` server.

To do this, follow these steps:

1. **Make a directory on your system called** `Chapter1`.

2. **In that directory, create a text file named** `Counter.idl`.

3. **In the text file** `Counter.idl`, **describe the** `Counter` **server as follows:**

```
interface Counter {
    long GetNextValue();
};
```

Throughout the chapter, we repeatedly say stuff like "create a file" and "enter this." If you don't want to go to all that trouble, you can simply copy the file from the CD-ROM and open it:

1. **Copy the whole** Examples\Chapter1 **directory from the CD-ROM onto your system.**

2. **Open the** Counter.idl **file so you can see what's in it.**

That's it. Not too bad so far. The IDL describes a single object (in IDL, an object is called an *interface*) named Counter. The object has one operation, GetNextValue().

At this point, you may be asking

1. How do I get from here to C++ classes and methods?

2. What are interfaces and operations?

3. Is it too early for lunch?

The answers to these questions are easy enough:

1. An *interface* corresponds to a C++ class.

2. An *operation* corresponds to a C++ method.

3. It's always lunch time somewhere in the world.

Generating C++ from IDL, or we're not in Kansas anymore

We're almost ready to leave IDL and travel to the land of our target language, the happy land of C++. Before we go, we must compile the IDL file with the IDL compiler.

At the command prompt, enter the following compiler command and press Return:

```
C:\Counter\> idl -B -h .h Counter.idl
```

The idl command compiles an IDL file. The command takes several command line options (the -B and -h .h options) an then the name of the IDL source file.

That's the way you compile it if you're using Orbix, like we do. The exact name and command-line options for your IDL compiler may be different.

The IDL compiler compiles the IDL file, and several new files appear in the directory. Resist the urge to edit or view these files. They're there for you to use, but not to read.

For Orbix users, these new files are `Counter.h`, `CounterS.cpp`, and `CounterC.cpp`. For other ORBs, you may have fewer or more new files after running your IDL compiler, and the names of the files probably are different.

IDL-generated files should be seen and not edited. If you accidentally edit these files, don't save your changes! If you think you may have saved these changes, don't panic! All you have to do is run the IDL compiler again to get fresh copies of the files.

Writing the Applications in C++

The `Counter` object is the server object for our example application. In the preceding sections we wrote the IDL definition for the object, and then compiled the IDL file. Whenever you create an application with CORBA, you begin by defining one or more server objects. After defining the `Counter` object in IDL and compiling it, we need to write the C++ code that actually makes it work:

1. **Write the C++ Code for the server (`Counter`).**

2. **Write a CORBA server application to make `Counter` available to other applications.**

3. **Create a CORBA client application that calls the `GetNextValue()` method in `Counter`.**

4. **Run them all to see what happens.**

Excited? You should be. It's much easier than being modest while playing Twister in a kilt.

Writing the C++ code for the server

The next step is writing the C++ class code for the `Counter` object. We need to create two files, one for the header and the other for the implementation of its services. These files are pretty much what you expect to see, with some CORBA stuff thrown in to make it all work.

Losing my header file over CORBA

If you are familiar with C++, creating this header file is a breeze. If you're not, then you need to rush right out and buy *C++ For Dummies*, read it, and then come back. A C++ header file contains the definition for one or more C++ classes.

To write the C++ class header file for the Counter object, follow these steps:

1. **Make a text file called** Counter_impl.h **in the same directory you were working in before (probably** Examples\Chapter1).

2. **Enter the following C++ class definition:**

```
#ifndef COUNTER_IMPL_H
#define COUNTER_IMPL_H
#include <Counter.h>

class Counter_impl : public virtual CounterBOAImpl {
public:
    // class constructor
    Counter_impl();
    // method for GetNextValue
    virtual CORBA::Long GetNextValue(CORBA::Environment&);
private:
    CORBA::Long MyCounterValue;
};
#endif
```

This example works with Orbix. Orbix requires that every method that implements an interface include an extra parameter at the end. This parameter must be CORBA::Environment&. You don't ever use it, but you must include it. If you're not using Orbix, you may not need this parameter.

As CORBA server classes go, the Counter class implementation is pretty typical. Things to notice about this class are

- ✔ **The whole thing is wrapped in an** #ifndef..#endif **block.** Like every good C++ header file, this block prevents multiple copies of the same class from being defined in case we include the header file more than once during a compile. Your compiler may support the more modern version of this block (#pragma once), which also works fine.

- ✔ **The** Counter.h **file that the IDL compiler generated is included.** This file contains a class named CounterBOAImpl that we must use. We subclass our Counter_impl class from this class in order to make it a CORBA object.

- ✔ **The C++ class definition does not use every letter of the alphabet.**

- ✔ **We use** _impl **in our class names.**

You may be wondering why we're ending our class name with `_impl`. After all, the IDL file just used `Counter`. Like death and taxes, this naming convention is yet another of those things that you just accept. The `_impl` on the end means this is the implementation for the IDL interface.

The `CounterBOAImpl` class we inherit from is the server skeleton that the IDL compiler generates. Understanding the skeleton is important, but for now just use it as we've described and you'll be fine.

Your IDL compiler may use a different name for its generated skeleton classes. Check the documentation that comes with your ORB to find out what it actually creates for you.

The IDL compiler generates the *IDL server skeleton.* The skeleton allows clients to gain access to each of the server's methods.

The `_impl` is used by convention to denote a file containing the implementation of an object. Follow this convention, and things will be much easier for you.

More things to notice about this file are

- ✔ **The class header file includes a class constructor.**

- ✔ **The method that corresponds to the operation in the IDL file is declared as a virtual method in the C++ class file.**

- ✔ **The class is a public virtual subclass of the skeleton class generated by the IDL compiler.** A very good technical reason exists for this convention, but fortunately, it really doesn't matter. You have to declare both the class and the method as *virtual* or the class doesn't work. So just do it.

- ✔ **The `CORBA::Long` type is a new thing.** This is the way you say `long` in CORBA. Because we use a `long` in our IDL, we use `CORBA::Long` here in the class header file. Like the preceding rule, you just need to do things this way.

- ✔ **The one private member variable is named `MyCounterValue`.** It's one of those `CORBA::Long` things. As you may expect, this variable stores the current counter value.

Attaching a body to the header

With the class header file complete, we press on to write the *class implementation,* which is the file that describes the behavior for the `Counter` object. In other words, the class implementation is where we flesh out the methods and make them real.

Virtual methods

Virtual methods are the C++ way to say "Polymorphism Happens Here." They tell the compiler that at run time, the program calls the method by using a base class pointer. However, what you really need is to have the actual subclass method called.

Because CORBA is the one that actually calls the implementation methods and it has only a pointer to the skeleton class, it needs your subclasses' methods to be declared virtual so that it can call them.

Aren't you glad you don't really need to know how this stuff all works?

To write the C++ class implementation file for the Counter object, follow these steps:

1. **Make a file called** Counter_impl.cpp **in the same directory you were working in before.**

2. **Enter the following C++ code:**

```
#include <Counter_impl.h>
// Constructor
Counter_impl::Counter_impl() {
    MyCounterValue = 0;
}
// GetNextValue method
CORBA::Long
Counter_impl::GetNextValue(CORBA::Environment&) {
    return ++MyCounterValue;
}
```

This program works with Orbix. Orbix requires that every method that implements an interface include an extra parameter at the end. This parameter must be CORBA::Environment&. You don't ever use it, but you must include it. If you're not using Orbix, you may not need this parameter.

The preceding example looks like pretty darn normal C++ code! That's one of the great things about CORBA — other than a few files that are included and those weird CORBA::Long types, things pretty much stay the same when you're writing the classes.

Things to notice about this file are

▶ **The header file where the** `Counter_impl` **class is defined is included.** In this case, it's `Counter_impl.h`.

▶ **The actual implementations of the constructor and the method are detailed.** The constructor sets the internal value of the counter (stored in `MyCounterValue`) to 0. The `GetNextValue()` method increments `MyCounterValue` and then returns it, just like you'd expect.

▶ No animals were harmed during the writing of this class implementation.

Writing the server application

You're probably feeling pretty good about this whole CORBA thing by now. After all, IDL looks sort of like C++, and other than remembering to include some files and the odd `CORBA_Long`, the C++ code looks pretty normal.

If you're the worrying type, you may be waiting for the other shoe to drop. Surprise! It really doesn't get much worse than this. From the server side of things, all we need to do is write the application that makes the server available to clients.

To create the server application, follow these steps

1. **Make a file called** `server.cpp`.

2. **Enter the following C++ code:**

```
#include <Counter_impl.h>
#include <stdlib.h>
#include <fstream.h>

int
main(int argc, char* argv[], char*[]) {
  try {
    // Create ORB and BOA
    CORBA::ORB_var orb = CORBA::ORB_init(argc, argv,
      "Orbix");
    // Orbix specific -- turn off Diagnostics
    orb->setDiagnostics(0);
    CORBA::BOA_var _myboa = orb -> BOA_init(argc, argv,
      "Orbix_BOA");
    // Create Counter object
    Counter_impl * counter = new Counter_impl;
    // Orbix specific -- must tell BOA object is ready
```

```
        _myboa->impl_is_ready("Counter",0);
        // Save reference
        CORBA::String_var s =
            orb -> object_to_string(counter);
        ofstream out("Counter.ref");
        if(out.fail()) {
            extern int errno;
            cerr << argv[0] << ": can't open 'Counter.ref': "
                << strerror(errno) << endl;
            return 1;
        }
        out << s << endl;
        out.close();


        // Run implementation - Orbix specific TIMEOUT
        myboa->impl_is_ready("Counter",
            CORBA::Orbix.INFINITE_TIMEOUT);
    }
    catch(CORBA::SystemException& ex)
    {
        cerr << "System error!" << endl;
        return 1;
    }
    return 0;
}
```

This program works with Orbix. Orbix requires that servers turn off diagnostics; otherwise, they print a bunch of messages to standard output when they run. Also, Orbix needs you to call impl_is_ready() before you create an object reference. We use the Orbix-specific version that does not wait (that's what the zero means) in order to indicate that Counter_impl is fully ready. Then we write the object reference. Finally, the last impl_is_ready() call uses an Orbix specific extension (CORBA::Orbix.INFINITE_TIMEOUT) that makes the server wait forever for a client. If you're not using Orbix, you don't need these items.

Before you run screaming from the room, hear us out: Only a couple of things in this file actually require you to think. The rest of the file's elements are basics that you do every time you create a sever application.

Take a look at what you must think about and do. We call this list the "You Musts" of creating the server application:

1. You must include the class implementation header file.

```
#include <Counter_impl.h>
```

2. You must create an object of that class.

```
Counter_impl * counter = new Counter_impl;
```

3. You must save a reference to that object.

```
CORBA::String_var s =
    orb -> object_to_string(counter);
// open file containing reference
out << s << endl;
```

4. You must get up and take a break because your leg has fallen asleep.

That's right. Just these lines in the listing would be different if you were implementing a server for a different object. The rest of the stuff is what makes CORBA work, and it's the same every time. Just do it (the rest of the stuff), and everything will work out fine.

Some of the things you have to do may vary slightly from ORB to ORB. For example, Orbix uses the names `orbix` and `orbix_BOA` to initialize the ORB and BOA variables. Your ORB probably wants some other names.

You have plenty of options when it comes to saving a reference to the object. Right now, take the simplest option of all: Write a magic string of information to a file. We talk about other ways to save a reference to an object in Chapter 3.

Writing the server application code is all very straightforward if you just follow the rules. The client application program is the same: If you follow the rules, nobody gets hurt. Unlike the server code, the client code contains some actual code that does something with the `Counter` object. That's what makes it a client application.

Writing C++ code for the client

The last programming step, but not quite the last step in the whole process, is to write the client application code. Like the server application code, the client consists of a bunch of CORBA stuff you have to do, as well as whatever you want the client to actually do.

In this case, we want the client to call the `GetNextValue()` method in `Counter`. The example uses a simple command-line interface, so it works for just about any operating system.

To write the client's code, follow these steps:

0. Take a deep, cleansing breath.

These deep-breathing exercises really do help.

1. **Create a file called** `client.cpp`.

2. **Enter the following C++ code:**

```cpp
#include <Counter.h>
#include <stdlib.h>
int
main(int argc, char* argv[], char*[]) {
   try {
      // Create ORB
      CORBA::ORB_var orb = CORBA::ORB_init(argc,
         argv, "Orbix");
      // Orbix specific -- turn off Diagnostics
      orb->setDiagnostics(0);
      ifstream in("Counter.ref");
      if(in.fail()) {
         cerr << argv[0] << ": can't open 'Counter.ref': "
            << strerror(errno) << endl;
         return 1;
      }
      char s[1000];
      in >> s;

      CORBA::Object_var obj =
         orb -> string_to_object(s);
      Counter_var Counter = Counter::_narrow(obj);
      // Main loop
      cout << "Enter 'n' for next counter" <<
         " or 'x' for exit:\n";
      char c;
      do {
         cout << "> ";
         cin >> c;
         if (c == 'n')
            cout << "Next counter value is: " <<
               Counter -> GetNextValue() << endl;
      } while(c != 'x');
   }
   catch(CORBA::SystemException& ex) {
      cerr << "CORBA Exception!" << endl;
      return 1;
   }
   return 0;
}
```

Because this example program works with Orbix, the same Orbix disclaimer applies here: If you're not using Orbix, you don't need to turn off diagnostic messages. You might think that diagnostic messages are off by default, but you'd be wrong.

Just as with the server, you have to actually think about only a couple of things in this file. The rest of it is stuff you enter every time.

Take a look at what you must think about and do. We call this list the "You Musts" of creating the client application:

1. **You must include the class header file (`Counter.h`) generated by the IDL compiler.**

```
#include <Counter.h>
```

2. **You must retrieve a reference to the server object.**

```
// open file containing reference
char s[1000];
cin >> s;
CORBA::Object_var obj = orb -> string_to_object(s);
```

3. **You must create an object of the class based on the reference.**

```
Counter_var Counter = Counter::_narrow(obj);
```

4. **You must do something with the object.**

```
Counter -> GetNextValue()
```

5. **You must jump up and down screaming, "The client is done!"**

Before moving on, take a closer look at what we did in this file.

✔ We initialized the ORB as we did for the server.

✔ We read the magic string of information from the file written by the server.

   Don't worry; much better ways of completing this step are available, and we tell you about those ways in Chapter 3.

✔ We tell the ORB how we like our coffee — two creams with a dash of cinnamon.

✔ We did another CORBA thing — we narrowed the object into a `Counter` object (see the nearby sidebar on "Narrowing objects" for the full scoop).

Narrowing objects

Typecasting is Hollywood's way of keeping Leonard Nimoy in pointy ears. Narrowing is CORBA's way of typecasting.

CORBA knows about the `CORBA::object` class. When you define a new interface in IDL, the generated C++ class skeleton you get from the IDL compiler is based on the `CORBA::object` class.

General operations like `orb->string_to_object(s)` return a `CORBA::object`. You know what class that object is supposed to be, but CORBA doesn't have a clue. Narrowing the object locks it into its specific class.

That's it for the CORBA part of the client application. The rest is plain old C++. In a loop, the program prompts for one of two characters, reads in a character, and then performs the selected operation.

Notice that when you call the method in the `Counter` object, it looks just like a plain old C++ method call instead of the gargantuan, really hairy monsters that would have to appear if you had to do all the CORBA stuff yourself. That's the power of CORBA.

And that's everything. We followed a few simple steps:

1. **Start with IDL to describe the object.**
2. **Use the IDL compiler to create some C++ files.**
3. **Write `Counter_impl.h` and `Counter_impl.cpp` to implement the object described in the IDL file.**
4. **Write `server.cpp` to implement the server application.**
5. **Write `client.cpp` to implement the client application.**
6. **Write Jodie Foster and tell her what good taste your neighbor has.**

Just two steps are left to do. We need to build executable files with our C++ compiler, and then we're ready to run the two applications (client and server) to see CORBA in action.

Building and running the applications

The subject of building and running the applications is another one of those cases where we do a lot of hand-waving when trying to tell you what to do. Actually, if you could see us as we write, you'd know that this hand-waving happens quite a bit. Not because we don't know what we're talking about, but because compiling C++ source files and linking them into runable executables is very different depending on your operating system, development tools, and ORB.

What we can suggest is that you review the documentation that came with your development environment and ORB. If your ORB has sample projects, take a look at them as well. In other words, the ball is back in your court. You're up at bat. It's fourth and goal. The puck's in play. You get the idea.

Compiling and linking and bears, oh my!

As we said before, we use Visual C++ 5.0 and Windows NT. The following code shows what the commands look like when we build the example on our C: drive in a directory named Counter. The stuff we enter appears in bold. To compile the C++ files, we use these commands:

```
C:\Counter\> cl /c /nologo -DWIN32_LEAN_AND_MEAN  -DWIN32
    -DEXCEPTIONS -DUSE_INIT -MD -GX -I. -Ox -TpCounterC.cpp
C:\Counter\> cl /c /nologo -DWIN32_LEAN_AND_MEAN  -DWIN32
    -DEXCEPTIONS -DUSE_INIT -MD -GX -I. -Ox -TpCounterS.cpp
C:\Counter\> cl /c /nologo -DWIN32_LEAN_AND_MEAN  -DWIN32
    -DEXCEPTIONS -DUSE_INIT -MD
    -GX -I. -Ox -TpCounter_impl.cpp
C:\Counter\> cl /c /nologo -DWIN32_LEAN_AND_MEAN  -DWIN32
    -DEXCEPTIONS -DUSE_INIT -MD -GX -I. -Ox -TpClient.cpp
C:\Counter\> cl /c /nologo -DWIN32_LEAN_AND_MEAN  -DWIN32
    -DEXCEPTIONS -DUSE_INIT -MD - GX -I. -Ox -TpServer.cpp
```

Icky, huh?

These commands are shown broken across several lines, but when you actually enter them, you need to put the entire command on a single line before pressing Return. If you're familiar with the make (or mmake, if you're using Windows) utility and Makefiles, then feel free to use Makefiles instead of compiling each file from the command line. Using make is a much more convenient way to build the application.

The Examples\Chapter1 directory on the CD-ROM includes a Makefile that you can use as a starting point for creating your own Makefile.

After the source files are compiled, we link them (along with the CORBA libraries supplied with the ORB) into two executables. You can include the link step in your Makefile, or do it by hand. We link them with the following link commands (again, the part that we enter is in bold type):

```
C:\Counter\> LINK  /MAP Client.OBJ CounterC.OBJ
   /OUT:client.exe initsrv.lib ITM.LIB
   Wsock32.LIB advapi32.lib user32.lib
C:\Counter\> LINK  /MAP CounterS.OBJ Counter_impl.OBJ
   Server.OBJ /OUT:server.exe initsrv.lib ITM.LIB
   Wsock32.LIB advapi32.lib user32.lib
```

We're done! The two executables are ready to go. We could just print them out and wear them as party hats, but that doesn't look very good on a status report. Instead, we'll try them out.

Running with scissors in your hand

Before running the application, you must have installed your ORB and started any ORB servers that you need in order to run CORBA applications. Your ORB may require registering your Counter server with the Implementation Repository (IR). Sounds official, doesn't it? Registering just means that you run a program that is supplied with the ORB. The IR tells the ORB the name of the server and how it's supposed to be used. If you must register the server, register it with the name Counter and define it as a *persistent* server. For Orbix, for example, you use this command to register:

```
C:\Counter\> putit Counter -persistent
```

Figure 1-1 shows the three applications running in their own windows. We're using Windows NT and running the server with two clients in this figure.

To run the applications yourself, follow these steps:

1. **Open three command prompt windows or console windows.**

   If you're using Windows 95/98 or NT, open three or more command/MS DOS prompt windows. In each window, change the directory to the directory where you created the programs. If you're not using Windows, you need to open two or more console windows.

2. **Run the server first in one window. Use this command:**

```
C:\Counter\> server
```

3. **Run each client in its own window. Use this command:**

```
C:\Counter\> client
```

4. **In one client, enter n and press Return to get the next counter value.**

   You see Next counter value is :1.

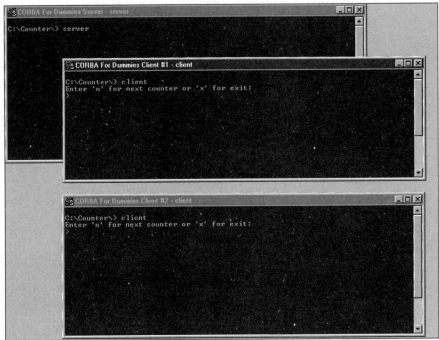

Figure 1-1:
Counter
server and
two clients.

5. **Go to the other client and repeat Step 4 to get the next counter value.**

    You see `Next counter value is :2.`

    Notice how the number goes up by one every time? That's because the counter value is stored in the server, and the server is the one place that remembers the counter value. CORBA lets you use that same server application from both clients.

6. **Enter x and press Return to quit both clients, but don't terminate the server.**

7. **Run a client again, and get the next counter value (by entering n and pressing Return).**

If you close the client and then close the server, the counter starts back at 0 the next time you run the server.

You can make the server remember its values, but don't concern yourself with that right now. If you must, Chapter 21 is all about adding persistence (the ability to remember values) to servers.

You've made it! You can say you've built a CORBA application. Even if you just followed along as we built it, you can say that. We won't tell.

Chapter 2
CORBA Basics

• •

In This Chapter

▶ Understanding the need for CORBA

▶ Getting an overview of the CORBA architecture

▶ Exploring the Object Request Broker (ORB) and its parts

▶ Taking a brief look at IDL

▶ Creating a simple application

• •

*I*n this chapter, we explain what CORBA is and why you want to spend time getting to know it.

We provide a very brief overview of the Object Management Group (OMG) and how it relates to CORBA. Next, we talk about CORBA's architecture — specifically the Object Request Broker (ORB). The ORB is the heart of any CORBA system. We continue with a discussion of the Interface Definition Language (IDL), without which the ORB would be lifeless. Finally, we end the chapter with the steps involved in creating a simple CORBA application.

Talking about all of this may sound like a tall order to undertake, but it isn't as hard as you may think. In fact, we believe that after reading this chapter, you'll be able to

✔ Explain why CORBA is really needed.

✔ Describe the OMA and CORBA architectures.

✔ Say the acronym without thinking about the cobra snake.

✔ Apply your newly acquired knowledge to the creation of a CORBA compliant application.

✔ Give a five-minute presentation, complete with overhead slides, on the migration patterns of computer techies to Framingham, MA — the home of the OMG.

Not a bad return on an investment of just reading.

The Real Need for CORBA

CORBA (Common Object Request Broker Architecture) is a standard for the development of distributed heterogeneous applications.

A *distributed application* has parts that exist in different processes. These processes may exist on the same machine or located across networked machines. A *heterogeneous application* is one whose parts are located on machines that vary by hardware, by operating system, or by programming language.

What's really important about CORBA, however, is that it provides a way for the information technology industry to move from creating applications in the way it does now to creating applications in a new and improved way. At this point, you must be asking, "What way is that?"

Take a moment to look at the practice in use today, and then we'll prognosticate. No, we don't mean anything concerning a bodily function. To *prognosticate* is to foresee into the future. We just wanted to use a fancy word to see whether you're still paying attention.

Where we are today

Today's software industry has two problems that CORBA addresses. Okay, the industry has more than just these two problems, but we want to keep our book to a reasonable size. In any case, the problems are

- ✔ Platform–and language–dependent software.
- ✔ Monolithic applications.

We talk more about these problems in the next two sections.

It's a sticky business

For the most part, software created today is specific to hardware platforms, operating systems, and programming languages. Software developers choose their combination and create their own fiefdoms of software. This approach has several drawbacks:

- ✔ **Consumers must pick a platform, network, or whatever and stick with it.** Switching hardware and operating systems is way too expensive.
- ✔ **Developers must reinvent the wheel repeatedly because they can't use pieces of software written by other developers.** They, too, are stuck.

> ✔ **Most of today's software is not distributed.** Sure, it's distributed to stores in shrink-wrapped boxes, but that's not what we mean. We mean that although client/server software is out there and becoming more commonplace, it has implementation problems that are holding it back. So distributed heterogeneous applications aren't exactly ubiquitous these days. In other words, most software is designed as single stand-alone applications that run on only one machine.

We just had to use the word *ubiquitous*. We've never read a technical computer book that didn't use it at least once. Although this isn't a really technical book, it does have techie stuff in it, so we think it qualifies. Ubiquitous (pronounced *u-bick-wit-us*) means *all over the place*.

Bigger is not always better

Another dilemma that prevents the software industry from zooming into the next millennium is the tendency to create large, monolithic applications. We're not talking about Stonehenge here. But monolithic applications can be just as hard to arrange and understand.

Take a look at the consumer side of things. These days, when you buy a software package, like a word processor, you get a bunch of options and features that you don't ever use. You know, stuff like a talking complaint-letter wizard.

Having all these "extra" features makes it harder for you to use the features that you really want and takes up valuable disk and memory space. Besides, we don't know about you, but being forced to pay for things that we don't want really rubs us the wrong way.

The situation doesn't look much better on the developer's side either. Today, developers must maintain monolithic software that engulfs all the features the software needs in order to be competitive. The "keeping up with the Joneses" effect has made it nearly impossible for developers to create focused applications. Instead, they must be able to say, "We have that, too" in order to succeed in today's marketplace.

Where we'll be tomorrow

The new era of computing promises to be more flexible, leaner, and more global in nature.

We know that tomorrow's applications are going to be distributed and heterogeneous. Many efforts are underway today, including CORBA, to make this happen. But what about the size problem? The answer lies in an approach called *plug and play*.

Plug and play components

The plug and play approach relies on something called *component technology*. The idea is to create applications from self-contained pieces that plug together and play the software tune that you want. These pieces are called *components,* and they can be objects, bigger components (comprised of groups of objects), pieces of applications (like spelling checkers), or entire applications (like a word processor as part of an office application).

Plug and play components are sort of like the special-order idea in a fast-food restaurant. Remember the "Hold the pickles, hold the lettuce, special orders don't upset us . . ." jingle? Well, that's basically what we're talking about. With plug and play, you, the software consumer, will be able to get applications that are your very own special order, without having to take the onions.

On the developer side of things, component technology promises to revolutionize the way the industry does business. Developers will no longer create and maintain a single, humongous application. Instead, they will create discrete components that, when combined, provide just the right set of features for the consumer.

The vision is to have software components from one developer seamlessly work with components from other developers. Components may physically reside in Ohio, in France, or on your own PC. They may be written in any language and use any operating system.

The ultimate vision for component technology is to have *smart components*. Smart components would have the facilities to do things like versioning, security, and self-testing. Versioning is the ability to create and maintain several variations of a component. In addition, their interfaces would allow such things as scripting, event reception, and transaction processing. Scripting allows a high-level language to invoke the operations of components. Event reception concerns the acceptance of events and the modification of behavior according to what they say. Transaction processing deals with grouping multiple actions into a single atomic action that is either committed or rolled back so that resources are not left in inconsistent states.

In a nutshell, the components would work autonomously and perform tasks that are required in order to be their own boss. Instead of always being told what to do, components would do what is needed, when it is needed, with little direction from the outside. In most science fiction books, this is when computers take over the world.

This vision of software applications leads to a radically different way of developing software from the methods used today.

Back to the future

So how is this future vision going to take place? Believe it or not, the answer lies in the past.

For more than a quarter of a century, hardware engineers have been doing what software developers are only now dreaming about — using a bus. Yes, for the last 25 years or so software developers have been transportationally challenged.

A *bus* is a framework that components can be plugged into so that they can talk to other components. When we say talk, we simply mean they can invoke operations, provide information, and get information back from other components.

A hardware bus is simple to understand. Inside your computer are one or more slots into which you plug cards for things like your modem and monitor. When you change your modem, you simply swap cards. The slots are your computer's hardware bus.

CORBA also provides services and facilities for developing and using these components. In other words, CORBA provides (or will provide) the ability to plug and play as you please — and that's where the future is going to be.

The OMG and CORBA

The Object Management Group (OMG) is responsible for creating and promoting CORBA standards. Here are six things you may want to know about it:

- ✔ It's a non-profit organization.
- ✔ It's a consortium of over 800 organizations that span the globe.

Application Programming Interface (API)

Software developers have been trying to duplicate the general idea of a hardware bus with software components. The closest they've come is the *application programming interface* (API). An API is a set of functions that can be called to perform actions. The APIs for the UNIX, Windows, and Macintosh operating systems contain thousands of functions. Instead of laboriously re-creating these functions, programmers can pick and choose the functions they want to use. However, this model isn't exactly what the software developers are looking for. This is where CORBA steps into the limelight. CORBA is an architecture for a software bus on which components can communicate with each other. These components can be written in different languages, use different operating systems and machines, and be distributed across networks.

- ✔ It aims to reduce the complexity, accelerate the development time, and lower the costs of new software applications.

- ✔ It is dedicated to maximizing the interoperability, reusability, and portability of software.

- ✔ It aims to help you rack up some really big frequent flyer miles by attending OMG meetings.

The "abilities" of CORBA include the following:

- ✔ **Interoperability** is the ability of a component to be invoked across networks, languages, operating systems, and tools. For CORBA, interoperability means the ability of objects and applications to exchange requests via ORBs — in other words, the ability to make requests and respond to requests on the same machine or across a network that uses the CORBA standard.

- ✔ **Reusability** is the ability of a system to grow in functionality through the extension of existing components and the ability to combine existing components in heretofore unforeseen ways in order to create new components.

- ✔ **Portability** is the ability to transfer a program from one hardware or software environment to another.

The OMA

The OMG produces a specification, not an executable system. Part of this specification is the Object Management Architecture (OMA). (You can combine these two acronyms to get a really neat yogic chant, "OMAOMG . . . OMAOMG.") Figure 2-1 illustrates the OMA.

The OMA is the way that the OMG sees the specifications, services, facilities, and everything else that is CORBA fit together to create one big happy architecture, or master plan. Without a plan, the OMG would just have a bunch of disconnected pieces.

CORBAservices

CORBAservices augment the core CORBA capabilities. These services make it easier for developers to produce and share their objects, components, and applications. Services are provided to

- ✔ Create objects.

- ✔ Control access to objects.

- ✔ Maintain relationships between objects.

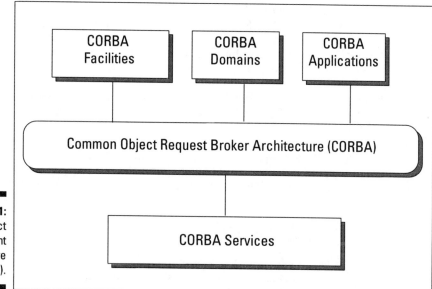

Figure 2-1:
The Object
Management
Architecture
(OMA).

Examples of services include the Persistence Service, the Naming Service, the Event Service, and the Transaction Service. CORBAservices are discussed in Chapters 18 through 22.

CORBAfacilities

CORBAfacilities are groups of components that provide additional capabilities that are more useful to application-specific tasks, such as dealing with user interfaces and work flows. They also support application development by providing higher-level capabilities for multistep tasks such as printing and electronic mail.

CORBAfacilities are *not* groups of white porcelain receptacles containing water.

CORBAdomains

CORBAdomains provide capabilities for developing applications in specific areas such as medicine, telecommunications, and finance. CORBAdomains are discussed in Chapter 17.

CORBAapplications

CORBAapplications are groups of objects or components developed specifically for particular applications. Basically, any application that anyone writes that uses CORBA counts as a CORBAapplication. So when you become proficient in developing CORBA applications, you are actually extending the OMA. Congratulations! That's a nice item that you can use for this week's status report.

Because the OMA is an architecture and not an executable system, CORBAservices and CORBAfacilities are specifications of collections of IDL-defined objects and not runable programs. However, you can buy implementations of some of these object services right off the shelf and use them with your CORBA application.

IDL is the acronym for *Interface Definition Language*. It's the declarative language used by CORBA to define the interface to objects.

The central item in the OMA is CORBA. It is the infrastructure, the framework, the bus, the heart and soul, the end all and be all — CORBA is the reason for this book and why you're spending your time reading about it. So take a closer look at CORBA and find out what all the hubbub is about.

The CORBA ORB

Like the OMA, CORBA is also an architecture — notice the *A* in its name. CORBA isn't an executable system, it's a specification of a standard. The OMG decides what goes in the standard and then lays it out piece by piece so that software vendors can create Object Request Brokers (ORBs). After an ORB exists, other software developers can use it to create servers, clients, and applications that are CORBA-compliant.

This explanation leads to the question, "What exactly is an ORB?" An ORB is

- ✔ Responsible for the communication between distributed heterogeneous applications.
- ✔ Something that sits between servers and clients and lets them talk.
- ✔ A really shiny glass ball that people look into to see the future.

An ORB allows applications to communicate with one another no matter where they are located or what kind of system they are running on. More simply stated, an ORB makes the whole thing work.

To be more specific, an ORB makes communication between objects transparent with regard to where the objects are located, their programming languages, their operating systems, and ultimately their internal implementations. It also whitens your teeth. Now that's what we call a deal.

The ORB is discussed in just about every chapter in this book because it's the heart of CORBA. Figure 2-2 shows the architecture for the CORBA ORB.

The client

A *client* is an object, component, or application that makes requests for services from other objects, components, or applications (also called *implementation objects* or *servers*). A given object, component, or application can be a client for some requests and a server for other requests.

The client isn't part of the ORB; instead, it uses the ORB. That's why it's shown above the dotted line in Figure 2-2. We include it in the figure so that you can see the ORB pieces that interact with clients.

An object implementation (server)

An *object implementation* (also called a *server*) provides a response to requests for services from other objects, components, or applications. A given object, component, or application can be a server for some requests and a client for other requests.

Servers aren't part of the ORB either. But as with clients, we include them in Figure 2-2 so that you can see their interactions with ORB pieces.

Object implementation is a more general term for *server.* We use the term *server* when discussing object implementations because it's easier to read. Whenever you see *server,* think object implementation.

The ORB core with IIOP

The *ORB Core* is responsible for communicating requests. It encompasses the entire communication infrastructure necessary to

- ✔ Identify and locate objects.
- ✔ Handle connection administration.
- ✔ Support ET phoning home.
- ✔ Deliver data.

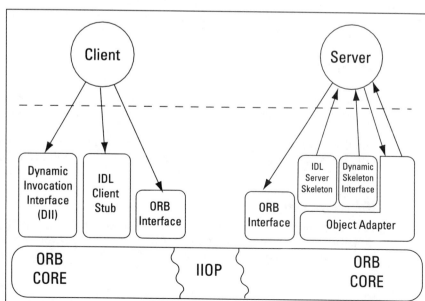

Figure 2-2:
The
Common
Object
Request
Broker
Architecture
(CORBA).

The ORB Core and its capabilities are discussed in detail in Chapter 3 and throughout the book.

The *Internet Inter-ORB Protocol* (IIOP) is a standard protocol for communication between ORBs on TCP/IP-based networks. ORBs are required to support IIOP in order to be considered CORBA-compliant. ORB developers can also support other protocols as long as IIOP is supported.

The IIOP is based on the General Inter-ORB Protocol (GIOP) standard. The GIOP standard is based on the Pyrotechnic Longitudinal ORB Protocol (PLOP) standard, but that acronym was just too gross to use. CORBA initially specified the GIOP standard, which is neutral with respect to networks. Because the GIOP is a generalized protocol, it can't be implemented directly, which means that ORB developers must specialize the GIOP standard. To ensure that ORBs from differing developers can interoperate, the IIOP standard was made mandatory.

IDL client stubs

An *IDL client stub* is automatically generated by the IDL compiler. It's a piece of code that allows a client to invoke an implementation object's services. IDL client stubs are the stodgy but much more common alternative to the DII. Client subs are often called *static* because they provide a complete yet fixed way for clients to invoke an object's services.

Dynamic Invocation Interface (DII)

The *Dynamic Invocation Interface* (DII) defines the client's side of the interface that allows dynamic creation and invocation of requests to objects. It's just the ticket for clients that want to impress their friends with peppy behavior. The DII offers a way to invoke a server's operations other than the static client stub invocations. The DII is discussed in Chapter 14.

ORB interface

The *ORB interface* is a collection of operations that provides services common to object implementations and clients. These services include ORB initialization and facilities to obtain the necessary object references.

The ORB interface provides functions that don't depend on which Object Adapter is used. These operations are the same for all ORBs and all object implementations. We cover the ORB interface in more detail in Chapter 3.

IDL server skeletons

The IDL compiler automatically generates *IDL server skeletons*. The server skeleton is code that provides the means by which a server's operations can be accessed. Like your skeleton, it keeps the server from collapsing.

The Dynamic Skeleton Interface (DSI)

The *Dynamic Skeleton Interface* (DSI) provides a run-time binding mechanism for servers who were not statically defined at compilation. Like the DII, the DSI is only used by the really cool, popular servers. The DSI looks at the parameter values of incoming requests and determines the target object and operation. The DSI is discussed in Chapter 14.

The Object Adapter

An *Object Adapter* is the primary mechanism by which a server object has access to ORB services. An Object Adapter performs many functions, including generating object references; invoking methods; dusting, mopping, and other light housekeeping; and providing basic access security. Object Adapters are discussed in Chapters 3, 6, 8, and 11.

It's Just Not CORBA without IDL

It's high time we talk a bit more about what IDL is and what you can do with it.

Interface Definition Language (IDL) is how CORBA defines an object (an *interface* in CORBA speak). IDL states an application's or object's contract to its potential clients. A *contract* is an application's or object's

- ✔ Constants (those things that remain the same throughout an application, like pi = 3.14159).
- ✔ Data types (the kinds of data stored, passed, and used).
- ✔ Favorite TV shows (anything with people wearing large animal costumes).
- ✔ Attributes (data that is stored by the object).
- ✔ Exceptions (red flags that can be thrown when something unexpected happens).
- ✔ Inheritance structure (the family tree of objects from which this object inherits).
- ✔ Operations, including its parameters, types, and return value (the services provided by the object).

Without IDL, CORBA can't describe the actions that objects can take and how those actions are invoked. CORBA would be lifeless without IDL. Chapter 4 details IDL.

Creating a Simple Application

An application's design can use either static invocations or dynamic invocations (or some combination of the two.) We're going to talk about the static approach here and leave the dynamic approach to Chapter 14.

When we say "static invocations" or "dynamic invocations," we're talking about how clients call methods in a server. When you're not using CORBA, you usually have a definition of the object that you're trying to call when you compile and link an application. Because the resulting executable program can't change the form of the call (the name or number of parameters), it's called a static invocation.

Dynamic invocations don't look like regular method calls at all. The client can determine, at run time, the names of the available server operations and the number and types of their parameters. The client then constructs a call.

Seat of your pants application development

To simplify creating an application, we have made the following assumptions:

- ✔ **The target language is Java or C++.**
- ✔ **The persistent server model is used.** Server models are discussed in Chapters 3 and 11.

Follow these steps to create an application in CORBA quickly:

1. **Perform object-oriented analysis and design to determine the distributed objects.**

2. **Use the CORBA IDL to describe the objects.**

3. **Compile the IDL file(s).**

4. **For each interface described in the IDL file, write a target-language implementation.**

5. **In your chosen target language, write a main program that instantiates the implementation objects (servers).**

6. **In your target language, write the client application(s) that will use these server objects.**

   Be sure to incorporate the client stub information in the implementation. The "how-to" of this step varies by target language.

7. **Compile all source files, including stubs and skeletons, and then link the executable files.**

8. **Run the server application created in Step 5, and then run as many kinds of clients as you need, as many times as you need them.**

Part II

Who Put the ORB in CORBA

The 5th Wave

By Rich Tennant

"Ms. Pembroke, the Sun and Microsoft reps are here."

In this part . . .

Part II is where the CORBA rubber hits the distributed object road! You see the nitty-gritty details of how a CORBA Object Request Broker (ORB) works. We take you inside the Interface Definition Language (IDL) so that you can see just how easy it is to define stuff in CORBA. We present three big examples in this part — one in C++, one in Java, and one in Java that works on the Web.

You get everything you need to use the basic CORBA features in C++, Java for the desktop as an application, and Java for the Web as an applet.

Chapter 3

A Big-Picture View of the ORB

An Object Request Broker (ORB) is responsible for the communication between clients and servers. It strives to make this communication as transparent as possible with regard to:

- Location
- Programming languages
- Operating systems
- Phases of the moon
- Internal implementations

Keeping these things behind the scenes lets you, the developer, use normal programming language constructs for calling a server's methods from clients.

The intent of this chapter is to give you a clear picture of what occurs when a client makes a request of a server. A request is simply CORBA's version of a method call. After all, the ORB really doesn't do much more than translate a request from a client into an actual method execution in a server.

Sometimes you'll see the term *object implementation* as a more general term for server. The CORBA specification uses this term to refer to an object without making any judgments as to whether it acts solely as a server, as a client, or both. We use the term *server* when referring to an object implementation because it's shorter, so whenever you see *server,* you should think *object implementation.*

Opening Up the Magic Box

An ORB can be implemented as a single component, as a collection of components, as a perfect glass sphere, and in several other ways. The underlying representation isn't important. Instead, what really matters is that the ORB provides the interface that is specified in the CORBA standard.

You can consider the ORB to be sort of a magic box. You don't really need to know how it works in order to use it. It's like driving a car for most people. We just get in and turn the key, then drive off, blissfully unaware of exactly how internal combustion engines work.

The ORB Core itself is not directly accessed. Instead, the ORB Interface component (refer to Figure 2-2) is the intermediary between objects and the ORB. The ORB Interface is a collection of operations that provides services that are common to clients and servers.

We aren't going to list all the operations that the ORB can perform. You can look at the OMG specification for that. Instead, we decided to list some of the operations that we use in our examples:

- object_to_string(): Converts an object reference to a string
- resolve_initial_references(): Finds well-known server objects
- object_overboard(): Sends an object reference into the foamy brine
- string_to_object(): Converts a string to an object reference
- BOA_init(): Returns an object that is a Basic Object Adapter (see Chapter 11)
- accept_apology(): Converts an apology into a weekend skiing vacation

You can get the full specification for your ORB's Interface component from the documentation that comes with your ORB. We are using Orbix from Iona Technologies, PLC., so our documentation can be found on the CD-ROM that accompanies this book in the Eval\Iona\Docs\ProgrammersReference.pdf file.

Taste the rainbow of ORB flavors

Numerous ways to implement an ORB are at your disposal. Regardless of the underlying representation, the ORB will be CORBA compliant, as long as the ORB provides the standard interface.

Here are several flavors of ORBs:

- **Client and Implementation Resident ORB:** ORB resides in the client application and the object implementation application.

- **Server-based ORB:** ORB exists as a separate process, which acts as a server that routes communications between clients and object implementations.

- **System-based ORB:** ORB is like the Server-based flavor except that the ORB is actually part of the operating system, an arrangement that enhances security.

- **Carbon-based ORB:** ORB is a big glass ball that resides on Zelda's tabletop, where it connects her with those in the great beyond.

- **Library-based ORB:** ORB is like the Client and Implementation Resident flavor except that it's implemented using shared libraries.

The implementation of the ORB is usually a greater issue for the ORB administrator than for the developer. If you're a developer, your ORB's flavor may affect the way in which you compile and link your files. If you're an ORB administrator, be sure to inform your developers of any other ways that the ORB's implementation affects their tasks.

This list gives you an idea as to how easily you can use the ORB's capabilities. You use them as you would any other application that has a well-defined interface.

Static on the Line

When a client sends a request to a server, the ORB performs certain activities to actually make the request happen. These activities vary depending upon the static and dynamic aspects of the request and of the interface definitions.

Static and *dynamic* have to do with when the ORB finds out the information it needs.

The advantages of the static approach are the following:

- ✔ It's the easiest way to program.
- ✔ A remote method call looks just like a local method call.
- ✔ The target language's type checking is enforced at compile time.
- ✔ Application execution can be faster.

The advantages of the dynamic approach are the following:

- ✔ It's flexible — it allows new object types to be added to an application at run-time.
- ✔ Application execution can be faster.

We are definitely not taking a stand on this issue. In this chapter, we use the static approach. For more information about the dynamic approach, see Chapter 14.

Getting the Handle on Objects

An ORB acts as the ferry for transporting requests and replies between clients and servers across the great ocean of the network. A *request* is a language-independent method call. A *reply* is simply the result of a request. Before a server's method can be called, a client needs to know which server to call. *Getting the handle on an object* means finding a reference by which the object can be uniquely identified for communication. In CORBA, this handle is called an object reference.

An *object reference* is similar to the ORB in that it, too, is a magic box. Inside the box is all the information about where an object is located and what information is required in order to communicate with it. In other words, an object reference is the unique information about an object that allows other objects to locate it and make method calls. You can think of it as a postal address with a bit more information attached to it — like the color of the house and how many bushes it has out front.

A request includes

- ✔ An object reference.
- ✔ The name of the method to be invoked.
- ✔ All the method's parameters.
- ✔ The type of the return value for the method.

All the parts of the request are written in a target language, of course, because nothing is implemented in IDL (Interface Definition Language).

In C++, the general form of a request is

```
value = obj->methodName(param0,...paramN);
```

From `methodName` on, the form is pretty standard C++ stuff. The CORBA part is buried in `obj`. This example shows you the way to use an object reference — by placing it in a request. But how do you get the object reference in the first place?

CORBA supports several ways to get an object reference:

- ✔ The `object_to_string()` operation
- ✔ The directory server
- ✔ Zelda's connection to the "other side"
- ✔ The Naming Service
- ✔ `resolve_initial_references()` operation

The four methods of getting an object reference listed above are expanded in the next sections.

The object_to_string() ORB operation

Server objects are made by creating a new instance of a server implementation class. After a server object exists, it can create a string reference to itself by calling an operation in the ORB Interface named `object_to_string()`. The server object then prints or writes this string version of its reference to a file or to a console.

Like most of today's political media coverage, this string is not intended for you to understand. You must simply accept it and presume that it's useful, which it is — the string version of the object reference, of course. We certainly didn't mean the media coverage.

The client can either read the string version from the file or accept it as a command line argument. It then turns the string reference into a reference that is used in a method call by using the ORB Interface operation called `string_to_object()`.

Chapter 1 shows an example in C++ of both a client and a server that use these functions.

The directory server

Some objects have methods that return other object references. If a client knows the object reference to one of these objects, it can call that method and receive object references for new and different objects.

For example, a server object can act as a directory object that looks up a name and returns the associated object reference. If a client knows the object reference for the directory server, it can call this method with a name and receive the object reference for a new server object.

The directory server was such a nifty idea that the OMG decided to create a CORBAservice called the Naming Service.

The Naming Service

Server objects use this bona fide CORBAservice to register their object references and name. Clients then look up the known name to get the object reference. Chapter 18 delves much deeper into the Naming Service.

This approach to getting an object reference works well if the server objects already know the reference to the Naming Service. But what if they don't know how to get the handle on the Naming Service itself? After all, they aren't created with this knowledge, and they can't use a service if they can't find it.

It's the chicken-and-egg problem — a client needs to know the object reference of the Naming Service in order to get the object reference of the Naming Service. What's a client to do? Another handy-dandy ORB Interface operation comes into play here — the `resolve_initial_references()` operation.

The resolve_initial_references() operation

The ORB Interface knows of several key server objects by name. The `resolve_initial_references()` operation provides object references to these servers. This operation is intended to help clients find the object references they need to get started.

One of these references is the Naming Service. As soon as a client gains access to the Naming Service for the first time, it can call that service's methods in order to locate other servers that have registered with the service.

Turning Method Calls into Requests

When a client receives an object reference, it packages the reference along with the method's name, its parameters, a nice bouquet of flowers, and the type of the return value. This package is then transformed into a language-independent request that the ORB sends. You can consider the transformation of a method call into a request as being done by elves. You don't need to know how it's done because CORBA takes care of all the details for you. If you really must know, see "Making requests out of method calls."

When the ORB receives a request, it is responsible for doing the following four things:

1. Finding the server for the request
2. Preparing the server to receive the request
3. Communicating the data making up the request
4. Delivering the return reply

Making requests out of method calls

You know that ORBs handle language-independent requests and that clients make method calls in a particular target language. But how do the twain meet? (Golly, we always feel like William Shakespeare when we use words like *twain*.)

The steps involved in transforming a language-specific method call into a request are as follows:

1. **The client obtains an object reference for the server.**

2. **The client packages this reference along with the method's name, its parameters, and the type of return value.**

3. **The client executes the server's method by calling the corresponding method in the client stub.**

4. **Inside the client stub, the call is turned into a request.**

5. **Because ORBs deal in requests, an ORB Interface operation is called to pass the newly created request to the ORB.**

Points to know about the above statements include the following:

✔ **The object reference is obtained by using one of the approaches described in the "Getting the Handle on Objects" section.**

✔ **When a client calls a server's method, it actually makes a call into the client stub for that server.** The client stub was automatically generated when the server's IDL definition was compiled. This stub is generated in the target language of the client.

✔ **The call is made as if it were a local method call.**

✔ **The way in which the method call turns into a language-independent request in the client stub (Step 4) can only be performed on nights with full moons.**

Figure 3-1 shows the steps involved after a client's method call has been transformed into a request that the ORB can send.

All these steps are done transparently. As a developer, you always treat a method call as if it were a local call — although the actual server may be located on an itty-bitty machine in the basement of a candy store owned by a group of computer zealots, who need the candy to stay awake all night so they can play computer games on the Web.

Where oh where can my little server be?

You can consider this step to be a lot of hand-waving and hand-shaking. What's important is that CORBA deals with the details, and you don't.

So you really want to know what happens, do you? What happens depends a bit on the ORB implementation, but the general rule is that the ORB uses the information in the object reference to locate the server object's computer on the network. Additionally, it determines the specific port number that the server object is accepting connections on. Basically, the ORB figures out everything it needs to know in order to establish a low-level network communications channel (a *socket,* if your ORB is using TCP/IP), based on the information in the object reference.

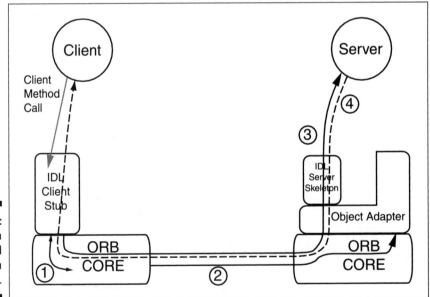

Figure 3-1:
Sending a
request and
receiving a
reply.

On your mark, get set, . . .

Next, the ORB sends a message to the server's Object Adapter via the Internet Inter-ORB Protocol (IIOP). This part is Step 2 of Figure 3-1.

An *Object Adapter* provides the means by which a server accesses ORB operations. It's also the part of CORBA that defines how a server is activated so that it can be used. Chapter 11 discusses Object Adapters.

The message that is sent from the client's ORB to the server's Object Adapter is "Okay, get ready to receive a request." It is intended to either start up (activate) the server or to ensure that the server is already up and prepared to receive the call.

The actual steps that occur to start up the server depend on the activation policy for the server.

An *activation policy* is simply the set of conditions under which a server is started so that it can begin to receive method calls.

CORBA has defined the following activation policies by which servers are activated for use by clients:

- ✔ Shared server
- ✔ Unshared server
- ✔ Server-per-method
- ✔ Persistent server

Communication and the IIOP

Message communication within and between ORBs is done via the Internet Inter-ORB Protocol (IIOP). The IIOP provides a standard mechanism by which message communication occurs within and between ORBs on TCP/IP-based networks. Because IIOP is standard and all ORBs use it, interoperability is achieved.

You can tell when two ORBs are interoperating because they each give a small sigh of relief when they find they can speak the same language!

Whenever we talk about messages and data being sent between ORBs, we are talking about using the IIOP.

Shared server

In the shared server policy, multiple objects reside in one server application. It's your basic college dorm room model. The first time a request is made on any object in the server, the Object Adapter activates the server — like when a pizza is delivered to that dorm room and everyone takes a slice.

Unshared server

In the unshared server approach, each server application has only one object — like a fraternity house where everyone has his own room. A new server is activated the first time a request is made and whenever a request is made of an object that is not yet active.

Nobody shares anything here. Everyone gets his own pizza.

Server-per-method

In the server-per-method policy, a new server application is activated each time a request is made. This approach is like sharing a room with someone who has multiple personalities. Several servers can be active for the same object or the same method. After the request is complete, the server automatically deactivates.

With this policy, you need multiple pizzas to satisfy one person.

Persistent server

The persistent server approach uses an external agent like a scheduler (or even a manual process) to activate servers. Something outside the Object Adapter activates the server application, so CORBA assumes that the server application is always active. The Object Adapter treats all communications to objects as if they were using the shared server policy.

This approach is like a commune. People in the commune believe that their pizza has always existed (in some form), so they never need to order it.

Go!

As soon as the ORB receives an "okay" message from the server's Object Adapter (this step is not shown in Figure 3-1), things get very busy.

1. **The client's ORB takes all the necessary information in the request, packages it nicely, and passes a magic wand over it.**

   In CORBA terms, this process is called *marshaling*.

2. **The client's ORB sends the data to the server's ORB, through its Object Adapter, and to its server skeleton.**

3. **The server skeleton turns the data into a target language-specific method call.**

4. **The server skeleton performs the call on the server implementation.**

✔ **Marshaling** is just a fancy way to say that the ORB converts a request or a reply into a form that can be transferred across a network. The procedure changes the data, which is in the format of the local machine, into platform-independent data. A client existing on a Macintosh machine, for example, can invoke methods on a server located on a UNIX machine without getting its integers scrambled.

✔ **Unmarshaling** means changing the data that passed across the network back into a form that the local machine understands.

RSVP

The last step in Figure 3-1 is the delivery and receipt of the return reply from the method call. After all, making method calls all day is pointless when you don't get anything in response.

Delivering the return reply involves marshaling the return value or values and then sending them across the low-level network connection, back to the client ORB and, ultimately, to the client stub.

The reply backtracks

1. Through the server skeleton

2. Through the server's ORB

3. Across the network via IIOP

4. To the client's ORB

5. Through the client stub

6. Back to the client itself

That's all there is to a method call. These things happen behind the scenes. You don't need to worry about the details.

Instead, you can use CORBA to make clients and servers who have radically different backgrounds and social positions talk with each other — without conflict.

Pass Me That Value

When passing information,

> ✔ **Operation parameters and return values are always passed by value.**
>
> ✔ **Server objects are always passed by reference.**

Feeling Independent

CORBA provides both language independence and platform independence. CORBA-compliant applications run on many different kinds of machines, but they can easily interoperate.

Language independence

CORBA is language-independent because

> ✔ It uses the Interface Definition Language (IDL) fixed-size data types.
>
> ✔ It uses IDL to describe interfaces (objects).

Platform independence

How does CORBA let a client on one platform (combining with hardware and OS) communicate with a server on a different platform?

> ✔ Before sending any local-format data across a network, the ORB marshals the data into a general form.
>
> ✔ The ORBs talk by using the Internet Inter-ORB Protocol (IIOP).
>
> ✔ After receiving data the ORB unmarshals it into the local platform format.

Marshaling isolates the ORB from the whims of network machines.

When the data for a request from a client is marshaled, that data is rearranged into the CORBA-specified form. When it reaches the destination machine, the process (now called unmarshaling) is reversed. What starts out as a long on the client machine is still a long on the server machine.

Every ORB that's CORBA-compliant has to be able to "talk" IIOP. Because all ORBs speak the same protocol for communicating requests and replies, an ORB on one platform can talk to an ORB on a different platform.

Chapter 4

Describing Objects with IDL

· ·

In This Chapter

▶ Going from an IDEA to IDL

▶ Sweating the details: case sensitivity, syntax, and comments

▶ Taking a closer look at the IDL elements

· ·

*I*DL is one of those three-letter acronyms that seem to pop up like mushrooms on a damp fall day in Silicon Valley. The acronym stands for Interface Definition Language. That sounds pretty complex, but in fact, it's very straightforward. Because CORBA is not tied to any specific programming language, operating system, or hardware platform, it needs its very own way of specifying objects. IDL is the CORBA way to do just that.

In this chapter we walk you from an idea to an actual working CORBA application. It's not as bad as it sounds because the application has a single object. First, we explain a bit about IDL. Then we go through the example. Finally, we discuss the elements of IDL that you use to create all your CORBA applications.

IDL

The IDL serves two important purposes in CORBA:

> ✔ **You use IDL to define the objects and modules that make up applications.** IDL creates definitions in a platform- and language-neutral way. You can read more about how IDL defines objects in Chapter 1.

> ✔ **IDL creates the server skeletons and client stubs that are automatically generated when an IDL file is compiled.** You use the stubs and skeletons to implement servers in a target language of your choice. An IDL client stub is a piece of code that allows a client to invoke a server's services. You use an IDL server skeleton to implement a server's services.

So that you can get a grip on how IDL is used, we're going to take you through the process of going from a rough idea for an object to its legal IDL definition. Before we start, we need to establish the house rules.

CORBA is available on a wide range of operating systems, and you can use just about any development tool to write your code. That's wonderful for you, but such variety makes it hard for us to describe simple things like creating a text file with IDL in it or compiling the text file with an IDL compiler. So keep the following points in mind when we tell you to do something:

✔ We use Microsoft Windows NT 4.0, Microsoft Visual C++ 5.0 Professional, and Orbix from IONA Technologies, PLC for Windows NT when working the examples.

✔ We use general terms when talking about filenames, editors, and other things that may be different for you, depending on your operating system and development tools.

✔ If you're using different tools, the names and quantities of files may be different.

✔ We use filenames that make sense to the application. If you prefer to use different names, go right ahead.

✔ If the name we use isn't legal for your operating environment, then by all means use a different name that works correctly.

✔ Check your environment's documentation if you have any questions.

From IDEA to IDL

When you make a new server or application for CORBA, you always start by using IDL to describe its interface. Because IDL is an object-oriented language, this process is very similar to writing a class definition in C++ or Java.

Before you can write the IDL, you need to know

✔ What the objects are.

✔ What each object is named.

✔ When the boss wants the IDL finished.

✔ What data each object deals with.

✔ What each object is supposed to do.

In this section, we show you a simple way to get from an idea to IDL. You can use our way, or you can use your favorite formal approach.

Our creative juices flowed, and we came up with the Random object. We are going to randomly create objects! No, not really. Our project is much more pedestrian than that. We are going to create an object that returns a random number.

When we give the project some thought, we realize that we need some way to seed the object so that it always produces the same sequence of random numbers when given the same seed number. We're not sure why this is a good idea, but those folks doing computer modeling seem to like it.

Of course, along the way we determine the objects and their names, operations, attributes, and return values.

The steps we take in order to get from a rough idea to IDL are as follows:

1. For each object, use pseudo-code to name the object and to list its attributes and operations.

2. Refine the pseudo-code by using the real IDL elements such as the keyword interface and curly brackets.

3. For each operation, decide the types of the return values and the types of the parameters, if this has not already been done. Use IDL to define these values and parameters. This turns the remaining pseudo-code for the operations into real IDL.

4. Add comments concerning such things as the object's behavior.

For now don't worry about such terms as pseudo-code and attributes. We explain them as we go along. As a matter of fact, our first step makes clear what pseudo-code is.

We begin by opening a new text file in our favorite editor. We name the file MYSTEP1.IDL. Now we're ready to describe an object in IDL.

When we say stuff like "create a file" and "enter this," you don't really have to do those things to follow along. If you want to save all that typing, you can simply copy the file from the CD-ROM and open it in your editor. The MYSTEP1.IDL file is in the Examples/Chapter4 directory of the CD-ROM.

In the text file, we enter the following:

```
Random number object
   Seed random number
   Get random number
```

We've just written the beginnings of the IDL for this object! This type of intuitive half-code is often called *pseudo-code*. It's a nice way to get started when you don't have all the details of a problem or its complete solution.

The idea is to write something down, just so you can get past that blank-screen stage of programming. In this case, we wrote down the three things we know so far.

The next step is to refine the pseudo-code a bit so that it looks more like IDL. We do this by using the real IDL elements. We talk all about these elements in the remainder of this chapter. For now, just follow along, and we discuss each change as we go.

Returning to the text file, we begin changing the pseudo-code into IDL. We start with the object's interface definition itself.

We change the text in our file to the following:

```
interface RandomNumber
{
    Seed random number
    Get random number
};
```

We did the following:

> ✔ Added the keyword `interface`. The keyword `interface` at the beginning of a line indicates to the IDL compiler that what follows is the definition of an object's interface.

> ✔ Removed the pseudo-code word *object* and combined two words, Random and Number, to create a name for this object.

> ✔ Played five rounds of our favorite computer game.

> ✔ Added curly braces and an ending semicolon.

We combined the two words *Random* and *Number* for the object name in order to capture the important information about this object in its name. You can use nonsense names instead, but then six months down the road, you'll be stuck trying to figure out what the `WhizBang` object does.

The naming seems easy enough to understand, but what about the curly braces and the ending semicolon? These items relate to the syntax that IDL expects. In other words, IDL has rules concerning how things are put together. In this case, the curly braces aid the compiler in knowing the beginning and ending of the object's interface. The semicolon signals the end of the definition.

IDL also has some additional rules about capitalization, commenting, and keywords. Before we can complete this definition in IDL, we need to spend a bit of time explaining some of these nitpicky details.

Boring but Important Details

IDL is a programming language of sorts, and it ends up compiled as part of the long trip from a neat idea to a working CORBA program. Because it does get compiled at some point, and because compilers remain far less bright than the average dog, a few rules are in effect that make life for the IDL compiler simpler and life for you just a tad harder.

Case sensitivity training

You can use capital letters and lowercase letters for the names of interfaces (object names), user-defined data types, exceptions, operation names, parameters, and so on. However, you must be consistent about the use of capitalization throughout your definitions and declarations. If you declare a data type called MyType, for example, you must always refer to it as MyType and not mytype or myTYPE. That's because IDL is case-sensitive. *Case-sensitive* doesn't mean that your code develops a rash when upper- and lowercase letters are mixed, but that the use of capital and lowercase letters is significant in IDL.

We use these capitalization rules:

  ✔ Name things in IDL by using English words run together.

  ✔ Use no more than three words.

  ✔ Capitalize the first letter of every word.

  ✔ Never use a state capital as an object name.

For example, an operation that adds a new stock to a portfolio could be named AddStock(). As with all our other rules, these aren't cast in stone. You can break them if you feel really strongly about it. Some people like to start object names with a capital letter and operation names with a lowercase letter. There's just no accounting for taste.

Although IDL is case-sensitive, you can't do something really crazy like use two names that differ only in their case to mean two different things. For example, if you try to define two operations as MyFunOperation() and myFUNoperation(), you get an error when compiling. You must use unique names, not names that differ only in case.

IDL keywords

Keywords are certain words that have special meaning to IDL. When defining interfaces, you must not use keywords as names of objects, application, operations, and so on. These are the IDL keywords:

any	attribute	boolean	case	char	const
context	default	double	enum	exception	FALSE
fixed	float	in	inout	interface	long
module	Object	octet	oneway	out	raises
readonly	sequence	short	string	struct	switch
TRUE	typedef	unsigned	union	void	wchar
wstring					

The use of capital and lowercase letters is significant in IDL, so you need to stick with lowercase when you use one of these keywords.

Syntax: Brace yourself for semicolons

As you may expect, a set of rules govern actually combining the parts that make up an IDL definition. These rules are called the IDL *syntax.*

The syntax of IDL is straightforward. An IDL file consists of a series of declarations and definitions, each of which has a beginning and an end. You indicate the beginning of a declaration or definition with one of the IDL keywords.

Because the IDL compiler isn't very smart, it likes to have a little help finding the end. A semicolon indicates the end of a declaration or definition. This convention is useful because it enables you to split up a very long declaration or definition across several lines.

If you forget a semicolon, you get a syntax error when you compile the IDL file.

Some data types, interfaces, and modules can contain a variable number of items. To help the IDL compiler along, these items are enclosed in curly braces ({ }). In addition, just to be sure that the IDL compiler knows what's going on, each closing brace (}) also has a semicolon after it. You'd think the compiler could tell that the definition was over just by the curly brace, but you'd be wrong. A definition just isn't over until the compiler sees that semicolon.

Our example uses a single IDL keyword (interface), and it meets the syntax requirements for IDL. The next step is to take those two sentences inside the curly braces and make them into operations.

We change the text of our file to

```
interface RandomNumber
{
  long SeedRandomNumber(in long seed);
  long GetRandomNumber();
};
```

We did the following:

✔ Combined three words — Seed, Random, and Number — to create a name for the first operation

✔ Added the keyword `long` and the weird stuff after the `SeedRandomNumber`

✔ Liked those first two changes so much that we did them again for `GetRandomNumber`

Now we have a legal definition of an object (er, interface). We had to make some decisions when we converted the pseudo-code for the operations into actual operations. We had to decide the types of the return values and the types of the parameters.

You can't really tell what this object is doing based solely on the IDL, can you? Well, you can either agree to personally explain this object to every programmer who uses it from now on, or you can add comments to your IDL that explain what the object does.

Your comments are welcome

You can never go wrong with comments in CORBA. Comments are one of the single most important things you can do to make your CORBA objects usable. Why? Because you use IDL to define the interfaces for objects. These objects, in turn, are likely to be used by other objects, potentially objects that are written by other programmers.

Although IDL is relatively easy to read, it's sure not English. Chances are, you have some important information in your head while you're writing the IDL for an object. You know what we mean. Little things like

✔ Services provided

✔ Input values

✔ Related objects

Information like this is hard to get just from the IDL, so you can leave comments in the file to record this stuff.

IDL features the same types of comments as C++ and Java do:

- ✔ **Block comments** begin with /* and continue even across multiple lines until reaching */. These comments don't *nest*. This doesn't mean that they don't like to hang around the house like the rest of us, but rather that you can't have a comment block inside of another comment block.

- ✔ **Line comments** are preceded by //, which indicates that everything from the // to the end of the line is a comment.

- ✔ **Constant Comment** doesn't do much for explaining your code, but a cup of it makes a great pick-me-up.

Use block comments at the top of every IDL file to describe its contents. Also use them before every module and object interface to give a description of what the module or object's main purpose is in life. Use line comments to explain what specific definitions do, such as each of the operations of an object.

We're going to add some comments to the example. We change the file so that it looks like this:

```
/*
    A random number generator object.
    This object provides a pseudo-random number based
    on a seed value. If it is seeded with the same
    value it repeats the same sequence of numbers.
*/

interface RandomNumber
{
    // return old seed, set new seed
    long SeedRandomNumber(in long seed);
    // return next pseudo-random number
    long GetRandomNumber();
};
```

Here we see that SeedRandomNumber() actually returns the old seed value when it is called to change to a new seed. Without a comment, that little gem of information is not at all obvious from the IDL.

We just completed a short trip from IDEA to IDL, and you went along for the ride! Along the way, we performed what technical folks call a *stepwise refinement* of an idea into a full IDL specification of an interface — which means that we started with a rough idea, and we worked to refine it one step at a time.

IDL Elements

Defining on object's interface is one of the primary uses of IDL. What you may be asking yourself is, "What exactly is an interface?" We're glad you asked. Simply stated, an interface is an element of IDL.

We don't mean elements like earth, wind, fire, and water. *Elements* in this case are just the building blocks that you can combine into a complete interface definition.

IDL consists of four categories of elements. The elements, from least-complicated to most-complicated, are described in the following list:

- ✔ **Data type:** A data type is a description of the accepted values and format of data. Data types are used to describe an object's attributes, its exceptions, and the parameters and return values for its operations.

- ✔ **Operation:** An operation is an action that an object performs. In other words, it is a service that clients can invoke. An IDL operation is similar to a member function in C++ or a method in Java. Operations have zero or more parameters and can return values. The definition of these parameters and return values in IDL is called an operation's *signature*. A signature can also declare one or more exceptions. *Exceptions* indicate that the operation did not perform successfully.

- ✔ **Interface:** An interface declares an object's data as well as its operations. It's like a class definition in C++ and Java without the implementation part. It provides the object's name, its attributes, and the operations that it supports.

- ✔ **Module:** A module is a group of interfaces. A module provides a *name space* for a set of interfaces. Having more than one interface enclosed in a module means that you can collectively refer to those interfaces. Within a module, all non-nested interfaces, exceptions, data types, and constant names must be unique. However, you can use the same name for an interface in two different modules.

Like all good works of engineering, IDL starts from a strong base of elementary building blocks — the data types. These data types are then used to help define operations. Operations can then be grouped to create interfaces. Multiple interfaces can also be grouped to create modules.

A sample IDL definition using the four major elements is shown in Figure 4-1.

Module   Interface

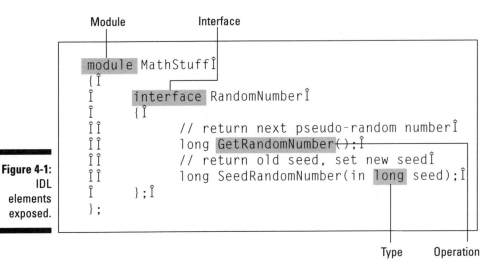

```
module MathStuffÎ
{Î
Î        interface RandomNumberÎ
Î          {Î
ÎÎ              // return next pseudo-random numberÎ
ÎÎ              long GetRandomNumber();Î
ÎÎ              // return old seed, set new seedÎ
ÎÎ              long SeedRandomNumber(in long seed);Î
Î          };Î
};
```

Figure 4-1:
IDL
elements
exposed.

Type   Operation

Are you my data type?

Like C++, IDL has three categories of data types, each of which has more aliases than a thief in a pulp mystery novel. These categories are

- ✔ Primitive (alias basic).
- ✔ Constructed (alias user-defined).
- ✔ Container (alias template).

IDL data types are based on the types in C++. If you know C++ data types, then you know most of what you need to know about IDL.

Very primitive types

Primitive types lack conversational skills and enjoy fire-gazing after a long day's hunt in the wild. This information doesn't help you understand the intricacies of IDL, but it sure explains a lot about their lack of dates on Saturday nights.

Primitive data types can be combined to create constructed types that are more complex. They can also be used in container types. IDL's primitive types can be broken down into *integer, floating point,* and *other* categories:

- ✔ Integer
    - `short` **and** `unsigned short`
    - `long` **and** `unsigned long`
    - `long long` **and** `unsigned long long`

✔ Floating point

- `float`
- `double`
- `long double`

✔ Other

- `char` **and** `wchar`
- `boolean`
- `octet`
- `void`

Integer

Although it would seem a nice thing to do, IDL doesn't define a plain integer type. Instead, it provides a cornucopia of six types.

Hopefully, having so many types ensures that you can specify everything exactly as you need to. Overkill? Maybe, and then again, maybe not. Consider that IDL is trying to be an "everything for everybody" language, so it has to provide ways to define things a bit more precisely than a single stand-alone language does.

The six primitive integer types are signed and have different ranges of values. Table 4-2 shows these values:

Table 4-2	Primitive Integer Types
Type	*Size*
`short`	16 bits signed
`unsigned short`	16 bits unsigned
`long`	32 bits signed
`unsigned long`	32 bits unsigned
`long long`	64 bits signed
`unsigned long long`	64 bits unsigned

The type of integer you choose depends on the range of values that you expect an attribute, parameter, or return value to be. If you choose a type that is too small, then the value is truncated. Truncating values causes major problems that you don't want to deal with. On the flip side, if you choose a type that is way too big, then you're wasting precious memory and sending and receiving more data than you need. Wasting memory can also cause major problems that you don't want to deal with.

Floating point

The floating point type is used to represent real numbers. IDL provides two floating point types:

- The float type is comparable to the C++ and Java float type. It represents the IEEE (Institute of Electrical and Electronics Engineers) single-precision (32 bits) floating-point value.

- The double type corresponds to the C++ and Java double type. It represents the IEEE double-precision (64 bits) floating-point value.

- The long double type represents an IEEE extended double-precision floating-point value. Try saying that three times fast! The long double has an exponent of at least 15 bits and a signed fraction of at least 64 bits. It's big. Use long doubles to represent the national debt — or your bank account, if you're Bill Gates.

A literal is a letter, number, or symbol that represents a particular constant or quantity. A *floating-point literal* consists of an integer part, a decimal part, a fraction part, the letter e or E, and an optionally signed integer exponent. Recall that an integer exponent is the power to which the floating-point literal is to be raised.

876.54e and .987E10 are typical floating point values in IDL files.

Char and Wchar

The char type is an 8-bit quantity that stores a single character value. As you may expect, it maps directly to the char type in C++ and Java.

A *character literal* is one or more characters enclosed in single quotes, such as 'c'.

The wchar (or *wide character*) type has an implementation-dependent width that is likely to be 16 bits. However, it is important that you check with your ORB documentation to verify the size of wchar in your implementation. For the most part, you probably won't use wchar. It is primarily useful when representing alphabets that are longer than the English 26 characters. If you plan to represent something in Cantonese or if you're developing software for international markets, however, wchar is just the data type you need.

Many programmers use the char type to hold 8-bit binary values. This practice isn't a good idea with CORBA, because the char type can be converted in unexpected ways when the client and the server are running on different hardware platforms. You should use octet for 8-bit values, not char.

Boolean

Boolean is a data type that can have only one of two values: TRUE or FALSE.

The Boolean data type is named after George Boole (1815-1864). He invented the system of logic that expresses values as TRUE and FALSE. A couple of hundred years later, someone else thought that you could do other interesting things with just two values (0 and 1), and the digital computer was born. All because of this guy named Boole. He at least deserves a data type named after him.

Octet

When data is transmitted across a distributed system, some kind of conversion usually takes place. The octet type is an 8-bit quantity that is guaranteed not to undergo any kind of conversion during communication.

Use octet for 8-bit values, not char. A value of type octet is not converted in any way when it is transmitted between a client and a server who are running on different hardware platforms.

Void

The void type in IDL is the same as the void type in C++ and Java. This data type is used when an operation doesn't return a value. The void type is like when you void a check — after that the check has no value either!

Types you construct yourself

If you were stuck with just the primitive data types, not only would you reconsider your current social circle, but you would also not get very far in creating applications worth using. You need some ways to create types that are more application-specific. IDL provides three data types to help you:

- ✔ Enumerated
- ✔ Structure
- ✔ Union

Enumerated

The enum (enumerated) type provides a way to create a user-defined type that holds a set of predefined values. Here's an example:

```
enum AfternoonActivities {
    Nap,
    ReadPaper,
    Exercise,
    VisitWithFriends
};
```

You need to know three things about IDL's version of the enum type:

- ✔ **If you know the enum type in C++, you know this type.**

- ✔ **Although the identifiers comprise an ordered list with ordinal values, IDL doesn't use the ordinal numbering.** This fact means that you shouldn't use the ordinal values for comparisons. Besides, even if IDL did pay attention to the ordinal values, attempting to use ordinal numbering across languages wouldn't work.

  The *ordinal value,* in case you're wondering, is the actual position (the first being 0 or maybe 1, the second being the next number, and so on) of an identifier in the list.

- ✔ **Unlike C++, enum defines the type name for you.** For example, you can use AfternoonActivities as a type name anytime after you define it by using the enum definition.

Structure

The struct (structure) type provides a way to create a user-defined type that holds a set of values of differing types. Here's an example:

```
struct RingDescription {
    short NumberOfStones;
    string KindOfStones;
    long KaratOfDiamond;
};
```

Unlike in C++, struct defines the type name for you, so you can use the struct name anytime after it defining it. For example, you can use RingDescription as a type name.

Union

The union type is the duck-billed platypus of IDL. It's a cross between IDL's struct type, a C union type, and a Pascal variant record:

- ✔ It's like an IDL struct type in that it provides a way to create a user-defined type that holds a set of values of differing types.

- ✔ It's like a C union type in that it can hold, at most, only one of its values at a time. That's because the data values are conceptually overlaid in the storage allocated to the union.

- ✔ It borrows part of the syntax of Pascal's variant record, specifically the use of the word case.

- ✔ It has a big flat tail and webbed feet.

Quite the conglomeration, eh? We combine everything outlined above, except the tail and webbed feet, into a single example of a union type in IDL:

```
union AnyNumber switch (long)
{
    case 1: long i;
    case 2: float f;
    case 3:
    default: string s;
};
```

In this case (get it?), the user-defined data type is `AnyNumber`.

To use this data type, you store a `long` into `AnyNumber.i`, or a `float` into `AnyNumber.f`, or a `string` into `AnyNumber.s`.

Still confused? Don't worry. Unions are hardly ever used. Instead, the much more popular concepts of objects, inheritance, and polymorphism have made unions a bit unfashionable and unfathomable these days. Unions were really important when memory (both RAM and disk) was very expensive, and saving a few bytes per object was worth the trouble. Now, that's not the case.

Unlike in C++, `union` defines the type name for you. For example, you can use `AnyNumber` as a type name anytime after you have defined it.

Is the container half full?

All modern programming languages provide a means by which to group multiple values of a similar type. IDL is no exception. It has the following container (sometimes known as *template*) types:

- ✔ Array
- ✔ Sequence
- ✔ String
- ✔ Wstring
- ✔ Fixed

Array

We wish that an IDL array was "a drop of golden sun," but instead it's just your usual data type. Specifically, an array stores a known length of values, all of which have the same type. Arrays are multidimensional with explicit sizes for each dimension.

For example, the following declaration is of an array with five dimensions:

```
long MyWeirdArray [5] [3] [4] [2] [3];
```

The first dimension has five elements. Each of these elements is an array of three elements (representing the second dimension), and each of these elements is an array of four elements, and so on.

We don't know about you, but thinking past three dimensions causes us to crave *The Twilight Zone* reruns, so we don't do it much.

A few things to know about arrays:

- ✔ If you know the array type in C++, you know this type.
- ✔ Arrays can hold elements of any IDL data type, including user-defined types.
- ✔ If you know a guy named Ray, you can find out whether he's multi-dimensional — unless he's an invisible Ray.

Sequence

The sequence type is a dynamically sizable array of one dimension. You use the sequence type, rather than the array type, when you want to be able to change the size of the array as needed.

Like an array, a sequence can hold elements of any IDL data type, including user-defined types.

When declaring a sequence, you can provide a maximum length. Declaring a maximum length is called *bounding*. If you don't provide a maximum length, the sequence is said to be *unbounded,* which means you can expand (or contract) it as needed. A bounded sequence is similar to an array because it has a fixed maximum size. Unlike an array, a bounded sequence may be smaller than the maximum size.

String

The string type stores a known number of 8-bit character values, except the NULL character. When declaring a string, you must include the maximum size that the string can be. For example, the following declaration represents a string that can be, at most, 11 characters long:

```
string[11];
```

A *string literal* is a sequence of characters enclosed by double quotes, such as "this is a string". A string literal can't contain the character '\0' because that's the NULL character.

Neither C nor C++ has the equivalent of a string type. In C, a string is represented by using the array type with elements of the type char. In C++, a string is a class. Of course, you can still use char * or char arrays in C++.

WString

The wstring (or *wide string*) type is akin to the string data type except that its elements are of type wchar instead of char. The string in this case is terminated by a wide character NULL.

Fixed

The fixed type represents a fixed-point decimal number that holds up to 31 significant digits. When declaring data to be of this type, you include the total number of digits and the number of digits after the decimal point.

For example, the following declares MyNumber to be a fixed decimal number with a total of five digits, two of which come after the decimal point:

```
fixed MyNumber<5,2>; // An example of this is: 123.45
```

When using fixed-point literals, the leading and trailing zeros are factored out — so 011.430 is considered to be 11.43 with a fixed < 4,2> type.

Any other types?

The any type is the IDL equivalent of the TV show *The X-Files*. The truth is out there . . . and it's your job to find out what it is.

You use the any type when the type of a parameter or return value isn't known. It means that any IDL type is valid. Here's an example:

```
void DisplayObject (in any ObjectToShow);
```

In this case, the DisplayObject() operation accepts a parameter called ObjectToShow. ObjectToShow can be any valid IDL type. It makes sense, then, that the operation's job is to find out the actual type so that the parameter can be dealt with properly.

I take exception to that

We would all like to believe that everything will go well when our programs run — especially when the boss is watching. Unfortunately, it is the nature of the beast that programs have problems, so IDL includes an error-handling capability. The exception data type is an integral part of this process.

Does anybody really know what typecode it is?

An IDL pseudo-type called *typecode* is often used in conjunction with the any type. But typecode isn't really an IDL type. You never use it with IDL. Instead, you use it when you implement an operation that takes a parameter of the any type. Chapter 14 discusses the any and typecode types.

When an operation's input parameter is of type any and that operation is called during execution, some way of identifying the type of parameter is necessary. Well, like a barroom hustler in the disco era, you can spend the day asking, "Hey, baby, what type are you?" or you can use typecode.

CORBA assigns a unique typecode to every data type (both standard and user-defined). This information can then be used at run-time to determine the type of an any parameter.

When something goes amiss during the execution of an operation (or *method*), the method takes three actions:

1. Stops what it is doing

2. Raises an exception

3. Returns to the calling object

When the calling object catches the exception, it can either handle it or pass it along to another object and take the rest of the day off as "personal time."

Exceptions come in two flavors:

- CORBA standard exceptions
- User-defined exceptions

Standard exceptions are provided by CORBA and are automatically raised when an error occurs so you don't have to specify each standard exception every time you create an operation. Programmers usually need to release aggression, so they call the act of raising an exception *throwing an exception*. Can't you just see that poor exception plastered to the cubicle wall?

You may want to throw a standard CORBA exception from within your own implementations. Doing so is both legal and encouraged. When was the last time you heard that throwing something was encouraged?

Your ORB documentation should include a complete list of standard CORBA exceptions — all 29 of them. If you can't find them in your documentation, a text file on the CD-ROM named Exceptions.txt lists their names and meanings.

How the whole exception-handling gizmo works

Let's take a look at how exception handling works so that you can see it in action.

Say that you have a server object for an engine control system called Engine. One of its services is the ability to supply the current revolutions per minute (rpm) for the engine. This operation is called Rpm( ). If a problem occurs during the execution of this method, a user-defined exception called EngineError is raised. The server interface and exception is declared in IDL and compiled. The compilation produces a client stub (an .h file) that holds tons of information, including stuff about the exception.

At some point during the execution of a client, the Rpm( ) method is called. When the target language is C++ or Java, calling the Rpm( ) method is done inside a try statement so that the client can handle the exception.

Unfortunately, at the time of the call, the engine was off, so the server object raises the EngineError exception.

This exception is returned to the client. The client knows about this user-defined exception because the .h file containing the client stub is included in the implementation file of the client. The exception is handled by the code that implements the client's behavior.

User-defined exceptions are just what they sound like. They are exceptions that you think your methods will throw when they are running. You get to make them up yourself.

The exception type can contain values of differing types. It looks and acts a lot like a struct type. An example follows:

```
exception FileError {
   short ErrorCode;
   string FileName;
};
```

Because CORBA already provides such a large selection of exceptions, you can probably get away with using standard exceptions in many cases instead of creating your own. Once again, CORBA is making your life easier.

Things that look like C

Think about some things that look like C. Here are some of our favorites:

- ✔ A really big ear
- ✔ Your kid's new nose ring

✔ The `typedef` declaration

✔ The ability to make forward declarations

We don't have much to say about the ear and nose thingies, but we probably should talk a bit about declarations.

Typedef

A `typedef` declaration in IDL is the same as the one in C. You use the `typedef` keyword to associate a name with a data type, making your code much easier to understand. Here's an example:

```
typedef string[2] PayCode;
```

This declaration means that instead of using `string[2]` in your code, you can now use the word `PayCode`. In effect, `PayCode` has become a synonym for `string[2]`.

The IDL `typedef` declaration provides a way to create your own user-defined data types. Creating user-defined types can also be done using the `enum`, `struct`, and `union` types.

Forward declarations

"Hey baby . . . want to go out tonight?"

"I bet you get winked at a lot."

"Even though we've only just met, can I have your phone number?"

These are forward declarations if we've ever heard them! Fortunately, IDL doesn't make such inappropriate advances to your sensibilities. Instead, *forward declarations* mean that IDL, like C and C++, allows an interface to be referenced before it has "officially" been declared.

A forward declaration informs the IDL compiler that the referenced interface will be defined later and to just keep its pants on and roll with the flow for now. For example, a forward declaration for an interface named `DefinedLater` is

```
interface DefinedLater;
```

This declaration appears anywhere in the IDL file before the name `DefinedLater` is used. Forward declarations often appear at the beginning of the IDL file.

Operations

An IDL operation is comparable to a member function in C++ or a method in Java. It's an action that an interface (an object in IDL) performs. Collectively, all the operations defined for an interface constitute that interface's behavior.

Operations are services that clients request. If you're familiar with methods or messages in object-oriented programming languages, you have the general gist of operations.

IDL is only a declarative language. For operations, this distinction means that

- ✔ The definition is done in IDL.

- ✔ Using an operation, calling an operation, and making a request of an operation are never done in IDL.

- ✔ The implementation of an operation is done in your chosen target language.

- ✔ You make requests and generally boss things around in the implementations of the server and clients that you write.

Defining an operation is straightforward. First you get a patient, then you get a scalpel . . . well, for those of you with weak stomachs, we won't continue.

The way to define an operation is through its signature — like the signature used in Java. The general form of a signature for an operation is as follows:

```
<ReturnType> <OperationName> (modifier0 type0 param0, ...,
modifierN typeN paramN)
[raises (exception0, ..., exceptionN)]
```

When declaring the return type and operation name, you don't include the angle brackets. Likewise, you don't actually include the square brackets for the "raises" part. Just to be tricky, the OMG does require you to use all the parentheses.

What's this thing with the square and angle brackets? It's based on something called *EBNF (Extended Backus-Naur Format) notation.* EBNF is just a way to express the syntax of a language. You can think of it as a means to create a template. In this case, we declared the form that an operation in IDL generally takes. You won't create any EBNF, but if you ever read the official CORBA specification, you'll become quite familiar with it.

In English, the general form of a signature includes the following items:

- ✔ <ReturnType>: Type of return value for the operation. If the operation returns nothing, then the void type is used.

- ✔ <OperationName>: The unique name of operation within an interface.

- ✔ (modifier0 type0 param0, ..., modifierN typeN paramN): Optional list of parameters, including their modifiers and data types. A modifier indicates the direction in which the information flows, with respect to the object performing the request. You use in, out, or inout. As you may expect, the data type denotes the type of data for the parameter.

- ✔ [raises (exception0, ..., exceptionN)]: Optional raises exception list that denotes which user-defined exceptions may be raised. An exception is an indication that an operation's execution was not performed successfully. The exceptions listed here are the user-defined exceptions that can be signaled to terminate a request for this operation. You don't have to list the CORBA standard exceptions here.

A signature looks something like this example:

```
void ProduceReport (in long NumberOfMonths,
    out long double TotalSales,
    inout string Status)
    raises (ReportError1, MonthSalesError);
```

This ProduceReport() operation doesn't return a value, so the void type is used. The operation takes in two parameters (NumberOfMonths and Status) and returns two parameters (TotalSales and Status). Notice that Status was both sent into the operation and sent out. Two user-defined exceptions are raised.

Interfaces

The primary thing you do with IDL is to describe interfaces. An interface is a user-defined data type that defines an object. Specifically, an interface describes the services provided by a CORBA object. Interfaces don't do any real work. The real work is done in your target language.

If you're familiar with any of the following, you know what an interface is:

- ✔ A class definition in object-oriented terms
- ✔ A class header file in C++ that contains a class definition
- ✔ A surface forming a common boundary between adjacent regions
- ✔ A Java interface type (except that IDL interfaces can contain attributes)

When dealing with interfaces in IDL, you can think of them as object references. Interfaces can be included in data structures, used as the type of parameters to be passed by operations, and used as the type of results returned from operations.

The syntax used to define an interface is as follows:

```
interface <interfaceName> :
       <Inherit0>,...<InheritN> {
  type0;...typeN;
  constant0;...constantN;
  attribute0;...attributeN;
  exception0;...exceptionN;
  operation0;...operationN;
};
```

 When declaring the interface name and inheritance names, you don't include the angle brackets.

An example is an object called BigBox. It inherits from the Box interface and defines two attributes and two operations:

```
interface BigBox : Box {
  attribute float HeightOfBox;
  attribute float WidthOfBox;
  string GetContents (in BoxNumber);
  long GetNumberOfItems (in BoxNumber);
};
```

The following parts make up an interface's definition:

interface	Keyword that starts the definition.
<interfaceName>	The name of the interface (that is, the object).
:<Inherit0>,...<InheritN>	Base interfaces. The colon must precede the list of base interfaces, if any are listed.
constant0;...constantN;	Zero or more constants for this interface.
type0;...typeN;	Zero or more data types.
attribute0;...attributeN;	Zero or more attributes.
exception0;...exceptionN;	Zero or more exceptions.
operation0;...operationN;	Zero or more operations.

Inheritance

In IDL, as in C++ and Java, your interface can inherit from one or more base interfaces. When an interface inherits from another interface, the interface from which it is derived is called a *base interface*.

Attributes

An *attribute* is a piece of data that can only be accessed through access or operations. These operations get and set the value of the attribute. The general syntax for the declaration of an attribute looks like this:

```
attribute <AttributeType> <AttributeName>;
```

Constants

Constants are like variables, except that they hold one unchanging value. The general syntax for the declaration of a constant is as follows:

```
const <ConstType> <ConstIdentifier> = <const_exp>;
```

If you understand constants in C++ and Java, you understand them in IDL.

We provide plenty of examples of interface definitions throughout the book and on the CD-ROM. Take a look at them — they won't bite, we promise.

Modules

A module is just a collection of interfaces that are somehow related. If objects relate in a cohesive way, you can indicate this relationship by using a module. Some reasons to group objects into modules include objects that

✔ Use each other's operations.

✔ Operate on related information.

✔ Are related by time.

Here's an example of a group of objects that define a payroll system:

```
module Payroll {
    typedef short PayID;
    interface Account {
    };
    interface AccountsPayable : Account {
    };
    interface AccountsReceivable : Account {
    };
};
```

Chapter 5

If Only We Had Some C++ Code

*O*ne of the nifty things about CORBA — on paper, at least — is that you can use it with many different programming languages. All this talk about COBOL client programs making use of Smalltalk server programs is very impressive, and in some outposts, people still use C, but most everyone who slings code for a living does so with C++ or Java.

Getting in a Bind

We're going to focus on C++ in this chapter, using the C++ binding for CORBA to write the interface implementations for the server objects. Remember that phrase — you'll want to use it at a cocktail party some day. We wrote a simple application in Chapter 1, and it wasn't so bad. In this chapter we create a more detailed system that draws on many of the features of the C++ language binding.

A *binding* is

✔ Something you discreetly try to fix — like a wedgie.

✔ Something that ties CORBA to a specific implementation language.

Bindings are the language mappings between IDL (Interface Definition Language) and target language constructs. For example, a `long` in IDL maps to (or is bound to) a `CORBA::Long` in C++. Without bindings, you can't do much with all your nice IDL code. CORBA supports several different language bindings.

We're not going to bore you with long tables showing how this or that IDL type maps to a C++ type. You can find that information in your ORB documentation. Instead, we're going to solve a meaty but not overly complex problem with CORBA and C++. Along the way, we encounter most of the keys that you need to know to solve your own problems.

The procedure for creating a CORBA application follows these general steps:

1. **Think about the application to be built and decide on a solution in terms of objects and their names, data, behavior, and distribution.**

2. **Use the CORBA Interface Definition Language (IDL) to describe the objects.**

3. **Compile the IDL file(s) to generate client stubs and server skeletons.**

4. **For each interface described in the IDL file, write a target-language implementation, usually consisting of a class definition (header file) and class implementation file.**

5. **Write, in your chosen target language, a main program that instantiates the implementation (server) objects.**

6. **Write, in your target language, the client application(s) that use these server objects.**

7. **Compile all source files, including stubs and skeletons and link the executable files.**

8. **Run the server application created in Step 5, and then run as many kinds of clients as you need, as many times as you need them.**

In this chapter, we cover Steps 1 through 4. We cover Steps 5 through 8 in Chapter 6.

Before we begin a down-and-dirty analysis of a problem and the design of the solution, you must understand what we mean by *clients, servers,* and *object references* and the ways in which these objects interact with a target language and CORBA.

Back in the good old days when you didn't have to worry about messy issues like distributed objects, you could design your applications using just C++ object method calls. Now, with distribution in mind, you need to think about how objects are located and what kind of functions they perform.

An *object* is an instance of a C++ class. When we say *class,* we're talking about the definition of an object (that is, a non-runable specification), not about it's social position. When we say *object,* we mean an instance of a class.

Any time a call goes out to a method in an object, the caller is the client and the callee is the server. In C++, these calls take two forms:

`someValue = serverObject->service();` is used when you have a reference to a server object, and `someValue = serverObject.service();` is used when you have an instance of a server object.

Is it real, or is it just a reference?

- ✔ **Reference:** An object reference means that you know where to find the object, but you don't actually have the object in hand. A reference is called a pointer in C++.

- ✔ **Instance:** An object instance is the proverbial bird in the hand. Not only do you know where to find the object, but you also have the whole object right there in some variable.

Whoever makes a method call is considered to be a client, and whoever processes the call is considered to be a server. In the preceding examples, the server is the object `serverObject`, and the client is the main program.

You're thinking, "This is all very interesting, but what does it mean?"

- ✔ If you're already using objects in C++, you're halfway to using CORBA.
- ✔ A server in the hand is worth two in the bush.
- ✔ Method calls are the key to object communication.
- ✔ The client is the consumer; the server is the producer.
- ✔ Have your people call our people, and we'll do lunch.

When writing CORBA applications, you need to think in terms of objects. To get from plain old C++ to CORBA, you just need to add a little distance (in both time and space — think *The Twilight Zone* here) between the client and the server. When you add that distance, some things have to change. That's just life. CORBA makes those changes as minimal as possible.

With CORBA, clients always use references to talk to server objects. References are things that look and act like pointers, but in fact they are little helper classes generated from the IDL. If you think about it, the concept of having an instance of a distributed object in a client application just doesn't work. Those objects are, by definition, not in your application — they are distributed somewhere else in the network. That's why you always use references. References keep client method calls looking very normal, like this one:

```
someValue = serverObject->service();
```

The call looks normal — except that `serverObject` is going to be a reference to a CORBA server object, instead of being a pointer. Other than that, the call works the same as it always did.

Here are some simple rules for deciding whether or not you have a server on your hands:

✓ If it performs actions for other objects, then it is a server.

✓ A client object that provides services has to be treated as if it were a server object. That's because clients that never act as servers are just application programs.

✓ If it wears a waiter's uniform, then it's probably a server.

✓ Objects that get called from many clients and want to hang out on the network are server objects.

We could use the term *object implementation* here to mean *server object*. That term is used throughout the CORBA specification as a more general term for *server*. *Server* is easier to read over many pages, though, so whenever you see *server* in this book, think *object implementation*.

Identifying Objects and Services

You use IDL to describe servers (and clients that are also servers), and then you implement them as C++ classes.

Normally, you follow a formal approach to identifying objects and their services. For now, however, we recommend that you think about the problem at hand and decide

✓ What the objects are.

✓ What each object is named.

✓ What data each object deals with.

✓ What behavior each object exhibits.

For example, say that you're hired to create a Portfolio Management System (PMS) for a brokerage firm. You meet with the folks at Giant Huge Funds (GHF), and they give you the list of requirements for the new system.

If you've ever done requirements work, you know that you actually drag the requirements out of the folks at GHF over several months, using exotic torture techniques, and the resulting list of requirements still isn't exactly right. But that's a different book.

Here are the requirements:

- ✔ GHF has multiple customers and needs to be able to add new ones as it grows its business.
- ✔ Each customer can have many stocks and can add new stocks to his or her portfolio.
- ✔ A customer can buy or sell units of a stock that he or she owns.
- ✔ Everything must run faster than Mercury conveying a message to Dionysus on a Saturday night.
- ✔ GHF wants to be able to limit its own employees to either adding customers or updating their stocks. (In other words, it wants to limit access to information in the system.)
- ✔ GHF wants its employees to be able to access the information from any machine on the network.
- ✔ Having spinning globes on the main window of all the client applications would be cool.
- ✔ Someday, all of this system may need to be accessible via the Web. (This statement is actually a teaser for you to read Chapter 9, where we talk about Java.)

Fortunately, CORBA is a perfect match for this kind of application. What else would you expect?

After our meeting with GHF, we have a GHH (Giant Huge Headache). The only thing that helps alleviate the pain is to get the job done. We begin by picking through the requirements to find our objects. After minutes of hard work, we come up with some objects. Our whiteboard looks like Figure 5-1.

The objects in Figure 5-1 — Customer and Stock — seem to address the requirements of GHF. All we need are some applications to do the tasks of adding customers and buying and selling stocks. (We talk about implementing client applications in Chapter 6.) We decide to create two client applications, each of which can do only those tasks allotted to one of the two different types of users at GHF. Employees can't use the Customer application, for example, to enter Buy and Sell orders.

This scenario is just an example. A real system would have many more requirements and be much more complex. If you're hoping to get a real commercial-quality Portfolio Management System (PMS) out of this chapter, you will be sorely disappointed. So just nod and wink along with us as we skip over obvious "real world" issues. Focus on what we're doing with CORBA. That's the important part, after all.

At this point, we're ready to move on to the second step — writing the IDL for the objects.

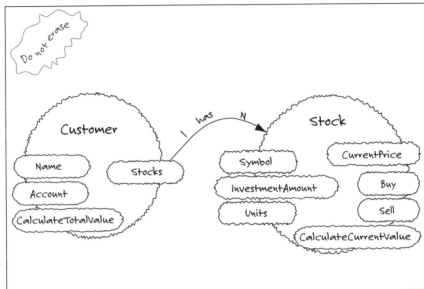

Figure 5-1:
Portfolio
Management
System
objects.

What about inheritance?

We're not going to kid you and tell you that implementing inheritance in CORBA is a breeze. However, figuring inheritance into the solution can be done, and in fact, we did it for this example. The first time we talked to the folks at GHF, they told us that their customers can have multiple assets. An asset is a stock, bond, certificate of deposit (CD), or mutual fund. Customers buy and sell units of the assets they hold. Units may be shares of stock or of a mutual fund, or (as in the case of CDs), they may be the entire asset. That simple expansion (from customers just having stocks to customers having assets that may be stocks, CDs, mutual funds, or stuff that GHF hasn't even thought of yet) cries out for a solution that uses inheritance.

It turns out that creating a solution that takes inheritance into account is very doable in CORBA, but it's not a simple topic and therefore not doable in this book. We already incorporated inheritance into the solution, so we include the full "multiple asset inheritance polymorphic monster portfolio" version, along with a very detailed README.TXT document, on the CD-ROM that accompanies this book. You can dive into that version after you understand everything we're doing in this chapter.

Describing Objects in IDL

When you write an IDL file, you can do a couple of things at the beginning that make the rest of the process easier. These include

- ✔ Using forward declarations for all interfaces in the file.
- ✔ Creating `typedef`s for complex type declarations.

The gory details of the IDL syntax are covered in Chapter 4. The gory source code of this example is contained on the CD-ROM in the `Examples\Chapter5` directory. The `Portfolio.idl` file contains the IDL for the objects. We look at it one section at a time.

We like making things easy on ourselves, so our IDL files always start out with the same stuff. In this case, our IDL file begins like this:

```
interface Customer;
interface Stock;
typedef sequence<Customer> CustomerList;
typedef sequence<Stock> StockList;
```

We always start with forward declarations for all the interfaces that we're using in the file. Using forward declarations means that we don't need to worry about which interface to write first. (See Chapter 4 for more information about forward declarations.)

Next are the `typedef`s we need. `Typedef`s are usually used in IDL to give a handy, short, descriptive name to some long, nasty-looking type expression. In this case, we gave the long, nasty expressions having to do with sequences of interfaces nice short names that end in "`List`."

Whenever you need to use a sequence of interfaces as an attribute, just use a `typedef` to give it a clear, descriptive name, and then use that name in your attribute definition. This tactic makes the interface much easier to read.

Defining interfaces

With all the preliminaries out of the way, we can now get started on the interfaces. The first interface is for the `Customer` object, and we write it like this:

```
interface Customer {
    readonly attribute string Name;
    readonly attribute string Account;
    readonly attribute StockList Stocks;
```

(continued)

(continued)

```
Stock AddStock(in string TheSymbol,
    in double InitialPrice);
double CalculateTotalValue(out double
    InvestmentChange);
};
```

This interface uses read-only attributes for the information we want employees to be able to access but not change. We're not being snobby, just careful — we wouldn't want just any client application to allow an employee to change a customer's account number. We also provide an operation to add a new stock.

The last operation is CalculateTotalValue(). This operation computes both the total value and the total investment change of all the customer's stocks. How can we return two values with just one operation, you ask?

You can use out parameters as a handy way to return additional values from an operation. Notice that the CalculateTotalValue() operation has an out parameter called InvestmentChange. The value returned in that parameter is the current gain or loss on the stock.

Have a look at the Stock interface next:

```
interface Stock {
    readonly attribute string Symbol;
    readonly attribute double InvestmentAmount;
    readonly attribute float Units;
    attribute double CurrentPrice;

    void Buy(in double AmountInDollars);
    double Sell(in float SellUnits);
    double CalculateCurrentValue(out double
        InvestmentChange);
};
```

The Stock interface has read-only attributes for its symbol, investment amount, and units because, just like Customer, we don't want employees changing these values directly. The current price attribute is not read-only, so an employee can change a stock's price.

The Stock interface also has Buy() and Sell() operations that change the investment amount and units values, as well as an operation to compute the current value of the stock called CalculateCurrentValue(). CalculateCurrentValue() is just like the customer's CalculateTotalValue() operation, in that it, too, returns a second value via an out parameter.

When defining interfaces, use

- Read-only attributes for stuff you want client application to be able to see but not change.
- Non-read-only attributes (that is, regular attributes) for stuff you want client applications to be able to both see and change.
- Operations to perform logical actions on interfaces.
- Out parameters to return more than one value from an operation.
- Most of the letters of the alphabet.

At this point, you may be tempted to say, "Enough already with the IDL. Let's get on to the C++." But we haven't yet addressed one problem. We review the interfaces we have and think about how a client application may use them.

We have Customers that have a list of Stocks.

Some questions come to mind: How do we enter new customers? How do we find existing customers? Take a moment to ponder these questions, and enlightenment follows. We'll give you a hint: You can always make more interfaces!

Adding a Broker

Here's one way to answer the questions posed in the preceding paragraph. We call it the Broker solution.

You can add an interface similar to the PortfolioBroker interface whenever you need some form of central directory or point of contact. Any time a group of objects needs to be located by name or ID, a PortfolioBroker-like object can be used for creating new objects and locating individual objects in the group. The PortfolioBroker acts like a one-stop shopping center for clients. It's the CORBA equivalent of the Quickie Mart.

We just add one more interface that enables us to create and find Customers:

```
interface PortfolioBroker {
    exception DuplicateCustomer {
        string ExistingCustomer;
    };
    Customer MakeCustomer(in string CustomerName,
        in string CustomerAccount)
        raises (DuplicateCustomer);
    Customer FindCustomer(in string CustomerAccount);
};
```

What about modules?

Multiple related interfaces can be inside a module. Putting them in a module is a really great idea if we're going to use them as part of some larger implementation that includes a bunch of other interfaces. We don't put these interfaces into a module for one simple reason: Adding a module wrapper around these interfaces just makes the C++ code more cumbersome to write and use, because a module adds another "layer" of names to every interface. Depending on your ORB, this wrapper may be something as simple as including a `namespace` declaration around your classes, or it may necessitate wrapping them inside one huge enclosing class.

Whether your ORB uses `namespace` or nested classes, the result is the same. If we include everything in the IDL file in a module named `Portfolio`, then the interfaces are mapped to class names like `Portfolio::Customer`. Including the class name in the interface name is nice sometimes because you can simplify your interface names and use modules to keep them from conflicting. Rather than subject you to a ton of code that includes such gems as `Portfolio::PortfolioBroker::DuplicateCustomer()`, however, we decided to forgo modules for this example.

The `PortfolioBroker` can make a new `Customer` object via the `MakeCustomer()` operation.

We want the `MakeCustomer()` operation to fail if a `Customer` with the same account number already exists. Some of the ways in which we can achieve this goal include

- ✔ Returning a weird value that we have to trust client applications to check to see whether it failed.
- ✔ Setting a flag in an `out` parameter that we still need client applications to check.
- ✔ Saying nothing at all — to heck with the client application anyway!
- ✔ Broadcasting the following message across the network: "Danger! The security system has been breached. Attempt to find the culprit."
- ✔ Defining an exception and raising it when this error occurs.

We stick with the last choice. We define an exception named `DuplicateCustomer` that is raised (or *thrown*) when a user enters a duplicate. This exception returns the existing `Customer`'s name. If no duplicate exists, a new `Customer` object is created and then returned.

We also create a FindCustomer() operation that looks up an existing Customer by account number (called CustomerAccount) and returns a reference to it. We need this operation so that client programs can find a Customer and then issue Buy and Sell orders.

So there you have it. We create a PortfolioBroker object in order to gain access to all Customers, as well as to add new Customers.

Generating Stubs and Skeletons in C++

Generating client stubs and server skeletons in C++ is Step 3 in creating a CORBA application. In this step, we compile the IDL and work on the C++ mappings for these interfaces. We use the IDL file to generate the client stub and the server skeleton C++ files. Recall that client applications use the client stub to access a server object, while the server skeleton is used when implementing the server object.

The precise name and number of these files varies from ORB to ORB. You can figure out how your particular IDL compiler works by reviewing the documentation that comes with it.

Our IDL compiler Orbix from IONA Technologies, PLC generates three files named Portfolio.h, PortfolioS.cpp, and PortfolioC.cpp when we compile the IDL file with this command:

```
C:\Portfolio\> idl -h .h -B Portfolio.idl
```

In this ORB, the generated IDL client stub is in the file named PortfolioC.cpp and the IDL server skeleton is in the file named PortfolioS.cpp. The one thing we need right now from the IDL compiler is the file named Portfolio.h. We need to include that header file in the implementation files for our server object because the header defines the interface to the server skeleton classes.

Think of the server skeleton file as a big box that you can't see into. Unless you like opening these kinds of boxes — if you do, then think of it as something else, because you should never need to open it. Oh, sure, if you really must open the server skeleton file, you can open it in your program editor, but only if you're interested in seeing some pretty complex C++ code. Take our advice and don't open it, because if you do, you may inadvertently change something, and that would be bad.

At this point, you need to figure out how your particular IDL compiler names the skeleton classes. The names usually are _sk_InterfaceName, or InterfaceName_sk, or InterfaceNameBOAImpl, or even POA_InterfaceName. Your compiler will follow some kind of rule for generating names — like always putting _sk_ as part of the class name. You need to check with your ORB documentation to find out what name to use.

For example, if your ORB is CORBA 2.2-compliant, it's supposed to use POA_InterfaceName. We're stuck with InterfaceNameBOAImpl because our ORB is only CORBA 2.1-compliant.

You use the names that the skeleton generates later in your classes as the base class names for each class that implements an interface.

A *base class* is a class from which another class is derived. It's also called *superclass, ancestor,* or *parent.*

Mapping IDL to C++ Classes

If we want these nifty interfaces to actually do something, we must implement the servers in a target language. This is Step 4 of the process of creating applications in CORBA. Because we're implementing our server objects in C++, the next step is to write in C++ the header file for the server class. We call it Portfolio_impl.h. It contains class definitions for all the classes in our IDL file.

We could, of course, spread the implementations out across several different header files. In fact, because we didn't use a module in the IDL file, we could have even split Portfolio.idl into several different files, one per interface. We're keeping this example simple, but just remember that splitting up is possible. If you do want to split stuff up, you need to include the appropriate header files in your header and implementation files.

The #include file preliminaries

Whenever we create a new class header file, we

- ✔ Wrap the whole thing in a #ifdef…#endif block or use #pragma once to prevent multiple inclusions.
- ✔ Include the IDL compiler-generated IDL server skeleton header file.
- ✔ Stand on our heads for a few minutes to stimulate our brains.

For Portfolio_impl.h, following these steps ends up being the following code:

```
#ifndef PORTFOLIO_IMPL_H
#define PORTFOLIO_IMPL_H
#include <Portfolio.h>
```

Mapping interfaces to C++ classes

For each interface in the IDL file, we need a corresponding C++ class in `Portfolio_impl.h`. You may recall that the interfaces are `Customer`, `Stock`, and `PortfolioBroker`. For each interface, we declare

- ✔ A class who's name ends in `_impl` that inherits from the IDL-generated skeleton class — we declare it by using `virtual public`.
- ✔ A virtual Get method in that class for each attribute in the interface.
- ✔ A virtual Set method in that class for each non-read-only attribute in the interface.
- ✔ A virtual method in that class for each operation in the interface.
- ✔ One or more class constructors.
- ✔ A class destructor, if it's needed.
- ✔ Class member variables, if they are needed.
- ✔ "I'm done, I do declare!"

Wow, that looks like a lot to declare when you read it in a big list. The last four items are stuff you do for any C++ class, though, so really only the first four are CORBA-specific.

TECHNICAL STUFF

What's up with all these virtuals?

CORBA's C++ binding uses inheritance and virtual methods to build a server object based on several subclasses. If you understand how virtual methods and virtual inheritance work to allow polymorphic behavior in C++, then you're all set. If you don't, then here it is in a nutshell: If you have a class that uses virtual inheritance to inherit from a base class, then when the methods of the base class are called, the actual code that gets executed is the code in your subclass. Neat, isn't it?

Virtual inheritance is practically mandatory to CORBA because much of what you write is built on top of many subclasses that CORBA already knows about. The connection between those classes and your classes is made using polymorphism.

Polymorphism literally means that a single organism can take on different forms. In C++, it means that you may have a pointer to an object that you believe is of a specific class, but in reality, it's an object of a subclass of that class. When you call a method of the base class, you actually end up executing the virtual method in the subclass.

Basically, CORBA is just one huge polymorphic mess. Luckily, though, you don't need to worry about how it all works. Even if you never figure out what `virtual` does or how polymorphism works, if you just declare all the methods that are mapped from your IDL interfaces as `virtual`, CORBA can do its polymorphic duties.

Customer_impl class definition

Our first interface requires most of the items in our checklist from the preceding section, so take a look at it bit by bit:

```
class Customer_impl : public virtual CustomerBOAImpl
{
public:
```

This class statement shows that we're inheriting from the public interface of `CustomerBOAImpl`. That's the skeleton class that the IDL compiler generated for the `Customer` interface. We don't name the class `Customer`, but rather `Customer_impl`, because the IDL client stub already declares a `Customer` class for us. That class is used to access the methods from the client's side. We're implementing the server side of the interface, so we need to use a different class name.

When implementing IDL interfaces as C++ classes, always declare your class with a different name. Also, always use `virtual` when you inherit from the skeleton class.

The actual name of the skeleton class is different based on your ORB. You need to look at the documentation or example files provided with your ORB in order to find out how the interface name (in this case, `Customer`) is mangled when the IDL compiler generates the server skeleton classes.

Mapping read-only attributes to Get methods

The `Customer` interface has three attributes. We define three methods in the class, using the same names as the attributes. These methods don't take any parameters, but they do return values. That's how a read-only attribute maps to a C++ Get method.

We define the three methods like this:

```
    virtual char * Name(CORBA::Environment&);
    virtual char * Account(CORBA::Environment&);
    virtual StockList * Stocks(CORBA::Environment&);
```

Because all the attributes in the `Customer` class are read-only, we don't need to define any Set methods.

This program works with Orbix from IONA Technologies, PLC. Orbix requires that every method that implements an operation or attribute include an extra parameter, `CORBA::Environment&`, at the end. You don't ever use this parameter, but you must include it. (Sounds like something the Orbix people could remove, doesn't it?) If you're not using Orbix, you probably don't need this parameter.

Take a look at those return types of char and StockList. The type you use for a C++ return value or parameter is based on the type you use in IDL.

Type mappings

The two IDL string attributes map to C++ char * types. For the C++ binding, CORBA always maps an IDL string to a C++ char *.

We don't define the StockList * return type for the Stocks() method; the IDL compiler generates it. Because the type was defined in the IDL file as an unbounded sequence, StockList is a subclass of the _CORBA_Unbounded_Sequence class that is provided with CORBA. That class supports specific operations on unbounded sequences. One of these classes is generated for each unbounded sequence that is defined in the IDL file.

Mapping operations to methods

The Customer interface has two operations. For each operation, we define a method in the class. Each method

✔ Uses the same name as the operation.

✔ Takes the same numbers and types of parameters (mapped to C++ types) as was used in the IDL definition.

✔ Returns a value that is the C++ type mapping of the CORBA type used in the IDL file.

✔ Causes a program to spontaneously recite the Pledge of Allegiance whenever a client application calls it.

✔ Is seldom a source of bugs in programs.

For our example, we define two methods:

```
virtual Stock_ptr AddStock (const char * TheSymbol,
    CORBA::Double InitialPrice,
    CORBA::Environment&);
virtual CORBA::Double
    CalculateTotalValue(CORBA::Double&
    InvestmentChange, CORBA::Environment&);
```

Notice that we use the same names for the parameters to the methods as we use for the parameters to the operations in IDL. Nothing specifically requires us to do this, but doing so makes the code easier to match up. In C++, you can use any name you want for method parameters, or even omit them completely. However, that kind of behavior just makes it harder for you to figure out what's going on.

When you look at the IDL for the AddStock() operation, you see that it has a return value of type Stock. Notice that the corresponding C++ type of the return value used in the class method AddStock() is Stock_ptr. That's because the IDL compiler automatically generates this type for us and puts it in the server skeleton.

Use _ptr types for return values and parameters of methods when those items are server objects.

We use CORBA::Double as the type in C++ everywhere we use double in the IDL definition. That's what you have to do for doubles in CORBA. You can use a CORBA::Double variable exactly the same way as you would a C++ double variable.

Notice that in CalculateTotalValue(), the InvestmentChange parameter is declared as a C++ reference. That's what the CORBA::Double& means — any change we make to InvestmentChange in the method is also made in the variable supplied as the parameter because the parameter is declared as out in IDL. The same thing would be true if the parameter were declared as inout.

Constructors and destructors

We declare the constructor and destructor for the class like this:

```
Customer_impl(const char * CustomerName,
    const char * CustomerAccount);
virtual ~Customer_impl();
```

You need to consider what information you need when you first create an instance of a server object. For the Customer_impl object, for example, you need two strings: the customer's name and the customer's account number.

Remember your mother telling you that you had to clean up your room before you could leave the house? Well, before deleting an object, you need to delete anything hanging around inside it. If data still remains, you need a destructor method in the object's C++ class. The Customer class needs a destructor in our example, so the last line declares the destructor.

Declaring member variables

Private member variables store a class's values that are not accessible by other classes. The private member variables for the Customer class are as follows:

```
private:
    CORBA::String_var MyCustomerName;
    CORBA::String_var MyCustomerAccount;
    StockList MyStocks;
};
```

Assigning to CORBA::String

You need to be careful when assigning `char *` values to `CORBA::String_var` variables. If the type of the `char *` is not `const`, then the `CORBA::String_var` "takes over" the `char *` rather than allocating a copy for you. You can either call `string_dup()` on the `char *` yourself in the assignment statement, or you can cast it to a `const char *`. For example, the following statement is totally, completely bad. It's a bug. You'd regret ever writing it:

```
CORBA::String_var str = "this
    is a problem";
```

This statement is a bad idea because the static string is just used by `str` and is deleted when `str` is deleted. The static string will, quite probably, crash the program. Change the expression to

```
CORBA::String_var str = (const
    char *)"This is OK";
```

Now everything works fine. Because you use a `const char *` in the assignment statement, the new memory is allocated and a copy is made inside of `str`. When `str` is deleted, its allocated `char *` is also deleted. No problem!

Here you find two `CORBA::String_var` variables. One stores the name (`MyCustomerName`), and the other stores the account number (`MyCustomerAccount`). We also declare a `StockList` named `MyStocks` to hold the sequence of object references for all the customer's stocks.

You decide the variable names to use here; no direct mapping from IDL exists.

You probably noticed that we use both `char *` and `CORBA::String_var` to manipulate IDL strings. These approaches work just fine. The `CORBA::String` type supplied with CORBA comes with three handy static methods of the CORBA class that are used for manipulating IDL strings:

- ✔ `string_alloc(ULong len)` allocates a new string that can hold `len` characters and the `NULL` terminator.

- ✔ `string_dup(const char *)` duplicates the string that's been passed in and stores it.

- ✔ `string_free()` frees the memory associated with the string.

In addition to these goodies, you get a type named `CORBA::String_var`, which is based on `CORBA::String`. The only thing the `_var` version adds is automatic deletion of the string when you're done with it. We use `CORBA::String_var` here so we don't need to delete the two strings explicitly after deleting the `Customer_impl` object.

When dealing with strings, keep the following points in mind:

- Use `CORBA::String_var` **as the type for** `char *` **variables that are mapped from IDL.**

- **Don't use** `CORBA::String_var` **for parameters to methods or constructors.**

- **Always use** `char *` **for** `out` **and** `inout` **parameters.**

- **Always use** `const char *` **for** `in` **parameters.** When you use a `const`, you're telling the compiler that you can't change the value of the `char *`. That's what an `in` parameter is all about, so use it.

- **Never approach a string when it is hurt or hungry.**

Stock_impl class definition

The remaining class definitions follow the same format. We're not going to go through them in as much detail as we have in previous sections of this chapter, but we point out the CORBA-specific stuff along the way.

The `Stock` interface has several read-only attributes, one non-read-only attribute, and three operations. The C++ class has methods that implement all these attributes and operations, as well as some member variables. Take a look:

```
class Stock_impl : public virtual StockBOAImpl {
public:
   virtual char * Symbol (CORBA::Environment&);
   virtual CORBA::Double
      InvestmentAmount(CORBA::Environment&);
   virtual CORBA::Float Units(CORBA::Environment&);
   virtual CORBA::Double CurrentPrice(
      CORBA::Environment&);
   virtual void CurrentPrice(CORBA::Double NewPrice,
      CORBA::Environment&);
   virtual void Buy(CORBA::Double AmountInDollars,
      CORBA::Environment&);
   virtual CORBA::Double Sell(CORBA::Float SellUnits,
      CORBA::Environment&);
   virtual CORBA::Double
      CalculateCurrentValue(CORBA::Double &
      InvestmentChange, CORBA::Environment&);
   Stock_impl(const char * TheSymbol,
      CORBA::Double InitialPrice);
```

```
private:
   CORBA::String_var MySymbol;
   CORBA::Double MyInvestmentAmount;
   CORBA::Float MyUnits;
   CORBA::Double MyPrice;
};
```

Note that we

- ✔ Don't define a destructor for `Stock_impl` because it doesn't need to delete anything when it's deleted.

- ✔ Use the binding for the `float` IDL type to the C++ type for the first time.

- ✔ Reveal our intimate thoughts and feelings in the `private` section.

- ✔ See how to deal with a non-read-only attribute.

We use `CORBA::Float` as the type in C++ everywhere we use `float` in the IDL definition. That's what you have to do for `float` in CORBA. You can use a `CORBA::Float` variable exactly the same way as you would a C++ `float` variable.

The rest of the class definition is much like what we've seen before. The only other new thing is that two `CurrentPrice()` methods are available. Why is that, do you suppose?

Whenever you declare an attribute in IDL, you have to declare a corresponding pair of methods in C++.

The Get method we've already seen — you always have one of these, even for read-only attributes. When an attribute is not read-only, you need to declare a second version of the same method. This version returns a `void` (in other words, it doesn't return a value), and it takes in one parameter that has the same type as the attribute.

PortfolioBroker_impl class definition

The `PortfolioBroker` IDL interface defines two operations that return interface references. The corresponding C++ methods return `_ptr` types of the C++ classes for those interfaces.

The IDL for the `PortfolioBroker` interface also includes a nested declaration for the `DuplicateCustomer` exception, and the `MakeCustomer()` interface indicates that it raises that exception. The C++ class definition for `PortfolioBroker_impl` doesn't seem to say anything about this. Take a look for yourself.

```
class PortfolioBroker_impl : public virtual
     PortfolioBrokerBOAImpl {
public:
   virtual Customer_ptr  MakeCustomer ( const char *
     CustomerName, const char *  CustomerAccount,
     CORBA::Environment&);
   virtual Customer_ptr  FindCustomer ( const char *
     CustomerAccount, CORBA::Environment&);
   PortfolioBroker_impl() {}
   ~PortfolioBroker_impl();
private:
   CustomerList MyCustomers;
};
```

The IDL compiler does all the work in creating an exception class based on an IDL exception type. The class is defined in the client stub and server skeleton for you. In this case, the exception is named `PortfolioBroker::DuplicateCustomer()`, because it was declared inside the `PortfolioBroker` interface.

Implementing the C++ Classes

We turn to the class implementation file named `Portfolio_impl.cpp`. It begins with the usual header inclusions:

```
#include <Portfolio_impl.h>
#include <math.h>
```

The `Portfolio_impl.h` class header file is what we finish working on in the preceding section. We need to include it or all of that hard work defining the classes goes to waste. We use some of the standard C++ math functions for the classes, so we include `math.h`.

Implementing classes for server objects

Implementing classes for server objects is much like implementing other C++ classes. In general, you do the same tasks you do with non-CORBA objects. The `Customer_impl` class isn't too tricky, except when it has to deal with the stored sequence of `Stock` object references like this:

```
We don't describe non-CORBA objects implementations.
            L&JCustomer_impl::Customer_impl(const char * CustomerName,
    const char * CustomerAccount) {
  MyCustomerName = CustomerName;
```

```
    MyCustomerAccount = CustomerAccount;
}
```

The constructor just stores the supplied name and account number into member variables.

Note that because the parameters are of type `const char *`, we didn't need to use `string_dup()` when storing them into the `CORBA::String_var`-type variables. That's why declaring `in` string parameters as `const char *` in your C++ methods is a good idea.

The two Get methods just use `CORBA::string_dup()` to return copies of the strings that store the name and account number, like this:

```
char *
Customer_impl::Name(CORBA::Environment&) {
    return CORBA::string_dup(MyCustomerName);
}
char *
Customer_impl::Account(CORBA::Environment&) {
    return CORBA::string_dup(MyCustomerAccount);
}
```

The `Stocks()` Get method also needs to make a copy of the unbounded sequence stored in `MyStocks` so that it can return the copy:

```
StockList *
Customer_impl::Stocks(CORBA::Environment&) {
    return new StockList(MyStocks);
}
```

Fortunately, among the constructors for this class (which the IDL compiler generated for us) is a copy-constructor that performs a "deep copy" of the supplied list. If we make a new `StockList` and supply an existing `StockList` to the constructor, the new list has copies of everything in the old list. So all we have to do is make a new `StockList`, with the existing one as the parameter to the constructor, and then return the copy.

Always return a copy of any allocated data from Get methods. Your client applications should delete the copies when they're done with them.

If you don't return a copy, you end up with corrupted memory — and usually a program that crashes. That's because CORBA deletes your supplied return value after it sends it to the client.

Creating new server instances

The AddStock() method actually creates new instances of Stock objects. These objects are server objects, so we need to be a little bit careful about how we do things. We look at the method in this and the next section.

First, we make a new instance of the Stock_impl class for client applications.

```
Stock_ptr
Customer_impl::AddStock ( const char *  TheSymbol,
    CORBA::Double InitialPrice, CORBA::Environment&) {
  Stock_impl * TheStock = new Stock_impl(TheSymbol,
    InitialPrice);
```

We call the constructor to make the new object. We get back a pointer to the new Stock server object, which we need to save somewhere. If we don't, we'll have a heck of a time trying to buy and sell units of it later!

Extending unbounded sequences

We store the new Stock object reference in the unbounded sequence variable MyStocks:

```
CORBA::Long size = MyStocks.length();
MyStocks.length(size+1);
MyStocks[size] = (Stock_ptr)TheStock;
```

Adding new elements to an unbounded list is a two-step process:

1. **Make the list longer by one.**

2. **Store the item in the newly added array position.**

To make an unbounded sequence larger, follow these steps:

1. **Call the unbounded sequence's** length() **method without supplying a value.**

   This step returns the current length.

2. **Add one (or more) to the value returned.**

3. **Call the unbounded sequence's** length() **method and pass in the new value.**

We cast the Stock_impl object into a Stock_ptr object before we store it in the sequence. This step is critical because the IDL-generated unbounded sequence type StockList only accepts objects of type Stock_ptr. It all works because Stock_impl is a subclass of Stock. All we need to do is return a reference to the newly created Stock object:

```
    return Stock::_duplicate((Stock_ptr)TheStock);
}
```

Implement server objects that save (or return) object references so they always save and return duplicates. That way, callers know that they can safely release any object reference passed in or received from a server method. That's why we return a duplicate of the newly created Stock object.

The CalculateTotalValue() method in the Customer_impl class does some computational work. It's a server object that uses an out parameter. Because this method calls methods of other server objects, it makes the Customer_impl object a server that acts like a client. Take a look at the code below, paying attention to the CalculateCurrentValue() method call. The CalculateTotalValue() method implementation is

```
CORBA::Double
Customer_impl::CalculateTotalValue(CORBA::Double &
    InvestmentChange, CORBA::Environment&e) {
  CORBA::Double TotalValue = 0.0;
  InvestmentChange = 0.0;
  CORBA::Long size = MyStocks.length();
  for (CORBA::Long i = 0; i < size; i++) {
    CORBA::Double ThisChange = 0.0;
    TotalValue += MyStocks[i]->
      CalculateCurrentValue(ThisChange);
    InvestmentChange += ThisChange;
  }
  if (fabsSInvestmentnμange) < 0.005)
    InvestmentChange = 0.0;
  return Totb ¼alue;
}
```

Releasing object references

The destructor has to deal with the object references stored in MyStocks as:

```
Customer_impl::~Customer_impl() {
  CORBA::Long size = MyStocks.length();
  for (CORBA::Long i = 0; i < size; i++)
    CORBA::release(MyStocks[i]);
}
```

We call CORBA::release() to release each stored object reference.

You must release object references when you're done with them so that CORBA can tell when the object is no longer used.

Implementing another class

The `Stock_impl` class is a simple C++ class that holds information about a stock.

The code below implements the methods of the `Stock_impl` class:

```
Stock_impl::Stock_impl(const char * TheSymbol,
      CORBA::Double InitialPrice) {
   MySymbol = TheSymbol;
   MyUnits = 0.0; MyInvestmentAmount = 0.0;
   MyPrice = InitialPrice;
}
char *
Stock_impl::Symbol (CORBA::Environment&) {
   return CORBA::string_dup(MySymbol);
}
CORBA::Double
Stock_impl::InvestmentAmount (CORBA::Environment&) {
   return MyInvestmentAmount;
}
CORBA::Float
Stock_impl::Units (CORBA::Environment&) {
   return MyUnits;
}
CORBA::Double
Stock_impl::CurrentPrice(CORBA::Environment&) {
   return MyPrice;
}
void
Stock_impl::CurrentPrice(CORBA::Double NewPrice,
      CORBA::Environment&) {
   MyPrice = NewPrice;
}
CORBA::Double
Stock_impl::CalculateCurrentValue(CORBA::Double &
      InvestmentChange, CORBA::Environment&) {
   CORBA::Double TotalValue;
   TotalValue = MyUnits * MyPrice;
   InvestmentChange = TotalValue - MyInvestmentAmount;
   if (fabs(InvestmentChange) < 0.005)
      InvestmentChange = 0.0;
   return TotalValue;
}
void
Stock_impl::Buy(CORBA::Double AmountInDollars,
      CORBA::Environment&) {
```

```
    MyUnits += (AmountInDollars/MyPrice);
    MyInvestmentAmount += AmountInDollars;
}
```

When you're making a server out of most C++ classes, the classes don't change much at all except for the use of CORBA types.

If a customer tries to sell more units than are available, we have a problem. Instead of returning an error code, we throw an exception.

```
CORBA::Double
Stock_impl::Sell(CORBA::Float SellUnits,
      CORBA::Environment&){
  if (SellUnits > MyUnits) throw
      CORBA::BAD_OPERATION(10,CORBA::COMPLETED_NO);
  MyInvestmentAmount -= (SellUnits * MyPrice);
  MyUnits -= SellUnits;
  return SellUnits * MyPrice;
}
```

We throw a CORBA standard exception if the number of units to sell is more than we have. We selected CORBA::BAD_OPERATION as the exception.

Before you create an exception type in your IDL file, check the standard CORBA exceptions to see whether you can use one.

Implementing the Broker class

The PortfolioBroker_impl class creates new Customers by using MakeCustomer(). It also looks up existing Customers in the FindCustomer() method. Because it maintains a list of Customers in a member variable, it also has a destructor to release the references when it's deleted. Here's the code for the MakeCustomer() method.

```
Customer_ptr
PortfolioBroker_impl::MakeCustomer ( const char * CustomerName,
      const char * CustomerAccount,
      CORBA::Environment& e) {
  Customer_var dup = FindCustomer(CustomerAccount, e);
  if (!CORBA::is_nil(dup))
      throw DuplicateCustomer(dup->Name(e));
  Customer_impl * TheCustomer =
      new Customer_impl(CustomerName, CustomerAccount);
  CORBA::Long size = MyCustomers.length();
  MyCustomers.length(size+1);
  MyCustomers[size] = (Customer_ptr)TheCustomer;
```

(continued)

(continued)

```
    return Customer::_duplicate(
        (Customer_ptr)TheCustomer);
}
```

We're taking advantage of the FindCustomer() method inside the MakeCustomer() method. We use FindCustomer() to look up the account number of the new Customer in our existing Customer list. If we find a match, we just throw our user-defined error. If not, we make a new Customer object, save it in our list, and return a duplicate of the reference. This is just like what we did in the AddStock() method of the Customer object in section "Implementing Classes for Server Objects."

The FindCustomer() method searches the unbounded sequence of Customer object references saved in MyCustomers to try to locate a Customer, given an account number. Here is the code for doing this:

```
Customer_ptr
PortfolioBroker_impl::FindCustomer ( const char *
        CustomerAccount, CORBA::Environment&) {

    CORBA::Long size = MyCustomers.length();
    for (CORBA::Long i = 0; i < size; i++) {
        CORBA::String_var act = MyCustomers[i]->Account();
        if (strcmp(act, CustomerAccount) == 0)
            return Customer::_duplicate(MyCustomers[i]);
    }
    return Customer::_nil();
}
```

We assign the string returned from Account() to a CORBA::String_var variable. We do this because the Account() method returns a copy of a string, and we want to make sure that copy gets deleted when we're done with it. The String_var type always deletes its memory, so putting the string there gives us exactly what we want.

If you don't delete the copy returned from a server object method, your program "leaks" memory, and that's never a good idea.

The PortfolioBroker destructor releases all the stored references to Customer objects when it's deleted, like the Customer object's destructor.

```
PortfolioBroker_impl::~PortfolioBroker_impl() {
    CORBA::Long size = MyCustomers.length();
    for (CORBA::Long i = 0; i < size; i++)
        CORBA::release(MyCustomers[i]);
}
```

Chapter 6

If Only We Had a C++ Application

*B*uilding server objects is fun. But unless you whip up some spiffy server and client applications, you never get to use those server objects. Using server objects with multiple clients is at the core of CORBA's flexibility. That's what this chapter is all about — creating server and client applications so that they can use the services of server objects.

It makes perfect sense to us (and, hopefully, to you) that before you can write the server and client applications, you need to fully implement the server objects. We cover implementing server objects in Chapter 5.

In the course of implementing the server objects, you get several important things that you need in order to create server and client applications. When the target language is C++, these items are

- ✔ A header file, generated by the IDL compiler, that defines the C++ classes that the client application uses

- ✔ A header file, which you write, that defines the C++ classes that the server application uses

- ✔ The server skeleton C++ file that is linked to your server application

- ✔ The answer to the eternal question, "What's a stub?"

- ✔ The client stub C++ file that is linked to your client applications

- ✔ Free tickets to an opera about the tribulations of a server and how it escapes its fate by hiding out on the Web

Chapter 2 defines a step-by-step approach to creating CORBA applications. This chapter discusses Steps 5 through 8:

5. Write a C++ server application that instantiates the server objects.

6. Write C++ client application(s) that use these server objects.

7. Compile all source files, including stubs and skeletons, and link the executable files.

8. Run the server application created in Step 5, and then run as many kinds of clients as you need, as many times as you need them.

For this chapter, we assume that you already have server objects written in C++. Our example server and client applications use the server objects of the Portfolio example that we develop in Chapter 5.

The IDL for the Portfolio example is in the Examples\Chapter6 directory on the CD-ROM at the back of this book. We also include the Portfolio_impl.h and Portfolio_impl.cpp server object implementations in C++ on the CD. The Server.cpp, Customer.cpp, and BuySell.cpp server and client application source files, as well as a Makefile, are there, too. In other words, all the files you need for this chapter's examples are in that directory.

Writing a Persistent Server Application

If you want client applications to use the server objects that you've written, you need to write a server application to actually serve them up. Think of the server objects as delicious dishes of food at a French restaurant. The persistent server application is like the waiter. It makes your tasty server objects available for consumption.

Why do we call it a *persistent server* when everyone knows that most waiters aren't?

   ✔ **Persistent Server Application:** A persistent server is implemented as a stand-alone application. Examples include an UNIX executable file or a Windows .exe file. A persistent server application is just one way to implement the activation policy for a CORBA server object.

   ✔ **Activation Policy:** An activation policy is a procedure by which a server object is made ready to process method calls from clients. Chapter 11 discusses server activation policies.

To write a server application, you need to

1. Decide on a server activation policy.

2. Identify which server objects must be created by the server application.

3. Decide how to make their references available to clients.

4. Decide whether you should get take-out French food for dinner.

We are using C++ with a persistent server activation policy. Using C++ changes the general steps to the following:

1. Include the server object implementation header file and any other header files you need.

2. Begin with a standard `main()` function.

3. Inside a `try` block, initialize the ORB and the BOA.

4. Create an initial instance of the desired server object or objects.

5. Make the reference to the server object available for clients.

6. Take a break for high tea.

7. Wait for clients.

Activation policy police

If you don't follow the steps for creating a persistent server application precisely, the activation policy police come to your cubicle and have a long talk with you. Fortunately, the first three steps are a breeze, so they've only visited us a few times. We had doughnuts on hand, so they went away happy.

You can find the complete source code for the server application in a file named `Server.cpp` on this book's CD-ROM in the `Examples\Chapter6` directory.

```cpp
#include <Portfolio_impl.h>
#include <SimpleNames.h>
#include <stdlib.h>
#include <fstream.h>

int
main(int argc, char* argv[], char*[]){
   try {
      CORBA::ORB_var orb = CORBA::ORB_init(argc,
         argv, "Orbix");
```

(continued)

(continued)

```
    // Orbix specific -- turn off Diagnostics
    orb->setDiagnostics(0);
    CORBA::BOA_var _myboa = orb -> BOA_init(argc,
        argv, "Orbix_BOA");
```

The server object implementation header file is `Portfolio_impl.h`. The `SimpleNames.h` header file defines a class we wrote that makes using the Naming Service a bit easier.

The `main()` is your basic C/C++ main function.

After `main()` is the beginning of the `try` block, followed by the ORB and BOA initialization calls. Just like we said!

This program works with Orbix. That's why we use `"Orbix"` and `"OrbixBOA"` in the two initialization calls. Orbix requires that servers turn off diagnostics; otherwise, a bunch of messages are printed to standard output when they run. If you're not using Orbix, these two elements are different in your code. However, you must then read all these reminders for the rest of the chapter. Aren't you tempted to just chuck it all and use Orbix?

Pick a server, any server

Solving forth-order differential calculus problems is easy — with the proper training. Identifying which server objects to create in a persistent server application is easy, too, and you don't need nearly as large a brain as you do for the calculus problems.

Follow these guidelines to identify which server objects to create:

- ✔ If you have just one server object, that's the one you need to create.

- ✔ If you have more than one server object, try to take advantage of their interrelationships to select key objects to create.

- ✔ If you're unsure of which server object to choose, select one at random. If it turns out that you guessed wrong, try again. Keep trying until someone points out the correct object at lunch.

- ✔ Think about how client applications need to get the information in the servers. Thinking about the problem in these terms usually makes which objects need to be created become apparent.

- ✔ If nothing seems to be appropriate, consider adding an additional server object that can act as a central access point for other objects. In other words, fake it.

The tree of references

Any time server objects contain references to other server objects, you can usually allow access to an entire "tree" of objects by just creating a server application for the "root" object.

For example, a hierarchical structure is often used for businesses. A company is made up of branches — branches have divisions, divisions have units, and so on. We're not sure where the root fits in for a business.

Say that this whole structure is implemented as a bunch of server objects. Each object at a given level (company, branch, and so on) has a list of references to the objects at the next level. You can serve the whole thing up just by creating a server application for the company object.

The `Portfolio` example has three server objects:

- ✔ `Customer` contains a name, an account number, and a list of `Stocks`.
- ✔ `Stock` contains a symbol, an investment amount, units, and a price.
- ✔ `PortfolioBroker` contains a list of `Customers`.

We know that the server object we need to create has to be one of those three! We need to create a server application for only one — the `PortfolioBroker` object. That object is used to create new `Customer` objects and to look up existing `Customer` objects. `Customer` objects can create new and return existing `Stock` objects. So if clients can get to the `PortfolioBroker`, they can get to other server objects. In other words, `PortfolioBroker` is the root of our tree.

All we need to do is allocate the `PortfolioBroker` server object, like this:

```
PortfolioBroker_impl * broker =
    new PortfolioBroker_impl();
// orbix specific code -- tell BOA it's ready
_myboa->impl_is_ready("Portfolio",0);
```

This program works with Orbix. Orbix needs you to call `impl_is_ready()` before you create an object reference. We use the Orbix-specific version that doesn't wait (that's what the zero means) in order to indicate that `PortfolioBroker_impl` is fully ready.

Object Adapters: What's a person to do?

You have to use the Basic Object Adapter (BOA) to implement a persistent server application. Unfortunately, versions of CORBA before 2.2 don't have a portable way to tell the BOA that a server object is ready but not to wait forever for clients. The object needs to not wait so that you can leave a reference to the server object for a client. Most ORB vendors supply a way to tell the server object not to wait with a vendor-specific extension to the BOA, but then you're stuck with nonportable code.

The OMG wants more portable servers, so in CORBA 2.2 more of the Object Adapter behavior is standardized in what is called the

Portable Object Adapter. POA really is better than the old BOA approach, but you'd be hard-pressed to buy an ORB product any time in 1998 that implements a POA. ORB vendors are slow to adopt new versions of the OMG specification for CORBA. As of this writing, most ORBs claim CORBA 2.0 or 2.1 compatibility, even though the CORBA 2.2 specification has been finalized since February 1998.

What are you to do? Simple! Use whatever your ORB vendor has (BOA, POA, TLA, and so on) and try to isolate the Object Adapter-specific code. We cover both the BOA and POA in detail in Chapter 11.

What's your handle, good buddy?

A client needs an object reference to access a server object. This reference has to be "left behind" by the server when the client is run, like a trail of bread crumbs. You can save a string version of the server object reference to a file. Clients read the file and get the reference; Chapter 1 shows an example of this form of saving an object reference. However, a far better way to leave behind an object reference in CORBA is called the Naming Service. The Naming Service

✔ Acts like a phone book for object references

✔ Uses a hierarchical (like a file directory) structure to organize names

✔ Calls other objects bad names

We discuss the Naming Service in Chapter 18. We also present a handy little helper class we wrote called `SimpleNames` that makes using the Naming Service very easy, because it takes care of all the details for you. We use the `SimpleNames` class in this chapter, without covering how it actually uses the Naming Service to do its work.

To use the Naming Service via our handy-dandy helper class, you need to

1. Put on your best suit.

2. Have a server object ready to name.

3. Think up a name consisting of zero or more subdirectory names and then the actual object name.

4. Stuff the name into a weird sequence called `CosNaming::Name`.

5. Call our handy-dandy `SimpleNames::bindToName()` object method to bind the object to the name.

6. Sit back and relax as we do all the hard work.

Here's what using the Name Service looks like for our server:

```
CosNaming::Name name;
name.length(3);
name[0].id   = (const char*) "Examples";
name[0].kind = (const char*) "CORBA_For_Dummies";
name[1].id   = (const char*) "Chapter5";
name[1].kind = (const char*) "CORBA_ For_Dummies";
name[2].id   = (const char*) "Broker";
name[2].kind = (const char*) "Object";
if (!SimpleNames::bindToName(orb, broker, name)) {
    cerr << "Could not bind PortfolioBroker to name."
        << endl;
    return 1;
}
```

Because `CosNaming::Name` is a CORBA unbounded sequence, we set its length first, and then we add pairs of string values for each subdirectory leading up to the actual object name. Then we add the object name.

We then pass the whole mess off to `SimpleNames::bindToName()`, where a team of highly trained technicians uses tiny silver hammers to craft it into a Naming Service entry. Those technicians give `PortfolioBroker` the name `Examples\Chapter5\Broker`.

Waiting for Godot

The server application is all but finished. All we need to do is wait for clients to use whatever objects we instantiated and named. Waiting may take a while, especially if the clients are vacationing at a spa resort and are enjoying themselves in the sauna and hot tub sections.

If our clients are hard at work, however, we tell the BOA to start processing requests for the server objects using the `impl_is_ready()` method:

```
      cout << "Portfolio server ready...\n" << flush;
      // Orbix specific code - disable timeout
      _myboa->impl_is_ready("Portfolio",
         CORBA::Orbix.INFINITE_TIMEOUT);
   }
   catch(CORBA::SystemException& ex) {
      cerr << "CORBA System Exception:" << ex << endl;
      return 1;
   }
   return 0;
}
```

Technically, the program never returns from this call. We close the `try` block and add a general-purpose `catch` section to catch and print any CORBA exceptions. That's all there is to writing the server application!

This program works with Orbix. The `impl_is_ready()` call uses an Orbix specific extension (`CORBA::Orbix.INFINITE_TIMEOUT`) that makes the server wait forever for a client. If you're not using Orbix, you don't need this item.

Writing an Abstract Client Application

We'd like to access the `Customer`, `Stock`, and `PortfolioBroker` objects from more than one client application. We want to have this access not to show off, but because that's what CORBA is really good at.

Why do you have multiple clients? You use multiple clients to

- ✔ Perform specific, limited tasks
- ✔ Demonstrate your prowess as a hunter/gatherer
- ✔ Operate on specific subsets of the available server objects
- ✔ Add but not edit information
- ✔ Read but not edit information
- ✔ Change all the information willy-nilly

Obviously, different clients do different things with a server. However, it may not be so obvious that some common things are always done.

If Picasso were to write these client applications, he might approach them from the abstract angle, which means that he might think about the fact that they all need to do the same thing "at the front end" before they get to the part that is specific to their function. He'd also make them have one big ear.

All client applications do the following:

- ✔ Remember the name of the object, or at least its telephone number.
- ✔ Stuff the name into a weird sequence called CosNaming::Name.
- ✔ Look up the server using the Naming Service via our handy-dandy class.

Because these steps are the same for every client application that uses the PortfolioBroker server object, we combine them into a function named FindBroker(). That way, we can reuse the function for every client, rather than rewrite it. Clever, aren't we?

Finding the PortfolioBroker

Finding the PortfolioBroker via the Naming Service is virtually identical to naming it. In the file named FindBroker.cpp, we create a function that looks up the name using our handy helper class and then does some error-checking to make sure that it gets a valid PortfolioBroker server object reference back.

```
#include <Portfolio_impl.h>
#include <stdlib.h>
#include <fstream.h>
#include <SimpleNames.h>

PortfolioBroker_ptr FindBroker(CORBA::ORB_ptr orb) {
    CORBA::Object_var obj;
    PortfolioBroker_ptr Broker = PortfolioBroker::_nil();
    try {
        CosNaming::Name name;
        name.length(3);
        name[0].id   = (const char*) "Examples";
        name[0].kind = (const char*) "CORBA_For_Dummies";
        name[1].id   = (const char*) "Chapter5";
        name[1].kind = (const char*) "CORBA_For_Dummies";
        name[2].id   = (const char*) "Broker";
        name[2].kind = (const char*) "Object";
        obj = SimpleNames::getReference(orb, name);
```

This operation is similar to naming the server, only this time we call SimpleNames::getReference().

We end up with a generic CORBA::Object reference in obj. That object may or may not be what we're expecting (in this case, a PortfolioBroker object reference), so we test it before we return it.

Narrowing the field

To get from a generic `CORBA::Object` reference to a specific server object reference, you use the IDL compiler-generated `_narrow()` method of the desired server class. That's a mouthful, isn't it? All it means is that each C++ class that corresponds to an IDL interface includes — for free — a static method named `_narrow()`. You plug in a `CORBA::Object` reference, and you get back a server object reference for that server.

We use the `narrow()` method to turn the `CORBA::Object` reference we get from the Naming Service into a `PortfolioBroker` object reference like so:

```
Broker = PortfolioBroker::_narrow(obj);
```

If the reference can't be narrowed because it's not really an object of that class, you get back a `CORBA::_nil` object.

The remaining code tests the object reference to see whether the object really exists. Sounds existential, doesn't it? The things we check are

✔ Did the `_narrow()` work?

✔ If so, does the object actually exist?

✔ If so, does it like French food?

```
    if (!CORBA::is_nil(Broker) &&
        Broker ->_non_existent())
            obj = CORBA::Object::_nil();
    }
catch(CORBA::SystemException& ex) {
    Broker = PortfolioBroker::_nil();
    }
```

Yoda says, "Using you are reference valid it is not."

Just because you have a reference doesn't mean you have a valid one.

That's because the server application may have left a reference (via the Naming Service or by writing the string version to a file) and then exited for some reason. In this case, you may well find a reference and even be able to use the `_narrow()` method to narrow it, but

it's not really valid. You don't get to discover this fact until you try to call one of the server object's methods. Then you get a `CORBA::OBJECT_NOT_EXIST` exception.

Rather than take that chance, use the `_non_existent()` method to test the object first, without calling any of its methods.

The IDL compiler adds the _non_existent() method to every server object for you. When you call this method, it tries to connect to the server. It's supposed to return TRUE if the object doesn't exist, but in some ORB implementations, it raises an exception instead. That's why we use it in an if statement, as well as wrap it in a try block. We're covered no matter what it does! By taking these steps, you can check to see whether the server is really there.

```
if (CORBA::is_nil(Broker))
    cout << "Could not find a PortfolioBroker object."
        << endl << "Run the server first!" << endl;
else
    cout << "Located the PortfolioBroker\n\n";

    return Broker;
}
```

If any problems develop along the way, we print an error message and return a nil object reference. If not, we return the narrowed, fully checked out PortfolioBroker object reference.

The Clients Are Here to See You

All clients follow the same basic steps:

1. Include the IDL-generated client header file and any other header files needed.
2. Create a main() function, and inside it create a try block.
3. Inside the try block, initialize the ORB (but not the BOA, because we're not acting like a server).
4. Get an object reference to one or more server objects.
5. Go on a mystery date.
6. Perform some client-specific operations using the server object.
7. Quietly exit under the cover of darkness.

We need to create two clients that perform two different actions using the PortfolioBroker server object. All the steps except Step 6 are implemented exactly the same in both clients.

In Step 6, the first client creates new Customer objects. The second client creates new Stock objects and edits Stock objects using the Buy() and Sell() methods.

Client #1, what is your name, please?

The complete source code for the Customer client application is in a file named Customer.cpp on the CD-ROM at the back of this book, in the Examples\Chapter6 directory.

The Customer application is a simple client that uses the FindBroker() function and accesses the PortfolioBroker and Customer server objects. It only does one thing, but it does it well: It lets you add new Customers. Steps 1 through 3 follow:

```
#include <Portfolio.h>
#include <stdlib.h>
#include <fstream.h>
PortfolioBroker_ptr FindBroker(CORBA::ORB_ptr orb);


int
main(int argc, char* argv[], char*[]){
   try {
      CORBA::ORB_var orb = CORBA::ORB_init(argc, argv,
         "Orbix");
      // Orbix specific -- turn off Diagnostics
      orb->setDiagnostics(0);
```

This program works with Orbix. That's why we use "Orbix" in the ORB initialization call. In addition, Orbix requires that clients turn off diagnostics. Otherwise, they print a bunch of messages to standard output when they run. If you're not using Orbix, these two things are different.

Our FindBroker() function performs Step 4, getting the object reference:

```
      PortfolioBroker_var Broker = FindBroker(orb);
      if (CORBA::is_nil(Broker)) return 1;
```

All we need to do is check to see whether it is a nil object. If it is, we just return from the main() and exit the program. We could print an error message, eject a floppy, emit a loud honking noise, or do something else to indicate a problem. But we don't.

In Step 6, we do something with the server object reference. We begin by using plain old C++ to let the user enter the new customer's name and account number:

```
      Customer_var c;
      char name[31], acct[31];
      cout << "Create new Customer\n";
      cout << "Customer Name: ";
      cin.getline(name,30);
```

```
cout << "Account number for " << name << ": ";
cin.getline(acct,30);
if (name[0] == 0 || acct[0] == 0) return 1;
```

Catching flack and exceptions

The `PortfolioBroker::MakeCustomer()` method creates a new customer server object and returns it. If the supplied account number already exists, the method throws a small hissy fit and then an exception.

We use a nested `try` block to catch a specific exception. In this case, it's the duplicate customer exception `PortfolioBroker::DuplicateCustomer`. If a duplicate is detected, we just print the name of the existing customer and return out of the `main()`, which ends the program.

```
try {
    c = Broker->MakeCustomer(name, acct);
}
catch (PortfolioBroker::DuplicateCustomer& ex) {
    cout << "Sorry, Account: " << acct << endl
        << "is already assigned to Customer: " <<
        ex.ExistingCustomer << endl;
    return 1;
}
```

If no exception occurred, the new `Customer` server object's two `Get` methods are called to get the customer name and account number, which are then printed.

```
CORBA::String_var cName = c->Name();
CORBA::String_var cAccount = c->Account();
cout << "\nCustomer: " << cName << endl
    << "Account: " << cAccount << endl;
}
```

Step 7 is the general CORBA error handler and the final return.

```
catch(CORBA::SystemException& ex)
{
  cerr << "CORBA Exception!" << ex << endl;
  return 1;
}


  return 0;
}
```

That's the end of the first client application!

We assign the strings returned from Name() and Account() to CORBA::String_var variables because these methods return a copy of a string, and we want to make sure that copy gets deleted when we're done with it. The String_var type always deletes its memory, so putting the strings in CORBA::String_var variables gives us exactly what we want.

If we didn't make sure that the copies of strings get deleted, we'd "leak" memory — allocating it but never freeing it — and that's never a good idea.

Client #2, what is your name, please?

We create a second client in the file named BuySell.cpp that supports adding new Stocks and buying and selling units of each Stock. Because much of the client is similar to the Customer client, we show only the key bits of code in this section.

The complete source code for the BuySell client application is in a file named BuySell.cpp in the Examples\Chapter6 directory on the CD-ROM that accompanies this book.

The BuySell application begins by prompting for an account number. After we enter the account number and it is stored into a variable named acct, we look up the customer using the PortfolioBroker:

```
Customer_var customer;
customer = Broker->FindCustomer(acct);
```

We get the list of Stock objects from the Customer server object. Next, we compute the total value of all Stocks.

```
StockList_var stocks = customer->Stocks();
CORBA::Double change;
cout << "Total Value: " <<
    customer->CalculateTotalValue(change) << endl
    << "Total gain or loss: " << change << endl
```

We use a class named StockList_var to hold the list of Stocks that the Stocks() method call returns. The IDL compiler defines this class for us as an unbounded sequence of Stock objects. The _var indicates that this class automatically deletes its contents and releases the object references at that time. Chapter 5 contains a detailed description of unbounded sequences, _var types, and releasing object references.

The Big Picture

The thing to notice about all the code in this chapter is not that it's a wonderful implementation of a Portfolio Management System (PMS), but rather that it really does look and behave like a normal C++ object-oriented program. Sure, you need to be aware of some key differences:

- ✔ You have to get the initial reference to a server object.
- ✔ You have to be mindful of the memory and object references that the server methods return.
- ✔ You have to brush your teeth before going to bed.
- ✔ You have to use exception handling.

None of those things is horribly difficult, except for brushing your teeth in C++.

Compiling and Running

It's time for the fun part! Compile and link the server and client applications, and then run the server application.

Before running the server, we're assuming that you've installed your ORB and started any ORB servers (including the Naming Service) that you need in order to run CORBA applications. Your ORB may require that your Portfolio server be registered with the Interface Repository (IR). If you must register the server, use the name `Portfolio` and say that it's a persistent server. For Orbix, we use this command:

```
C:\Portfolio\> putit Portfolio -persistent
```

To run the applications, follow these steps. The stuff you enter is shown in bold.

1. **Run the server first in one window.**

```
C:\Portfolio\> server
```

2. **Next, run the customer client in another window and enter some customer information:**

```
C:\Portfolio\> customer
Located the PortfolioBroker
```

(continued)

(continued)

```
Create new Customer
Customer Name: Kiera Lim
Account number for Kiera Lim: 1001


Customer: Kiera Lim
Account: 1001
```

3. Run the `buysell` **client and enter some stock information for the customer created in Step 2.**

```
C:\Portfolio\> buysell
Located the PortfolioBroker


Enter Customer account number (x to exit): 1001


Customer: Kiera Lim
Account: 1001


No Stocks.
a to add, x to exit: a
Stock Name: HAL
Current Price: 9.50
Enter amount in dollars to buy: 200
You bought 21.05 shares
```

After you enter a number of stocks, the output looks something like this:

```
C:\Portfolio\> BuySell
Located the PortfolioBroker


Enter Customer account number (x to exit): 1001


Customer: Kiera Lim
Account: 1001
2 Stocks
Total Value: $1451.74
Total gain or loss: $-48.26



Select Stock:
 1) HAL Total Value: $314.95 Change: $14.95
 2) SAL Total Value: $1136.79 Change: $-63.21
Enter 1-2, a to add, x to exit:
```

The information you enter is saved as long as the server application runs. Chapter 21 discusses ways to make server objects remember their values even when they're not running.

Chapter 7

If Only We Had Some Java Code

*I*f you've come to this chapter seeking refuge from the horrors of C++, take heart. Here you will find beauty, simplicity, and automatic memory management, thanks to Java. Seriously, if you've done some work with C++ and CORBA, working with the CORBA/Java combination is like a walk outside on a beautiful, sunny day.

CORBA works with numerous languages, and it works especially well with Java. The foremost reason is Java's automatic memory management. Because you, the developer, never need to delete anything yourself, many of the messy details of using CORBA just disappear like money in Las Vegas. The other big win for Java and CORBA is that Java already treats all objects as references — another big mess of details (at least when compared to C++) that you don't have to worry about.

This chapter focuses on using the Java binding for CORBA to write the interface implementations for server objects.

Bindings are the language mappings between IDL and target language constructs. For example, a `long` in IDL maps (or is bound to) an `int` in Java. Because CORBA contains multiple language bindings, you can use the same IDL files to create applications in several different languages.

In C++, types that you use in IDL are mapped to special classes supplied by CORBA. Unlike C++, IDL types are almost always mapped to native Java types. You can find detailed information on the Java bindings in your ORB documentation.

In this chapter, we solve a meaty but not overly complex problem with CORBA and Java. We also solve this problem using C++ in Chapter 5. Rather than redo all the work from scratch, we're going to use the same IDL that we present in Chapter 5, with one minor modification: We wrap the interfaces in a single module. We solve the same problem in both chapters not because we couldn't think of a different example for the Java chapter, but because seeing two different language bindings in action on the same problem is helpful.

Java is a lot like C++, except when it's different. That statement is half joke and half hard-won wisdom. Plenty of Java looks just like C++. Even parts that don't behave the same can look the same. Before we begin solving a problem with Java and CORBA, you need to understand what we mean by clients, servers, and object references and the ways in which these entities interact with a target language and CORBA.

Java is expressly designed to be used as an object-oriented language. It's also designed to be much smarter about memory. Specifically, Java takes care of

- ✔ Keeping track of memory in use
- ✔ Freeing unused memory

Steps in creating a Java/CORBA application

1. **Think about the application to be built and decide on a solution in terms of objects, their names, data, behavior, and distribution.**

2. **Use the CORBA Interface Definition Language (IDL) to describe the objects.**

3. **Compile the IDL file(s) to generate client stub(s) and server skeleton(s).**

4. **For each interface described in the IDL file, write a target-language implementation.**

   In Java, you just write classes.

5. **Write, in your chosen target language, a main program that instantiates the implementation (server) objects.**

   In Java, this program is a class with a `main()` method.

6. **Write the client application(s) that use these server objects.**

   In Java, these applications are classes with `main()` methods, applets, or application subclasses.

7. **Compile all source files, including stubs and skeletons, and link the executable files.**

   Surprise! You don't have a link step when you use Java.

8. **Run the server application created in Step 5, and then run as many kinds of clients as you need, as many times as you need them.**

In this chapter, we cover Steps 1 through 4.

✔ Remembering important birthdays

✔ Using pointers without ever seeing them

The first two bullets in the preceding list are usually combined and referred to as *automatic memory management* or *garbage collection.* We like the latter phrase because it fits our view of memory management — it's a messy job that we'd rather not deal with directly. Java cleans up memory that you used before but aren't using now, like the trash in the can at the curb. It outdoes the trash service by actually going through all your memory and finding the bits of memory that you're not using — like having the garbage collectors come into your house and gather up the trash for you, instead of your taking it out to the curb.

The last item in the bulleted list is a key one as well. Java uses the word *reference* to refer to an object pointer. Because every object pointer is wrapped inside a reference, you never actually see it, change it, mess it up, or otherwise play with it.

A *reference* means that you know where to find the object, but you don't actually have the object in hand. When you make a new instance of a class (using the new operator) in Java and then store that instance in a variable, the actual instance isn't stored in the variable. Instead, a reference is stored there.

When you design an application using Java, you structure it as a group of objects communicating via method calls. When you add CORBA to the mix, nothing changes, at least not when you look at the code. That's pretty darn neat!

Any time a call goes out to a method in an object, the caller is the client and the callee is the server. In Java, you always have a reference to an object, so these calls always take the following form:

```
someValue = serverObject.service();
```

Whoever makes a method call is considered to be a client, and whoever processes the call is considered to be a server. In the preceding examples, the server is the object `serverObject`, and the client is the `main()` in a class.

With CORBA, clients always use references to talk to server objects. Because Java does, too, things pretty much work the same way when you're calling methods in local Java objects as they do when you're calling non-local CORBA server objects. Using references keeps client method calls looking exactly the same, whether the server is a plain old Java object or a CORBA server object.

Rules to determine whether an object is a server

Use these rules to determine whether an object should be a server object:

✔ If it performs actions for other objects, then it's a server.

✔ A client object that can also be a server object has to be treated as if it were a server object.

✔ Clients that never act as servers are just application programs.

✔ If it wears a paper hat and asks whether you want fries with that, then it's probably a server.

✔ Objects that are only servers, that have many clients, and that are totally networked are server objects.

Identifying Objects and Services

First, you identify the objects that are in the application. Next, you use IDL to describe the servers (and clients that are also servers). After that, you implement the servers as Java classes.

Chapter 5 contains a description of a proposed Portfolio Management System (PMS) for GHF (Giant Huge Funds). The general requirements of that system are reproduced here:

✔ GHF has numerous customers and needs to be able to add new ones to the system.

✔ Each customer can have multiple stocks and can add new stocks to or delete stocks from his or her portfolio.

Object identification

A simplified approach for object identification is to discover

✔ What the objects are

✔ What each object is named

✔ What each object likes for breakfast

✔ What data each object deals with

✔ What behavior each object exhibits

 ✔ A customer can buy or sell units of a stock that he or she owns.

 ✔ Shorts, pants, longs, futures, pasts, and derivatives are not for sale at GHF.

 ✔ Access to information in the system is limited by job function.

 ✔ The information must be accessible from any machine on the network.

 ✔ The Vice President of Human Resources wants spinning globes on the main window of all the client applications.

Fortunately, the combination of CORBA and Java is a perfect match for this kind of application. My, that's a happy coincidence!

Describing the objects in IDL

The source code of this example is on the CD-ROM that accompanies this book, in the `Examples\Chapter7` directory. The `Portfolio.idl` file contains the IDL for the objects, and we cover the IDL syntax in Chapter 4. The IDL is essentially the same as we describe in Chapter 5. Refer to that description for the complete details.

The entire IDL file follows:

```
module Portfolio{

    interface Customer;
    interface Stock;

    typedef sequence<Customer> CustomerList;
    typedef sequence<Stock> StockList;

    interface Customer {

        readonly attribute string Name;
        readonly attribute string Account;
        readonly attribute StockList Stocks;

        Stock AddStock(in string TheSymbol,
            in double InitialPrice);

        double CalculateTotalValue(out double
            InvestmentChange);
    };
```

(continued)

(continued)

```
interface Stock {

    readonly attribute string Symbol;
    readonly attribute double InvestmentAmount;
    readonly attribute float Units;
    attribute double CurrentPrice;

    void Buy(in double AmountInDollars);

    double Sell(in float SellUnits);

    double CalculateCurrentValue(out double
        InvestmentChange);
};

interface PortfolioBroker {

    exception DuplicateCustomer {
      string ExistingCustomer;
    };

    Customer MakeCustomer(in string CustomerName,
         in string CustomerAccount)
         raises (DuplicateCustomer);

    Customer FindCustomer(in string CustomerAccount);
  };
};
```

This IDL describes three interfaces (Customer, Stock, and PortfolioBroker) that meet the requirements for the PMS.

The Customer interface contains

- ✔ The customer's name.
- ✔ The account number.
- ✔ The stock information.
- ✔ The Stocks attribute, which returns a sequence of all the Stock objects for the customer.
- ✔ The AddStock() operation, which is used to add new Stock objects to the customer.

The Stock interface contains

- ✔ All the information for a specific stock.
- ✔ The Buy() operation, with which you buy shares of a stock.
- ✔ The Sell() operation, with which you sell shares of a stock.
- ✔ The CurrentPrice attribute, by which you can change the price of the stock.

The PortfolioBroker interface

- ✔ Acts as a central access point for clients.
- ✔ Contains the MakeCustomer() operation, used to create entries for new customers. The MakeCustomer() operation raises the PortfolioBroker.DuplicateCustomer exception if a new customer account number duplicates an existing customer.
- ✔ Contains the FindCustomer() operation, used to find existing customers by account number.

The only change from the IDL file presented in Chapter 5 is that this IDL file wraps all the interfaces in a module named Portfolio. A *module* is a handy way to group a number of interfaces. When the IDL is compiled for a specific target language (such as Java), all the interfaces enclosed in the module include the module name somehow, a system that enables a module to provide a single name space for the interfaces. Exactly how the interface includes the module name varies based on the target language. For Java, all the classes that map to the interfaces in the module are grouped into a Java package.

Generating stubs and skeletons in Java

Step 3 in creating a CORBA application is generating stubs and skeletons. We compile the IDL and work on the Java mappings for these interfaces. We use the IDL file to generate the client stub and the server skeleton Java files.

The precise name and number of the client stub and server skeleton Java files varies from ORB to ORB. You can figure out how your particular IDL compiler works by reviewing the documentation that comes with it. When using Java, each interface generates its own set of stub and skeleton Java source files. If the IDL uses a module, then all the source files generated for that module are contained in a subdirectory with the name of the module. Furthermore, any time an interface includes a nested declaration of an exception or another interface, Java source files for those items are generated in a subdirectory — one that contains the name of the enclosing interface with Package appended to it.

We're using VisiBroker for Java, from Visigenics. The CD-ROM that accompanies this book contains a demonstration copy of VisiBroker.

We compile the IDL file by using this command:

```
C:\PortfolioJava\> idl2java -strict Portfolio.idl
```

Our IDL compiler creates a subdirectory named `Portfolio` because of the `module` statement in the IDL file. This folder contains 28 generated files and one subdirectory named `PortfolioBrokerPackage`. That's a lot of files! Like every other ORB, our compiler generates a bunch of files that we never use and some that are very important. The important files are the

- Client stub class for each interface
- Server skeleton class for each interface
- `Helper` and `Holder` classes for each interface
- Complete works of William Shakespeare
- `Helper` and `Holder` classes for every sequence
- Subdirectories for nested interface and exception definitions
- Implementation class and `Helper` and `Holder` classes for every exception

We never look inside any of these files, but that's what they're used for. The `Portfolio` package includes definitions for each interface class, which is how Java maps the `module` IDL statement. The key thing to know when we get ready to implement each of the server objects is that they are all in the `Portfolio` package.

Think of these files as toxic-waste Superfund sites. Knowing about them is good, but you don't want to spend a lot of time inside. You can actually discover quite a bit about the underlying guts of the ORB by poking around inside these files, but everything you need to know is available elsewhere. Never change anything in these files. If you do, then re-run the IDL compiler and regenerate them.

At this point, you need to check your ORB documentation to find out what name your IDL compiler gives to the skeleton classes, but `_InterfaceImplBase` is pretty standard for Java mappings. The generated names created in the skeleton are used later in your classes as the base class names for each class that implements an interface.

Mapping IDL to Java Classes

Step 4 of the process of creating Java applications in CORBA is the implementation of the server in Java. Here are the rules for implementing the server in Java:

- ✔ Each of the interfaces defined in the IDL file gets a matching class created for it.
- ✔ Each class is in its own file.
- ✔ Each filename needs to be exactly the same as the class name.
- ✔ Each class name must rhyme with the word *orange*.

We don't make up these rules ourselves; they're just the normal rules for Java.

The customer is always right, so we're going to start with the Customer server class. The CustomerImplementation class must be in a file named CustomerImplementation.java.

The CD-ROM at the back of this book contains the source code for the CustomerImplementation class in the Examples\Chapter7 directory in a file named CustomerImplementation.java.

Getting the class file preliminaries out of the way

Whenever we create a Java class file for a server object, we

- ✔ Import the classes we use
- ✔ Import the IDL compiler generated server skeleton class
- ✔ Stand on our heads for a few minutes to stimulate hair growth

For CustomerImplementation.java, we accomplish the necessary importing with the following code:

```
import org.omg.CORBA.DoubleHolder;
import Portfolio.Stock;
import StockImplementation;
import Portfolio._CustomerImplBase;
```

Here are some things to notice about this code:

✔ **In the IDL, we use a** `double` **as an** `out` **parameter to the** `CalculateTotalValue()` **interface.** Using a `double` means that we need to import the `DoubleHolder` class contained in the ORB-supplied `org.omg.CORBA` package. That's how an IDL `double` maps to a Java `double` when it's used as an `out` or `inout` parameter.

Any time you have an `out` or an `inout` parameter in an IDL operation, you need to use the corresponding `Holder` class in your Java implementation, because Java does not directly support passing a value by reference. The `Holder` classes hold a value that's passed by reference. The actual value is stored inside the `Holder` class, in `Holder.value`.

✔ **The** `Customer` **interface returns a** `Stock` **from** `AddStock()`, **so we need to import the** `Portfolio.Stock` **class.**

✔ **We need to create new** `Stock` **server objects in** `AddStock()`, **so we import the** `StockImplementation` **class.**

✔ **We import the IDL-generated server skeleton class** `Portfolio._CustomerImplBase`, **because we're subclassing our server class from it.**

You can choose to forgo all the imports entirely, if you're fond of typing in the complete class name for `Stock`, `DoubleHolder`, and so on every time you use them. Likewise, you can import whole packages (for example, `Portfolio.*` instead of `Portfolio.Stock` and `Portfolio._CustomerImplBase`) if you want. However, we think that importing just the classes that we use is much clearer.

Mapping interfaces to Java classes

Each interface in the IDL maps to a single Java class in its own source file. For each interface, we

✔ Declare a `final` **class whose name ends in** `Implementation`. The class inherits from the IDL generated skeleton class. We use "`extends`" to subclass the generated server skeleton class.

✔ Declare and implement a `Get` method in that class for each attribute in the interface.

✔ Declare and implement a `Set` method in that class for each non-read-only attribute in the interface.

✔ Declare and implement a method in that class for each operation in the interface.

✔ Declare and implement one or more class constructors.

✔ Declare and implement a class `finalize()` method, if it's needed.

> ✔ **Declare class member variables, if they are needed.**
>
> ✔ **Declare "We hold these truths to be self-evident."**

That's a fair number of items on the old to-do list. You're probably already used to doing the last four tasks for your Java classes anyway; only the first four are CORBA-specific.

Note that we're not going to bother creating a separate interface class and implementation class for the server classes. We could, but we don't need to. Interface classes are useful if you're writing classes with the idea that others (or even you!) will subclass them in the future. By making an interface class, you create a short, easy-to-read specification of a Java class's interface, much like a C++ class header file. However, we don't want these classes subclassed, so we don't need to make the interface classes for them.

CustomerImplementation class

The `Customer` interface requires most of the items in our checklist, so we take a look at it bit by bit.

```
public final class CustomerImplementation
   extends _CustomerImplBase {
```

This class statement shows that we're inheriting from the skeleton class `_CustomerImplBase` that was generated by the IDL compiler for the `Customer` interface. We name our class `CustomerImplementation` because the IDL client stub already declares a `Customer` class for us. That class is used to access the methods from the client's side. We're implementing the server side of the interface, so we need to use a different class name.

TECHNICAL STUFF

The final word on classes

CORBA's Java binding uses inheritance to build a server object based on several subclasses. Because the server implementation you write is the last subclass in that chain, you can make it a `final` class. Making it a `final` class has two effects:

✔ The class cannot be subclassed again.

✔ Instances of the class may execute a bit faster.

You don't have to make the server implementation a `final` class, but doing so lets the world (and the Java compiler) know that you don't really expect anyone else to make new classes based on that class. In many cases, making the server implementation can speed the execution of objects of the class.

When implementing IDL interfaces as Java classes, always declare your class with a different name. Any name will do, but the convention is to name it by using the same name as the IDL interface, with Implementation tacked on the end. Don't forget to make the filename match the class name — most Java compilers require you to do so.

The actual name of the skeleton class may be different based on your ORB. You need to look at the documentation or example files provided with your ORB in order to find out how the interface name (in this case, Customer) is changed when the IDL compiler generates the server skeleton classes. The stub file itself may be generated in a subdirectory (ours is in the Portfolio subdirectory) if you use a module statement in the IDL file.

Mapping read-only attributes to Get methods

The Customer interface has three attributes, so we define three methods in the class by using the same names as the attributes. These methods don't take any parameters, but they do return values, which is how a read-only attribute maps to a Java Get method. Here's how we define the three methods:

```
public String Name() {
    return MyName;
}

public String Account() {
    return MyAccount;
}

public Stock[] Stocks() {
    return MyStocks;
}
```

Because all the attributes in the Customer class are read-only, we don't need to define any Set methods. Each of these methods just returns the appropriate member variable. We haven't defined these yet, but that's not a problem with Java.

If you've already tackled using C++ with CORBA, you may be wondering why we don't return copies of the data in these three methods, like we do in C++. The short answer is "Because we don't have to." The long answer is "Because we use Java, we're exempt from the drudgery of managing memory. Java is so slick that it can make copies for us. It copies everything, all the time, just for fun. Sometimes, if you listen to a Java program while it's running, you can hear small popping sounds as it makes copies of stuff."

Determining type mappings

We seem to know almost by magic what to use for the return type for these methods, don't we? That's because the type used for a Java return value or parameter is based on the type used in IDL.

The two IDL `string` attributes map to Java `String` types. For the Java binding, CORBA always maps an IDL `string` to a Java `String`.

Because a Java `String` is never bounded (that is, fixed to a particular size) and can contain Unicode characters, trying to return a `String` from a Java server object that doesn't match the IDL specification for the interface is possible. When that happens, CORBA throws an exception. The possible exceptions are

- ✔ `CORBA.MARSHAL` if the `String` is longer than the bounded CORBA `string` specified in the IDL
- ✔ `CORBA.PULL_MY_FINGER` if the `String` is `"Uncle Fred"`
- ✔ `CORBA.DATA_CONVERSION` if the `String` contains Unicode characters that don't map to ASCII characters

The return type for the `Stocks()` method is just a plain old Java array of `Stock` object references. That's how bounded and unbounded sequences in IDL map to Java — they are just arrays of whatever type the sequence holds.

As was the case with strings, Java arrays are not bounded. Therefore, in the case of bounded sequences, trying to return an array that is larger than the bounds specified in IDL is possible. CORBA shows its displeasure with this turn of events by throwing the `CORBA.MARSHAL` exception and a flaming tantrum.

Mapping operations to methods

The `Customer` interface has two operations. For each operation, we write a method in the class. Each method

- ✔ Uses the same name as the operation
- ✔ Takes the same numbers and types of parameters (mapped to Java types) as used in the IDL definition
- ✔ Returns a value that is the Java type mapping of the CORBA type used in the IDL file
- ✔ Is the drink that picks you up and calms you down

The `AddStock()` method adds new `Stock` objects to a member variable inside `Customer`. Because these `Stock` objects are server objects, it pays to do things carefully. We look at the method in several chunks. Here's the first one:

```
public Stock
    AddStock(String TheSymbol, double InitialPrice) {
        StockImplementation TheStock = new
            StockImplementation(TheSymbol, InitialPrice);
```

Use the same names for the parameters to methods as you do for the parameters to operations in IDL. You aren't specifically required to use the same names, but doing so makes the code easier to match up to the IDL.

The IDL for the `AddStock()` operation has a return value of type `Stock`. The corresponding Java type of the return value that is used in the class method `AddStock()` is also `Stock`. This is always the case.

IDL methods that return interfaces map directly to Java methods that return object references.

Creating new server instances

In this method, we create a new instance of the `StockImplementation` class. It becomes a usable CORBA server just by creating the object in Java. The constructor is called to make the new object. We get back a reference to the new `Stock` server object that we need to squirrel away somewhere.

Extending unbounded sequences

We store the new `Stock` object reference in the array member variable `MyStocks`. We need to do a little work to make this array larger each time we add a new Stock object to it.

```
Stock[] newList = new Stock[MyStocks.length+1];
for (int i = 0; i < MyStocks.length; i++)
    newList[i] = MyStocks[i];
MyStocks = newList;
MyStocks[MyStocks.length-1] = TheStock;
```

Adding new elements to a Java array that represents an unbounded list is a four-step process:

1. **Make a new array that is one element larger than the current array.**

2. **Copy all the elements in the existing array into the new array.**

3. **Replace the existing array with the new array.**

4. **Store the item in the newly added array position, being sure to buff and polish the item before storage.**

You may think we need to cast the `StockImplementation` object into a `Stock` object before we store it in the array. After all, the array is declared to hold `Stock` objects, not `StockImplementation` objects. However, this is one of those times that inheritance (and a smart compiler) jumps in and saves us. Because `StockImplementation` is a subclass of `Stock`, Java does the right thing and silently does the cast for us. You can put an explicit cast in if you want to, but it's not necessary.

All we need to do to finish this method is return a reference to the newly created Stock object. Here's how:

```
    return TheStock;
}
```

If you've done the CORBA dance with C++, you're probably looking at that return statement and muttering something about duplicates, references, and how we must have goofed up somewhere. Nope. It's happy Java land, where all the hassles of remembering to return a duplicate reference melt away like the cream on a double cappuccino. In other words, don't sweat it — this is actually correct code. It really is just this simple.

Making servers act like clients

The CalculateTotalValue() method in the CustomerImplementation class actually does some computational work. It's an example of a server object that uses an out parameter. Because this method calls methods of other server objects, it makes the CustomerImplementation object act like a client. The CalculateTotalValue() method looks like this:

```
public double
CalculateTotalValue(DoubleHolder InvestmentChange) {
    double TotalValue = 0.0;
    InvestmentChange.value = 0.0;
    DoubleHolder ThisChange = new DoubleHolder();
    for (int i = 0; i < MyStocks.length; i++) {
        TotalValue +=
            MyStocks[i].CalculateCurrentValue(
                ThisChange);
        InvestmentChange.value += ThisChange.value;
    }
    if (java.lang.Math.abs(InvestmentChange.value) <
        0.005)
        InvestmentChange.value = 0.0;
    return TotalValue;
}
```

We use DoubleHolder as the type in Java everywhere that we use double in the IDL definition of an out or inout parameter. You use a DoubleHolder variable slightly differently than a plain old Java double variable. With a DoubleHolder (or any Holder object), you always use the Holder.value member variable to access or change the actual value held by the object.

You have to use a Holder class for any out or inout parameter in Java.

Hold everything, even the holder

We keep waving our hands and telling you to use Holder classes for out and inout parameters when you use Java. Here's why. Java always passes stuff to methods "by value." That means you always get a copy when you pass a parameter to a method. The whole point of an out or inout parameter is that changes made inside the method to the variable are reflected in the caller's supplied parameter variable. In other words, the variable is passed in "by reference" so that the method can use the reference to change the value of the caller's variable. In C++, this chore is usually accomplished via a pointer or reference type.

Guess which type is the only type passed by reference in Java? Yep, the object reference. Actually, Java passes a copy of the object reference even in this case, but the reference itself still points to the same object. CORBA uses this little factoid to come up with the Holder class solution to the out/inout reference problem. It's a little ugly, but it works.

CORBA generates Holder classes for every interface you define in IDL, as well as for every type usable in IDL. If you declare an out or inout parameter in IDL, it maps to one of these Holder classes in Java. All the Holder class does is wrap a member variable of the correct type, named value, inside a class. When you pass the class into a member function, it can change the value in the caller's Holder object. It's not exactly transparent to you, the developer, but it does work.

Think about those Stock objects we're using in this method to calculate the total value of the investments for the Customer. The MyStocks array holds references to the Stock server objects that were created via the AddStock() method. When we call the CalculateCurrentValue() method in each Stock object, it is actually a distributed object's method call using CORBA. In this case, the method call isn't a very long trip — after all, both the client (in this case, the Customer object) and the server (one of the Stock objects) happen to be on the same computer. Even if the Stock objects were on a machine in Algeria for some reason, this code wouldn't change. Sometimes, you just gotta love CORBA.

Writing constructors and destructors

We still need to write the constructor and destructor for the class, so here it goes:

```
public CustomerImplementation(String name,
     String account) {
   MyName = name;
   MyAccount = account;
   MyStocks = new Stock[0];
}
```

A constructor is your chance to initialize a new instance of a server object. For the `CustomerImplementation` object, we need two strings — the customer's name and the customer's account number. Within the constructor, these two strings are assigned to the corresponding member variables. We also initialize the array that holds the `Stock` objects added in the `AddStock()` method. We initialize this member variable with a zero-length array. That way, if a user calls the `Stocks()` method before any `Stock` objects have been added, he or she gets the correct result — a zero-length array.

Always initialize every member variable that is accessible via a `Get` method in the constructor, but don't initialize strings and arrays with nulls. Instead, use empty strings and zero-length arrays. Some implementations may throw an exception if you try to return a null string or null array.

```
public void finalize() {
    MyStocks = null;
}
```

The `finalize()` class method is as close as Java gets to a destructor. It may be called just before the object is garbage collected, but then again, it may not. You don't have to provide one because the objects that the class holds are also released when this object is garbage collected. We like to use them anyway, just so that we feel better about the whole thing. This destructor puts a null in the array member variable holding `Stock` object references, which lets Java know that we're not using those `Stock` objects any more.

Go ahead and add `finalize()` methods to your server implementations, if they hold other object references.

Declaring member variables

We use private member variables to store a class's values. By making them private, we're assured that other classes can't change these values on a whim. The private member variables for the `Customer` class are as follows:

```
private String MyName;
private String MyAccount;
private Stock[] MyStocks;
}
```

Of the two `String` variables, one stores the name (`MyName`) and the other stores the account number (`MyAccount`.) We also declare an array of `Stock` objects named `MyStocks` to hold the sequence of object references for all the Customer's stocks. Notice that the array declaration doesn't allocate an array — that's done in the constructor.

You decide the variable names to use here, because no direct mapping from IDL exists. We suggest names that are either really clear or really obscure.

StockImplementation class

The Stock interface has three read-only attributes, one non-read-only attribute, and three operations. The Java class has methods that implement all these items, as well as some member variables.

The source code for the StockImplementation class is on the CD-ROM at the back of this book in the Examples\Chapter7 directory in a file named StockImplementation.java.

Starting with imports

We always begin a server implementation class with the import statements:

```
import org.omg.CORBA.BAD_OPERATION;
import org.omg.CORBA.CompletionStatus;
import org.omg.CORBA.DoubleHolder;
import Portfolio._StockImplBase;
```

The first two imports are for the CORBA BAD_OPERATION exception we throw in the Sell() method. The first one is for the actual exception object, and the second is for the completion status value. Next comes one of those DoubleHolders, because the CalculateCurrentValue() operation in the IDL definition of the Stock interface uses a double as an out parameter. Finally, we import the IDL generated server skeleton for the Stock interface.

Implementing a class act

The class statement and the read-only attributes are implemented in Java pretty much the same way as they are implemented for the CustomerImplementation class:

```
public final class StockImplementation
    extends _StockImplBase {

  public String Symbol() {
    return MySymbol;
  }

  public double InvestmentAmount() {
    return MyInvestmentAmount;
  }
```

```
public float Units() {
   return MyUnits;
}
```

We don't have much new stuff to report here, except that the IDL float type that is used for the Units attribute maps directly to a Java float return type for the Units() Get method.

Mapping the non-read-only attributes

The CurrentPrice attribute isn't read-only, so it maps to a pair of methods in the Java class.

```
public double CurrentPrice() {
   return MyPrice;
}


public void CurrentPrice(double value) {
   MyPrice = value;
}
```

Whenever you declare an attribute in IDL, you have to create corresponding methods (called the Get and Set methods) in Java:

- ✔ If the attribute is readonly, you just create the Get method.
- ✔ If the attribute is not readonly, you also create the Set method.
- ✔ If you're feeling really wacky, you can add a Twiddle method that rearranges the current value and then returns it.

Primitive maps

Most primitive types in IDL map directly to Java types. These are the boolean, char, short, float, and double types.

A CORBA long maps to a Java integer, and an octet maps to a Java byte. In a weird twist of fate, the CORBA long long maps to a Java long. The remaining permutations of longs, shorts, and unsigneds, such as unsigned long long, map to a long, or an integer, or a short in Java.

Because Java doesn't have an unsigned type, these may end up being large negative values if the supplied unsigned value is larger than the largest positive value these types can hold in Java. Other than warning you, there isn't much we (or you) can do about this problem.

The Get method always returns a value of the same type (mapped to Java, of course) as the attribute. The Set method returns a void (in other words, it doesn't return a value) and it takes in one parameter that has the same type as the attribute. In Java, as in C++, having two methods with the same name that differ only in their return types or parameters is called *overloading*.

Three methods and a baby

The three methods for the StockImplementation class implement the Buy(), Sell(), and CalculateCurrentValue() operations. These operations are pretty standard Java methods, as you can see in the following example.

The Buy() operation looks like this:

```
public void Buy(double AmountInDollars) {
    MyInvestmentAmount += AmountInDollars;
    MyUnits += (AmountInDollars/MyPrice);
}
```

The Buy() method adjusts the values of the investment amount and units member variables to reflect the purchase of more stock. Nothing specific to CORBA here! As a matter of fact, if the Buy() method walked up to you on the street, you wouldn't be able to tell whether it was a method in a Java class, a CORBA class, or a kickboxing class, would you? Kind of comforting, isn't it?

Here's the Sell() operation:

```
public double Sell(float SellUnits) {
    if (SellUnits > MyUnits)
        throw new BAD_OPERATION(10, CompletionStatus.COMPLETED_NO);
    MyInvestmentAmount -= (SellUnits * MyPrice);
    MyUnits -= SellUnits;
    return (SellUnits * MyPrice);
}
```

The Sell() method adjusts the values of the investment amount and units member variables to reflect the sale of some stock. However, it throws a fit if the number of units to sell is more than are available. Well, at least it throws an exception — in this case, the CORBA standard BAD_OPERATION exception.

Whenever something undesirable happens in a server method, you can either throw an exception or return an error value. When you return an error value (like null or -1), you're betting that every client will check the returned value to see whether it's an error or not. When you throw an exception, you know that the client will find out that an error occurred. We suggest that you use exceptions.

Because we know that when we throw this exception, the operation isn't complete, we set the status to `CompletionStatus.COMPLETED_NO` to let the client know that nothing changed in the server.

When you're writing your IDL for an interface, you decide whether a particular operation can raise an exception. If you decide that an exception is needed, you can either define one in the IDL file or you can just use one of the CORBA standard exceptions. Often a standard exception does the trick just fine.

The `CalculateCurrentValue()` operation looks like this:

```
public double CalculateCurrentValue(DoubleHolder
    InvestmentChange) {
  double TotalValue;
  TotalValue = MyUnits * MyPrice;
  InvestmentChange.value = TotalValue - MyInvestmentAmount;
  if (java.lang.Math.abs(InvestmentChange.value)
      < 0.005)
    InvestmentChange.value = 0.0;
  return TotalValue;
}
```

The method implements an operation that uses a `double` (`InvestmentChange`) as an `out` parameter. Our method uses a `DoubleHolder` type for the parameter, so we need to be sure to use `InvestmentChange.value` to retrieve or change the value of the `double` everywhere in the method. Other than that, it's plain old Java!

Wrapping it up

To wrap up the `StockImplementation` class, we just need a constructor and the member variables. Because the class doesn't hold any references to other server objects, we don't need a destructor.

The constructor and member variables are written this way:

```
StockImplementation(String symbol, double price) {
  MySymbol = symbol;
  MyPrice = price;
  MyUnits = 0.0f;
  MyInvestmentAmount = 0.0;
}

private String MySymbol;
private double MyPrice;
private float MyUnits;
private double MyInvestmentAmount;
}
```

The constructor sets two member variables to the supplied values and initializes the other two (units and investment amount) to zero.

PortfolioBrokerImplementation class

The `PortfolioBroker` IDL interface defines two operations that return references to interfaces. The corresponding Java methods return references to the Java classes for those interfaces. Two imports are for the `Customer` class and the `Customer` implementation class, because we're allocating `CustomerImplementation` objects and returning `Customer` references. Finally, we import the server skeleton for the `PortfolioBroker` interface.

The source code for the `PortfolioBrokerImplementation` class is on the CD-ROM that accompanies this book in the `Examples\Chapter7` directory in a file named `PortfolioBrokerImplementation.java`.

The IDL for the `PortfolioBroker` interface includes a nested declaration for the `DuplicateCustomer` exception. Also, the `MakeCustomer()` interface indicates that it raises that exception.

Bringing in more imports

We see the effect of this nesting right from the start, in the import section of the class:

```
import
    Portfolio.PortfolioBrokerPackage.DuplicateCustomer;
import Portfolio.Customer;
import CustomerImplementation;
import Portfolio._PortfolioBrokerImplBase;
```

The first `import` statement is for the nested exception class that the IDL compiler generates. Notice that it's generated in its very own Java package, inside the `Portfolio` package.

Whenever you declare a nested interface, type, constant, or exception in IDL, the IDL compiler for Java generates a nested package with the same name as the interface, type, constant, or exception with `Package` appended to the name. All the Java classes generated by the nested declarations are in this package. The IDL compiler does all the work involved in creating an exception class based on an IDL exception type, so we just need to import the class and use it.

That old class magic

The class statement is implemented in the same way as it was for our other classes:

```
public final class PortfolioBrokerImplementation
   extends _PortfolioBrokerImplBase {
```

We just extend the skeleton class, creating a final class.

Coming up with more method madness

The MakeCustomer() method creates and returns a new Customer server
object. It also stores all the references in an array that it hands out:

```
public Customer
  MakeCustomer (String CustomerName,
      String  CustomerAccount)
      throws DuplicateCustomer {

   Customer dup = FindCustomer(CustomerAccount);
   if (dup != null)
      throw new DuplicateCustomer(dup.Name());

   CustomerImplementation TheCustomer =
         new CustomerImplementation(CustomerName,
         CustomerAccount);
   Customer[] newList =
         new Customer[MyCustomers.length+1];
   for (int i = 0; i < MyCustomers.length; i++)
      newList[i] = MyCustomers[i];
   MyCustomers = newList;
   MyCustomers[MyCustomers.length-1] = TheCustomer;
   return TheCustomer;
}
```

Unlike the Sell() method in the Stock class, we have to use the throws
modifier in the method declaration. This isn't a case of arbitrary enforcement by the Java compiler. In fact, the IDL generated server skeleton class
(or a class it inherits from) already specifies that it can throw any standard
CORBA exception. Because DuplicateCustomer is a user-defined exception, we can't throw it unless it's in the method declaration.

For all user-defined exceptions, you must use the throws modifier in the
method declaration.

We call the FindCustomer() method (defined next) to look up the account
number of the new customer. If we get back a match, we throw the exception, returning the name of the existing Customer. Otherwise, we create a
new Customer, extend our array holding the Customer object references,
add the new Customer object to the end, and then return it.

The last method is `FindCustomer()`:

```
public Customer
FindCustomer (String CustomerAccount) {
    for (int i = 0; i < MyCustomers.length; i++)
        if (MyCustomers[i].Account().equals(
            CustomerAccount)) return MyCustomers[i];
    return null;
}
```

This method scans the array of saved `Customer` objects. For each one, it retrieves the account number string and compares it to the test string. If it finds a match, it returns the string. If it doesn't find a match, it returns a `null`. This operation is one of those plain old Java methods, except that it's actually using a bunch of server objects (the `Stock` objects). So it's another case of a server object acting like a client.

Tie a yellow ribbon 'round the old Java class

To wrap the class up, we write our constructor, destructor, and member variables:

```
public PortfolioBrokerImplementation() {
    MyCustomers = new Customer[0];
}

public void finalize() {
    MyCustomers = null;
}

private Customer[] MyCustomers;
}
```

By now, you're a jaded Java CORBA developer, so you know what these variables do. We think the constructor allocates an empty array for the array holding the `Customer` object references. The `finalize()` method nulls out this array — a step that isn't really necessary but doesn't hurt. The only member variable is the `MyCustomers` array, which holds the `Customer` object references.

Chapter 8

If Only We Had a Java Application

• •

In This Chapter

▶ Writing a server application

▶ Writing client applications

▶ Building and running applications

• •

*P*retend, for a moment, that you have been handed several completely implemented server classes that are written in Java. You need to write the server application and some client applications that use them.

Writing a server application requires two bits of knowledge:

✔ The desired activation policy

✔ The constructor parameters for one or more server objects

There are four possible activation policies. For now, we stick with the simple *persistent server* policy: We write a single application that creates the initial server object instances a client may need and that then waits forever to serve client requests. Chapter 11 discusses all four activation policies.

To know the parameters needed for the server object class constructor, we need to take a peek at the server class implementation, beause that's the only place they're defined. We note the parameters needed in the server implementation constructor, so we can supply them when we create the instance of the server class.

You also want to write client applications for those servers. What are your next steps? Do you

A. **Decide on a server activation policy and write a server application in Java?**

B. **Carefully hunt for clues in the implementation class source code for the server objects?**

C. **Carefully examine the Interface Definition Language (IDL) file for the server objects to determine their interfaces?**

D. **Write one or more client applications, in Java or in any other language?**

The correct answers are A, C, and D. You never need to look at the implementation class source code to write a client application — that's what IDL is for!

Chapter 2 defines a general, step-by-step approach to creating CORBA applications. This chapter discusses Steps 5 through 8, as listed in Chapter 2:

5. Write a Java server application that instantiates the server objects.

6. Write Java client application(s) that use these server objects.

7. Compile all source files, including stubs and skeletons, and link the executable files.

   You don't have a link step when you use Java. Instead, you execute the compiled classes directly.

8. Run the server application created in Step 5, and then run as many kinds of clients as you need, as many times as you need them.

Because we open this chapter with the "let's pretend" game, you can probably guess that we're going to use pre-existing server classes. Rather than make up some new ones, we use the Java server objects of the `Portfolio` example that we develop in Chapter 7.

The IDL for the `Portfolio` example is in the `Examples\Chapter8` directory on the CD-ROM at the back of this book.

Writing a Persistent Java Server Application

If you pick the persistent server policy, as we do in this chapter, you have to write a persistent server application to go along with it. Server applications create server object instances that can then respond to client requests.

Knowing the terminology is always helpful, so keep the following definitions in mind:

- **Persistent Server Application:** A persistent server is implemented as a stand-alone application. In Java, a stand-alone application is a class with a `main()` method, run by using a Java interpreter before any clients are run. The Java interpreter may be `jview`, `java`, or another Java Virtual Machine (`VM`).

- **Activation Policy:** An activation policy is a procedure by which a server object is made ready to process method calls from clients. Chapter 11 discusses server activation policies.

Writing a server application in Java consists of the following steps:

1. **Deciding on a server activation policy.**

2. **Identifying which server objects must be created by the server application.**

3. **Deciding how to make the created server object references available to clients.**

4. **Sitting down to a nice hot cup of coffee and some of those really hard biscotti things.**

We are using Java with a persistent server activation policy. Our server application isn't going to do anything fancy like display a GUI (graphical user interface) window. Therefore, our general steps are

1. **Import the server object implementation class and any classes we need.**

2. **Create a class (named** `JavaServer`**) that has a single** `main()` **method.**

3. **In the** `main()` **method, inside a** `try` **block, initialize the ORB.**

4. **Create an initial instance of the desired server object(s).**

5. **Make the reference to the server object available to client applications.**

6. **Order a Mocha Java — we've earned it.**

7. **Wait for client applications.**

Caffeine activation

Simple server applications like the ones in this chapter are easy to write. Stay on the well-lit paths and you'll be safe. We get the first three steps out of the way quickly in the next bit of Java code.

The complete source code for the server application is in a file named `JavaServer.java` in the `Examples\Chapter8` directory of the CD-ROM that accompanies this book.

```
import PortfolioBrokerImplementation;
import org.omg.CORBA.ORB;
import org.omg.CORBA.Object;
import org.omg.CosNaming.NameComponent;
import org.omg.CosNaming.NameHolder;
import org.omg.CORBA.SystemException;
```

(continued)

(continued)

```
import SimpleNames;

public final class JavaServer {

    public static void main(String args[]) {
        try {
            ORB orb = ORB.init(args,null);
        ORB myOrb = new ORB();
                myOrb.init(args,null);
```

The server object class is `PortfolioBrokerImplementation`. Next are the `import` statements for the CORBA classes we need. Finally, the `SimpleNames` import is for a class we wrote that makes the use of the Naming Service a bit easier. The `SimpleNames` class is covered in Chapter 18.

We declare a simple `final` class with just a `main()` method. The `main()` is our basic Java main method. It gets executed when we run the class from a Java VM. Then we have the beginning of the `try` block, followed by the ORB initialization call.

Self-serving server selections

We're ready to serve up one or more of our server objects, but how do we know exactly which one to serve? This problem is the same no matter what language you're using, so rather than repeat the rules here, we ask that you head on over to Chapter 6 and read the section about activation policies.

There are three server objects for the `Portfolio` example:

- `Customer` contains a name, an account number, and a list of Stocks.
- `Stock` contains a symbol, an investment amount, units, and a price.
- `PortfolioBroker` contains a list of `Customers`.

Because the `PortfolioBroker` class is intended to be the initial access point for clients, its implementation is the one we are serving.

Creating an initial instance of the server takes just a few actions. This is Step 4 in our step-by-step process.

1. **Create an instance of the server class by using** new.

2. **Use** orb.connect() **to tell the ORB that the server is ready.**

Where's the BOA constrictor?

You may have noticed that we haven't mentioned a Basic Object Adapter (BOA) here. The Java language binding doesn't really specify one, and most ORB implementations seem to get by quite well without one. The usual method to indicate that an object is ready to serve is simply to create it.

Sometimes, however, you may want to do some additional initialization work with an object or create more than one server object before indicating that you're open for business. Even when a simple new is all it takes to activate a server object, ORB vendors usually provide some alternative setting or option to delay things until you're ready. As usual, we suggest that you look at your ORB documentation to answer this question.

Here's what the code looks like for creating an initial instance of the server:

```
PortfolioBrokerImplementation broker;
broker = new PortfolioBrokerImplementation();
orb.connect((Object)broker);
```

We're using the persistent server activation policy, so we need to use orb.connect() on the first instance. After that, any other server objects that are created are "automagically" connected for us. In fact, even this initial object is probably connected for us as soon as it's created. However, that behavior may vary based on your ORB vendor. Check the documentation of your ORB to find out exactly what you need to do to connect your server objects to the ORB.

Using the Naming Service

Just like their C++ brethren, Java servers and clients need some way of finding each other. The server application needs to leave some clues behind so that clients can find the server objects in it. The CORBA Naming Service remains the number one choice of clients for linking up servers and clients.

This is Step 5, making the reference to the server available to clients, in our step-by-step process.

The Naming Service is just another CORBA server. Servers can register their object references with it, supplying a name that looks very much like a directory path and filename. Because we are talking about CORBA, the OMG uses different names for these things. In the CORBA Naming Service, what look like directory paths and filenames are called Name Components.

We discuss the Naming Service in Chapter 18. The Naming Service is pretty easy to use, but it does take several lines of code to either register or look up a name. Rather than do that over and over, we wrote a class called `SimpleNames` that provides two static methods. The `bindToName()` method, which servers use, makes (or updates) an entry with the Naming Service. The `getReference()` method looks up a name and returns the associated reference. The `SimpleNames` class (in C++) is also described in Chapter 18.

The source code in Java for the `SimpleNames` class is in a file named `SimpleNames.java` in the `Examples\Chapter8` directory on the CD-ROM that accompanies this book.

Using the Naming Service with `SimpleNames` is simple:

1. **Have a server object ready to name.**

2. **Think up a name consisting of zero or more subdirectory names and then the actual object name.**

3. **Think up a nickname, just for fun.**

4. **Stuff the name into an array of `NameComponent` objects.**

5. **Use the `SimpleNames.bindToName()` static object method to bind the object to the name.**

6. **Rejoice in the knowledge that someone else is doing your work.**

Here's what these steps look like for our server:

```
NameComponent myName[] = new NameComponent[3];
myName[0] = new NameComponent("Examples",
   "CORBA_for_dummies");
myName[1] = new NameComponent("Chapter8",
   "CORBA_for_dummies");
myName[2] = new NameComponent("Broker",
   "Object");
if (!SimpleNames.bindToName(orb,
      (Object)broker, myName)) {
   return;
}
```

`SimpleNames` needs an array of `NameComponent` objects. You can think of the array as specifying the full path and name for the object. Each element in the array corresponds to a directory in the path, except the last one. The last element in the array is the actual object name. Each element is a `NameComponent` object that includes both the component `id`, and the component `kind`. For example, the first directory in our example code has an `id` of "Examples" and a `kind` of "CORBA_for_dummies". We create an array of length 3 and then add the three `NameComponent` objects to it.

We send the `NameComponent` array and the `PortfolioBroker` server object to `SimpleNames.bindToName()`, where it becomes a Naming Service entry. The result is that `PortfolioBroker` is registered with the Naming Service under the name `Examples\Chapter8\Broker`.

Although we show a Windows style directory path for the name of an object in the Naming Service, this is just a shorthand notation we use. In fact, there is no way to use a string such as "`Examples\Chapter8\Broker`" or "`Examples:Chapter8:Broker`" or even "`Examples.Chapter8.Broker`" to refer to a specific object in the Naming Service. The only way to do it is by using an array of `NamingContext` objects.

I'll wait for you if you'll wait for me

The last step is to wait. At this point, depending on your ORB vendor implementation, you either have to call the ORB `impl_is_ready()` method, or you don't. VisiBroker for Java uses tasks for server objects, so as soon as you use the `connect()` ORB method, a separate task that accepts connections for the server starts. The main thread (in the `main()` method) doesn't need to do anything other than not exit, as shown in the following example:

```
try {
    Thread.currentThread().join();
}
catch(InterruptedException e) {
    System.exit(1);
}
}
catch(SystemException se) {
    System.exit(1);
}
}
}
```

We try to `join` the `main()` thread to the server thread. If that attempt succeeds, then the `join()` call never returns and the program waits forever for client requests. If something bad happens, we just exit. The server application is done!

This program works with VisiBroker for Java. If you're using a different ORB, you may need to end the `main()` method with a call to `orb.impl_is_ready()` to wait for clients to connect.

Why multiple clients?

We can think of several really good reasons to use multiple client applications:

✔ They can be limited to specific tasks.

✔ You can impress your manager by creating several client applications instead of just one.

✔ Each client can operate on specific subsets of the available server objects.

✔ A client application can be designed to add but not edit information.

✔ A client application can be designed to read but not edit information.

✔ A client application can be a guest star in a science fiction TV show, and edit information before it even exists, due to temporal distortions.

Writing Generic Client Applications

We use a couple of client applications to access the Customer, Stock, and PortfolioBroker objects. That's the whole point of using CORBA, after all. You make the servers once, and then you access them from several different clients that do little bits of what you normally do in a large program without CORBA.

If each client begins by locating the same server object, then it is basically the same as all the other clients that work with the same server object. We call this behavior the *generic client,* because it does the generic stuff that all the clients accessing the server have to do.

All client applications do the following:

1. **Specify the name of the server object.**

2. **Stuff the name into an array of** NameComponent **objects.**

3. **Get a reference to the server object by using the Naming Service —** and our SimpleNames **class.**

We're writing two clients that use the PortfolioBroker server object. Each client needs the exact same code to do these three steps. We can either

✔ Repeat the code in both clients.

✔ Make a final class with a static method that does these steps, and then call the method from each client.

We opt for the last choice. If we ever need to write more clients that use the PortfolioBroker server object, we'll get even more use out of it.

Where is my PortfolioBroker?

The FindBrokerFn class is a little helper class that contains one static method named FindBroker(). Writing this class is a lot like writing a simple function in C++.

The source code in Java for the FindBrokerFn class is in a file named FindBrokerFn.java in the Examples\Chapter8 directory on the CD-ROM at the back of this book.

The method just uses the correct name to retrieve the object reference from the Naming Service by using our SimpleNames class. The method then does some error checking to make sure that it gets back a valid PortfolioBroker server object reference.

```
import Portfolio.PortfolioBroker;
import org.omg.CORBA.ORB;
import org.omg.CORBA.Object;
import org.omg.CosNaming.NameComponent;
import org.omg.CORBA.SystemException;
import SimpleNames;
```

Like every other Java class, we begin by importing all the classes we use. In this case, we use the PortfolioBroker class and, for the first time, the PortfolioBrokerHelper class. Next comes the usual collection of CORBA classes and, finally, SimpleNames.

```
public final class FindBrokerFn {
    public final static PortfolioBroker
    FindBroker(ORB orb) {
```

Next, we declare a final class, because we're not expecting to need to make subclasses. In the class, we create one static method.

```
Object obj;
    PortfolioBroker Broker = null;
    try {
        NameComponent name[] = new NameComponent[3];
        name[0] = new NameComponent("Examples",
            "CORBA_for_dummies");
        name[1] = new NameComponent("Chapter8",
            "CORBA_for_dummies");
        name[2] = new NameComponent("Broker","Object");
        obj = SimpleNames.getReference(orb, name);
```

With Java, you use a static method in a class when you want to be able to call the method without creating an instance of the class.

Next, we create the name we're looking for and then call
`SimpleNames.getReference()` to retrieve the object reference from the
Naming Service. That method returns a `CORBA.Object` reference, which we
store in `obj`. That object may or may not be a `PortfolioBroker` object
reference, so we test it before we return it. The testing process is described
in the next section.

A narrow escape with a helper

When you compile an IDL file into a Java binding, you get a `Helper` and a
`Holder` class for each interface in the file. For example, our example IDL file
generates a `PortfolioBrokerHelper` and a `PortfolioBrokerHolder`
class. The `Helper` class contains some stuff you never use and one method
that you do use:

```
    Broker = PortfolioBrokerHelper.narrow(obj);
  }
catch(SystemException ex) {
    Broker = null;
  }
```

The `narrow()` method in this class takes a `CORBA.Object` as its parameter
and returns an object of the desired class (for example, `PortfolioBroker`),
if the object is really of that class, or else returns `null`.

Always use the `narrow()` method in the IDL-generated `Helper` class to
convert a general `Object` reference into a specific server object reference.

We need to test the `Broker` variable to see whether it's `null`. If not, we also
verify that the server object is really there. We accomplish these two tasks
like this:

```
  if (Broker == null || Broker._non_existent()) {
    Broker = null;
    System.out.println("Could not find" +
      " a PortfolioBroker (java) object.\n" +
      "Run the server first!");
  }
  else
    System.out.println(
      "Located the PortfolioBroker\n");
  return Broker;
  }
}
```

If the Broker variable is not `null`, then we get a `PortfolioBroker` reference from the Naming Service. That's not quite good enough to return without one more test. This test checks to see whether the server object is currently running.

It's quite possible for a persistent server object to register itself with the Naming Service and then exit without removing that reference. If that happens and a client uses the Naming Service to get a reference to that server object, bad things happen. The client gets a reference and can even `narrow()` it, but the reference points to a server that's not running. If the client tries to call a method by using the reference, an exception is thrown. Fortunately, every server object class includes a method named `_non_existent()` that can test whether the server is really running. If it isn't, that method returns `true`.

If `Broker` is not `null`, we call its `_non_existent()` method to verify that it is really running. If it's not running, we set it to `null` and print an error message.

If `Broker` is `null` or some exception is thrown, we also print the error message. In any case, we return whatever we have, which is either `null` or a valid `PortfolioBroker` object reference.

You Can Never Have Too Many Clients

In this section, we write two client applications in Java. Because it's Java, you may be expecting cool GUI applications, but that's not going to happen here. Instead, we're making bare-bones Java classes with `main()` methods which use the standard input and standard output for a character-based interface. In other words, these applications are a close match to the C++ applications we develop in Chapter 6. We're not lazy, just incredibly crafty. We want you to see how to use CORBA in a Java client, not how to code cool GUIs in Java.

We write a GUI-based Java client that can run in a web browser in Chapter 9, so you can see how such a client impacts accessing the server objects.

The main thing to take away from these client applications isn't just how clever they are as Java examples, but rather how using CORBA hardly impacts their code. Keep these key differences in mind:

- ✔ The initial reference to a server object is required if you want to use the object.
- ✔ `Holder` classes are required if you want to pass `out` or `inout` parameters to server objects.

> ✔ Helper classes are required to narrow objects.
>
> ✔ Exception handling is necessary.

Considering all the power and flexibility that CORBA brings to Java, using CORBA to create distributed Java server and client applications is worth this small amount of effort. We talk about these differences in more detail in following sections.

Each client you write needs to do the following:

1. **Import the IDL-generated client stub class and any other classes needed.**

2. **Create a class that has a single** main() **method.**

3. **Inside a** try **block, initialize the ORB.**

4. **Get an object reference to one or more server objects.**

5. **Create an animated, spinning globe or other cute web animation.**

   Okay, technically your client application doesn't *need* to do this!

6. **Perform some client-specific operations by using the server object.**

7. **Exit stage right when complete.**

Because we're creating two clients that use the PortfolioBroker server object to perform two different actions, all the steps except Step 6 are implemented exactly the same in both clients. In Step 6, the first client creates new Customer objects. The second client creates new Stock objects and edits Stock objects by using the Buy() and Sell() methods.

Customers for nothing

The complete source code for the AddCustomer client application is in a file named AddCustomer.java in the Examples\Chapter8 directory on the CD-ROM at the back of this book.

All the AddCustomer client does is accept a name and an account number from the user. It then tries to make a new Customer object. If you've read Chapter 5, the first four steps probably look pretty familiar:

```
import Portfolio.Customer;
import Portfolio.PortfolioBroker;
import
    Portfolio.PortfolioBrokerPackage.DuplicateCustomer;
import org.omg.CORBA.ORB;
import org.omg.CORBA.Object;
```

```
import org.omg.CORBA.SystemException;
import FindBrokerFn;
import java.io.*;

public final class AddCustomer {
   public static void main(String args[]) {
      ORB orb = ORB.init(args,null);
      try {
         PortfolioBroker Broker =
            FindBrokerFn.FindBroker(orb);
         if (Broker == null) return;
```

The pure Colombian beans (Step 6) of the client is next. It starts with plain old Java code that prints some prompts and accepts the user entry for the customer name and account number:

```
BufferedReader stdin =
   new BufferedReader(
      new InputStreamReader(System.in));
Customer c;
String name, acct;
System.out.println("Create new Customer");
System.out.print("Customer Name: ");
name = stdin.readLine();
System.out.print("Account number for " + name +
   ": ");
acct = stdin.readLine();
if (name.equals("") || acct.equals("")) return;
```

That code was just a lot of standard Java console I/O programming. Next, we make a Customer object with the values that the user enters, and then we use PortfolioBroker.MakeCustomer() to create a new customer server object:

```
try {
   c = Broker.MakeCustomer(name, acct);
}
catch (DuplicateCustomer ex) {
   System.out.println("Sorry, Account: " + acct +
      "\n" +"is already assigned to Customer: " +
      ex.ExistingCustomer);
   return;
}
```

Because the PortfolioBroker doesn't like two Customer objects having the same account number, it throws an exception if we try to add a duplicate. Rather than have our general error handler catch that error, we create a nested try block to catch the duplicate customer exception DuplicateCustomer. If a duplicate is detected, we just print the name of the existing customer and use the return statement to leave the main() method, which ends the program.

The last statement displays the newly added customer information:

```
System.out.println("\nCustomer: " + c.Name() +
    "\n" +"Account: " + c.Account());
}
```

If no exception exists, the new Customer server object's two Get methods are called to print the customer name and account number.

To complete the AddCustomer client application, we write the general CORBA error handler and the final return statement. This is Step 7 in our step-by-step process:

```
catch(SystemException ex)
{
    System.out.println("CORBA Exception!" + ex);
    return;
}
return;
}
}
```

That's the end of the first client application!

Stocks for free

The second client supports adding new Stocks as well as buying and selling units of each Stock. Recall that only Step 6 in our seven-step process for building clients is different than the AddCustomer client we write in the preceding section.

We show only the key bits of code here, but the complete source code for the BuySell client application is in a file named BuySell.java on the CD-ROM that accompanies this book, in the Examples\Chapter8 directory.

The BuySell application begins by prompting for an account number, which it stores into a variable named acct. We then look up the customer by using the PortfolioBroker. Take a peek at the code:

```
Customer customer;
customer = Broker.FindCustomer(acct);
```

Then to compute the total value and investment change of all Stocks, we
retrieve the list of Stock objects from the Customer server object:

```
Stock stocks[] = customer.Stocks();
DoubleHolder change = new DoubleHolder();
double totalValue =
    customer.CalculateTotalValue(change);
if (stocks.length > 0) System.out.println(
    stocks.length + ((stocks.length == 1) ? " Stock" :
    " Stocks") + "\n" + "Total Value: $" +
    nf.format(totalValue) + "\n"+ "Total gain or loss: $"
    + nf.format(change.value) + "\n");
```

In the preceding code, the variable named nf was initialized to hold a Java
NumberFormat object in a section that isn't shown. We use nf to output
double values formatted with two digits following the decimal point.

Because CalculateTotalValue() uses a double out parameter, we need
to allocate a DoubleHolder in the variable named change and pass it in to
the method. We then use change.value to access the returned value from
the method.

At this point, the user makes a menu selection to add a new stock or work
with an existing stock.

If the user chooses to add a stock, the program prompts for a symbol, price,
and investment amount. It uses the AddStock() method in the Customer
instance to add the new stock. That method returns a reference to the new
Stock object, so the program uses that reference to call the Buy() method
to buy the desired number of shares.

```
Stock newStock = customer.AddStock(name, price);
newStock.Buy(amount);
```

If the user chooses to work with an existing stock, he or she may enter a
number that selects a particular stock. We use this number to retrieve the
selected stock from the stocks array:

```
Stock stock = stocks[isel];
```

The user then buys, sells, or changes the price of the selected stock. The
code for each action follows:

```
// buy
stock.Buy(amount);
// sell
try {
    stock.Sell(units);
}
catch (BAD_OPERATION& ex) {
    return; // did not have that many units
}
// set price
stock.CurrentPrice(price);
```

We used a nested exception handler to catch the CORBA standard exception BAD_OPERATION when we call the Sell() method. That's because the Sell() method throws this exception if the customer tries to sell short. Selling short is something we just don't condone!

Compiling and running the applications

It's time for the fun part! Compile all the classes that make up the server and client applications and then run the server application.

Before running the server, you must have installed your ORB and started any ORB servers (including the Naming Service) that you need in order to run CORBA applications. Your ORB may also require that your Portfolio server object be registered with the Implementation Repository (IR) before you run it. If you must register the server, use the name Portfolio and say that it's a persistent server. VisiBroker for Java doesn't need its servers registered with an Implementation Repository.

Helpful stuff on the CD-ROM

We've compiled all the classes for you, on the book's CD-ROM in the Examples\Chapter8 directory. We've also included a Windows batch file named vbmake.bat that compiles all the classes with VisiBroker for Java. The CD also holds four batch files that are used to run the Java applications:

✔ startns.bat starts the VisiBroker Naming Service.

✔ startserver.bat starts the PortfolioBroker persistent server.

✔ AddCustomer.bat runs the client that adds a new Customer.

✔ BuySell.bat runs the client that buys and sells stocks.

To run the applications, follow these steps. The stuff you enter is shown in bold.

1. Run the server first in one window.

```
C:\PortfolioJava\> startserver
```

2. Run the AddCustomer **client in another window and enter your customer information:**

```
C:\ PortfolioJava \> AddCustomer
Located the PortfolioBroker

Create new Customer
Customer Name: Kiera Lim
Account number for Kiera Lim: 101


Customer: Kiera Lim
Account: 101
```

3. Run the BuySell **client and enter stock information for the customer created in Step 2:**

```
C:\ PortfolioJava \> BuySell
Located the PortfolioBroker

Enter Customer account number (x to exit): 101

Customer: Kiera Lim
Account: 101

No Stocks.
a to add, x to exit: a
Stock Name: HAL
Current Price: 11.75
Enter amount in dollars to buy: 200
You bought 17.02 shares
```

You can continue to buy and sell stocks, add new stocks, and add new customers as long as you like. If you compare these programs to the ones developed in Chapter 6, you see that they behave exactly the same.

Our server doesn't save its data anywhere except in memory. That means that any information we enter is saved only as long as the server application runs. When we exit from the server (press Ctrl+C in the server windows for most operating systems, or just close the window), then all the information is discarded. Chapter 21 discusses ways to make server objects remember their values even when they're not running.

Chapter 9

The Web and CORBA

*Y*ou can use Java to implement CORBA server objects, server applications, and client applications. When you're writing applications in Java, you can decide to implement a *graphical user interface* (GUI) or a plain old *console* (often called a *command-line*) *interface.*

Chapter 8 describes how to write Java clients that use command-line interfaces. These interfaces are great for making "run anywhere" clients for your network. However, if you want to be hip and with it, dude, you need to get your clients on the Web.

Web-based Java clients are called *applets,* and they always have GUI interfaces.

An applet is a Java application that runs inside a web browser.

You need to address three basic problems with CORBA applets:

⬝ ✔ Performing ORB initialization

⬝ ✔ Getting initial object references

⬝ ✔ Getting around the Java security limitations placed on applets

Additionally, you need to keep compatibility in mind, because your applet may be running on several different machines. We spend the rest of this chapter addressing these issues, but first, a word from our coffee sponsors.

Getting a Quick Taste of Java

Because this book isn't about Java, we don't go into a great deal of detail about how to write Java applets in general. If you don't know how to write an applet that is accessible via a Java-enabled web browser, you need to get your hands on a copy of *Java Programming For Dummies,* 3rd Edition. What you do need to know before reading this chapter is that HTML is the language you use to create Web pages, and Java is the language you use to add program functionality to those Web pages.

Here's the decaffeinated process for writing and serving up a Java applet on the Web:

1. **Write a Web page in HTML that includes a special** `<applet>` **tag that specifies the class name for the applet.**

2. **Write an applet class that extends the standard Java** `Applet` **class.**

   You can, of course, write several other classes that your applet class uses to make your Web application cool.

3. **Add a little cream and sugar.**

4. **Compile the class(es).**

5. **Install the generated** `.class` **files, along with the HTML Web page, in a directory that is served by your web server.**

6. **Other people load the Web page by supplying its URL, or Uniform Resource Locator, to their web browsers.**

7. **They ooh and ahh over your wonderful applet.**

A CORBA-based applet is a Java applet first, so you need to do all the same things to it that you normally do for an applet. You do all the preceding steps in addition to the extra stuff you do for CORBA. Chapter 8 discusses writing non-Web-based CORBA applications in Java.

Accessing Web-Based Objects

Some fundamental differences exist between running a Java application on a computer and running a Java applet from within a web browser. These differences impact both the way your client is run and the way it is implemented.

Getting that extra initialization information

The first difference you notice when you go the applet route is that you don't have a command line handy when you run the applet. When your client is implemented as an application, you can use command-line options to supply vendor-specific settings used during ORB initialization. For Java, these settings are often related to things like the default context for the Naming Service. When you create an applet, you obviously don't have a command line around to use.

ORB vendors use the standard Java approach for supplying parameters to an applet. These parameters are in the form of param/value pairs supplied in the HTML file.

For example, VisiBroker has a number of optional settings that you can use in your HTML file, as shown in the following applet tag:

```
<applet
    code=AddCustApplet.class width=400 height=100>
    <param name=org.omg.CORBA.ORBClass
        value=com.visigenic.vbroker.orb.ORB>
    <param name=ORBservices value=CosNaming>
    <param name=SVCnameroot value=CFDExample>
</applet>
```

In this example HTML file, the `ORBservices param` specifies `CosNaming` as its `value`, indicating that the applet uses the Naming Service. When you initialize the ORB (by using `ORB.init()`), you pass in the applet to the method call, which lets the ORB access the parameters used in the HTML file. The `ORB.init()` method determines all the ORB-specific stuff and uses it to do the proper initialization. A typical ORB initialization performed in an applet class looks like this:

```
orb = ORB.init(this, null);
```

Each ORB vendor has its own set of optional settings. These settings are used to fine-tune performance, locate services, and perform other initialization tasks. Each vendor has similar options, but they always use different names for those options. The preceding example works with VisiBroker for Java. You need to consult your ORB documentation to find out the names and uses of its optional settings.

Getting the first server object reference

All CORBA clients, even Java applets, have to obtain a valid object reference to a server before they can call any of its methods. When creating a Web-based applet there are some slight differences to using the standard CORBA initial reference techniques that you need to be aware of.

We outline the various ways a client can get an object reference in Chapter 3.

When you're writing an applet, you can use the same techniques as for any other client. The main ways a client gets an object reference are

✔ Via the Naming Service.

✔ Via `www.pick.a.server.any.server.com`.

✔ By using string versions of the object reference.

Using the Naming Service

In many ways, using the Naming Service with an applet is a lot like using the Naming Service with an application. You use the exact same code, and it returns the same result. It's like low-impact aerobics — good for you, yet easy on your knees.

We're going to implement the `AddCustomer` Java client from Chapter 8 as an applet (named `AddCustApplet`) that uses the Naming Service. This client uses the `PortfolioBroker` and `Customer` server objects that we present in Chapter 7, along with the same persistent server application we present in Chapter 8. In other words, you're seeing the power of CORBA reusability in action. We can access the same server application from both Java applications and applets.

The `AddCustomer` GUI is very simple. It has two text fields, where the user enters the customer name and account number, and a button labeled `Add Customer`, which the user clicks to add the new customer.

The source code in Java for the `AddCustApplet` class that uses the Naming Service is in a file named `AddCustApplet.java` in the `Examples\Chapter9\NSVersion` directory on the CD-ROM that comes with this book. Also in that directory are all the other files you need from Chapters 7 and 8, so you have everything you need in one place.

To add a customer by using `AddCustApplet`, the user does the following:

1. **Fill in two text fields with the name and the account number.**

2. **When finished with Step 1, click the Add button.**

If the add succeeds, the text boxes are cleared and a dialog box displays the new customer's name and account number. If the account number is a duplicate, the text boxes are not cleared and a different dialog box displays an information message.

Importing classes for an applet

The `AddCustApplet` applet begins like any other Java file, with a straightforward series of `import` statements and the class declaration:

```
import Portfolio.Customer;
import Portfolio.PortfolioBroker;
import Portfolio.PortfolioBrokerHelper;
import
    Portfolio.PortfolioBrokerPackage.DuplicateCustomer;
import org.omg.CORBA.ORB;
import org.omg.CORBA.Object;
import org.omg.CORBA.SystemException;
import FindBrokerFn;

import java.io.*;
import java.awt.*;
import java.awt.event.*;
import java.applet.Applet;
import java.awt.Toolkit;


public class AddCustApplet extends Applet
        implements ActionListener {
```

In the preceding code, we

- Import the classes we use for the Portfolio server (`Customer`, `PortfolioBroker`, `PortfolioBrokerHelper`, `PortfolioBrokerPackage.DuplicateCustomer`) as well as the CORBA classes.
- Import the Java classes that we need for the applet.
- Declare a class named `AddCustApplet` that extends the `Applet` class and implements the `ActionListener` class.

That last bit is just the Java 1.1 way to implement GUIs. Because our applet includes a button, we need a way to do something when that button is clicked. Extending `ActionListener` enables us to add a method to the class that gets called when a user clicks the button.

This applet is a Java Development Kit (JDK)1.1 applet, which just means that it uses some of the newer Java features like ActionListener.

Viewing private parts

The first thing in the class is its private member variables:

```
private TextField _nameField, _acctField;
private Button _doAdd;
private PortfolioBroker Broker;
private ORB orb;
```

The first three variables hold the text fields and the button for the GUI. Next is the variable that holds the PortfolioBroker server object reference, and the last variable holds the ORB object.

Initializing the applet

The init( ) method of an applet is called just one time, when the applet is loaded off the web server. This makes the init( ) method the perfect place to do the CORBA initialization tasks that every client needs to do. The init( ) method is also the place to go ahead and get that first object reference for a client. That way, when the client has fully loaded and displayed its GUI, it's prepared with an initialized ORB and a reference to a server object.

The init( ) method does three things that get the applet ready for use:

1. **Create the layout portion of the GUI by using the Java AWT classes.**

2. **Initialize the ORB and retrieves the initial server object reference.**

3. **Fill in the GUI with either a form or a brief error message.**

Creating the GUI

The following code allows us to divvy up the applet window area into three panels in a 3 x 1 grid:

```
public void init() {
    Panel top = new Panel(new FlowLayout(
        FlowLayout.RIGHT,10,10));
    Panel bottom = new Panel(new FlowLayout(
        FlowLayout.RIGHT,10,5));
    Panel buttonArea = new Panel();
    setLayout(new GridLayout(3,1));
    add(top);
    add(bottom);
    add(buttonArea);
```

Initializing the ORB

In this second step, we initialize the ORB and then get a reference to the `PortfolioBroker` server object by using the `FindBrokerFn` class. We describe that class in Chapter 8.

```
ORB orb = ORB.init(this, null);
try {
    Broker = FindBrokerFn.FindBroker(orb);
}
catch(Exception ex)
{
    System.out.println("System Exception!" + ex);
    Broker = null;
}
```

Rounding out the GUI

Step 3 fills in the GUI with either a form or a brief error message:

```
if (Broker == null) {
    buttonArea.add(
        new Label("Sorry, could not connect to the"
        + " PortfolioBroker."));
}
else {
    top.add(new Label("   Customer Name"));
    top.add(_nameField = new TextField(30));
    bottom.add(new Label("Customer Account"));
    bottom.add(_acctField = new TextField(30));
    buttonArea.add(_doAdd =
        new Button("Add Customer"));
    _doAdd.addActionListener(this);
}
```

We want to display either a simple label indicating that we could not connect to the server, or the data entry form used to add new customers.

If we don't have a valid `PortfolioBroker` reference, we just put a single label in the topmost panel that displays an error message to the user. No buttons are on the form in this case, so the user can't do anything — which is fine, because we don't have any way to add a new customer.

If we do have a valid `PortfolioBroker` reference, we add a label/text field pair to the top and middle panels and a button to the lower panel. We add this class as the `ActionListener` for the button, which just means that clicking the button calls our `actionPerformed()` method. We're ready to add new customers!

Taking action

The `actionPerformed( )` method is where the action is, as far as applets with buttons are concerned. Most action routines do these types of, well, actions:

1. **Validate the input from the user.**

2. **Sing a song about youth in Seattle, where they drink plenty of coffee.**

3. **Attempt to call a method of a server object, supplying the entered data as parameters.**

4. **Update the GUI and display feedback of the result of the action.**

5. **Include general error handling.**

Our `actionPerformed()` method is no different. Take a look at how each of these steps is performed.

Validating Input

In the first step, we get the string contents of the two fields and verify that they're not blank. If they are, we display a simple error dialog box and return. This result leaves the data that the user entered in the fields, so the user can add whatever is missing. We show the code for `SimpleDialog` (our simple dialog box) a little later in this chapter.

```
public void actionPerformed(ActionEvent evt) {
    try {
        Customer c;
        String name = _nameField.getText();
        String acct = _acctField.getText();
        if (name.equals("") || acct.equals("")) {
            SimpleDialog d = new SimpleDialog(
                "Invalid Entry!",
                "Null name or account (" + name +
                ") (" + acct + ")");
            d.setVisible(true);
            return;
        }
```

Singing like a slacker

Sing the following in your finest flannel shirt: "Oh, my coffee is cold and I'm young! Dah Dah Dah!"

Calling home

Inside a nested `try/catch` block, we attempt to make a new customer with the supplied name and account number.

```
try {
   c = Broker.MakeCustomer(name, acct);
}
catch (DuplicateCustomer ex) {
   SimpleDialog d = new SimpleDialog(
      "Account number duplicate!",
      "Account: " + acct +
      " is already assigned to Customer: " +
      ex.ExistingCustomer);
   d.setVisible(true);
   return;
}
```

If all goes well, the catch statement is not invoked. If the catch statement is invoked, it means that the user entered a duplicate account number. We use the same SimpleDialog class to display the error message, and then we return. This result also leaves the data that was entered in the text fields so that the user can try another account number.

Updating the GUI

If nothing bad happens, then the new customer is added in the preceding code, and we just need to update the GUI.

```
_nameField.setText("");
_acctField.setText("");
SimpleDialog d = new SimpleDialog(
   "Made New Customer!", "Customer: " +
   c.Name() + " -- Account: " + c.Account());
d.setVisible(true);
}
```

We clear the two text fields and then use the returned Customer server object reference to retrieve the name and account number. We display this information, again using the SimpleDialog class, in a message that indicates that we added the new customer.

The user can now enter a new name and account number in order to add another customer.

Expecting the unexpected errors

The last little bit of code implements our error handlers. We don't do much here other than print an error message to the Java console.

```
catch(SystemException ex)
{
    System.out.println("CORBA Exception!" + ex);
    return;
}
catch(Exception ex)
{
    System.out.println("System Exception!" + ex);
    return;
}
return;
}
}
```

When writing Java applets that use CORBA, it's vital that you include try/
catch blocks so that you can detect the many different exceptions that
CORBA can throw. Unlike our example, you should provide feedback to the
user when your applet catches an error. A SimpleDialog box that notifies the
user of the problem may be sufficient.

A really simple dialog class

The SimpleDialog class has nothing to do with CORBA, but we do use it to
display error and information messages. It's just a subclass of the Java
Abstract Window Toolkit (AWT) Dialog class:

```
class SimpleDialog extends Dialog
    implements ActionListener {

  SimpleDialog(String title, String msg) {
      super(null, title, false);
      Panel top = new Panel();
      Panel bottom = new Panel();
      setLayout(new GridLayout(2,1));
      add(top);
      add(bottom);
      top.add(new Label(msg));
      Button b = new Button("OK");
      b.addActionListener(this);
      bottom.add(b);
      pack();
      Toolkit t = Toolkit.getDefaultToolkit();
      Dimension d = t.getScreenSize();
      setLocation(new Point(d.width/2, d.height/2));
  }
```

```
public void actionPerformed(ActionEvent event) {
    setVisible(false);
}
}
```

This class includes a constructor that makes a dialog box with a label and an OK button. When you call the constructor, you supply a string for the title bar and a string for the label.

You can use this simple dialog class in your applets for both error and information messages, just as we do in our applet.

Using string versions of object references

If the Naming Service seems like overkill for a Web-based applet, you can always go retro and use string versions of object references. That's usually accomplished by having the persistent server application write the string version of the object reference to a file and then having the clients read that file to get the reference. When the client is an applet running in some browser, reading a file involves using the Java URL class.

Avoiding the Naming Service speeds up your applet significantly if you're just getting one object reference. Reading the string reference off the server is much faster than using the Naming Service for just one reference because extra connections and messages are needed to locate and talk to the Naming Service.

When using string versions of object references with applets, follow these steps:

1. **The persistent server application creates a file containing a string version of the server object reference.**

   By convention, you name this file by giving it the class name of the server object with ".ior" appended.

2. **After starting the server, copy the .ior file into the correct directory on the web server.**

3. **The client applet reads the file from the web server, using the Java URL class.**

4. **Like Cinderella's Fairy Godmother at midnight, the client turns the string back into an object reference and goes on its merry way.**

The AddCustApplet that we develop with the Naming Service already does everything a Java applet client should do. In order to change it to use string references, we modify the AddCustApplet class to read a string reference file from the web server. Fortunately, we need to change only a little bit of the init() method, so you don't need to wade through a lot of new code! We also need to change the JavaServer persistent server application from Chapter 8 so that it saves a string reference to a file instead of using the Naming Service.

The source code in Java for the AddCustApplet class that uses string references is in a file named AddCustApplet.java. As you may expect, this file is in the Examples\Chapter9\StringVersion directory on the CD-ROM at the back of this book. Also in that directory are all the other files you need from Chapters 7 and 8, along with the modified JavaServer.java file, so you have everything you need in one place. We just show the changed portions of the two files here. Refer to the files on the CD-ROM to see the full class.

Stringy servers

In the server application's main() method, instead of registering the object with the Naming Service, we just create a file with the object reference:

```
ORB orb = ORB.init(args,null);
PortfolioBrokerImplementation broker;
broker = new PortfolioBrokerImplementation();
orb.connect(broker);
String ior = orb.object_to_string(broker);
try {
    OutputStreamWriter w = new OutputStreamWriter(
        new FileOutputStream("PortfolioBroker.ior"));
    w.write(ior, 0, ior.length());
    w.close();
}
catch (IOException ex) {
    System.out.println(
        "Could not write PortfolioBroker.ior: " + ex);
    return;
}
```

We use orb.object_to_string() to generate a string version of the object reference. We then do a bunch of Java footwork to write that string to a file named "PortfolioBroker.ior".

Our persistent server application just creates the .ior file in the same directory where it is run, which means that you need to remember to copy the .ior file into the proper Web server directory every time you run the server application. This procedure is the most general way to code the server application. A less general way is to hard-code the full path name to the Web server directory right into the server application. We're not saying that hard-coding is the better way, but that method certainly removes the "Oops! I forgot to copy the .ior file to the server" step in the process of running everything!

Stringy clients

The changes to the client are nearly as simple as the changes to the server. Instead of calling FindBrokerFn.FindBroker(), we read the file off the web server and turn it into an object reference:

```
URL u = new URL(getDocumentBase(),
    "PortfolioBroker.ior");
BufferedReader s = new BufferedReader(
   new InputStreamReader(new BufferedInputStream(
      u.openStream()))));
String ior = s.readLine();
s.close();
Object obj = orb.string_to_object(ior);
Broker = PortfolioBrokerHelper.narrow(obj);
```

This stuff is more Java than CORBA! The Java parts all deal with using a URL class to read the file off the server. We use getDocumentBase() to specify that the file is in the same directory on the server as the applet's Web page is. Then we use a bunch of Java classes to read the string by using the URL object. Hey, nobody said Java was intuitive!

Finally, we get to the CORBA part. We use orb.string_to_object() to convert the string reference into a CORBA Object reference. Then we use the PortfolioBrokerHelper class to narrow the resulting Object into the desired class.

The rest of the client is the same. When you run the applet, it even looks and acts the same. If you time it with a stop watch, the applet probably loads a bit faster than the one using the Naming Service, but that's the only difference you or your users see. Unless, of course, your users have special X-ray-like vision that enables them to see bits flying hither and yon.

Playing outside the Security Sandbox

An applet can do almost anything a non-Web-based Java application can do, with a few limitations. These limitations are imposed for security reasons and are sometimes called *sandbox security* in Java documentation because Java applets are limited to "playing in their own sandbox" when running in a web browser.

The security limitations for Java applets are that applets cannot

- ✔ Read or write files on the local machine.

- ✔ Open Internet connections to any server machine other than the web server it was loaded from.

Not reading and writing files on the local machine isn't a big deal for CORBA, but being limited to just one server machine is! After all, you may want to access servers spread across several machines, using a web-based applet.

You have several options for getting around the limitation of running on only one machine. You can

- ✔ Use a vendor-specific product that acts as a gateway for all applets.

- ✔ Give up and load every server object onto your web server machine.

- ✔ Sign trade agreements with machines on the Web so that you can exchange secret coffee-brewing information late at night.

- ✔ Sign all your CORBA applets, using the new JDK1.1 signing system.

- ✔ Design your own proxy server objects and run them on the web server machine.

The big easy

ORB vendors know that limiting Java applet access to just the Web server machine is a big issue, so most of them have very viable and transparent ways around the problem. Inprise has a product called GateKeeper that allows applets to access any server object on any machine on the network. IONA Technologies has a product called WonderWall that does the same thing. Our recommendation is to seriously consider using your vendor's workaround, if it supplies one.

The little easy

For some systems, running all your CORBA server objects on the same machine as your web server may be an acceptable solution. This avoids the problem completely, since you limit the Java applet to accessing just the Web server machine.

If you use this solution, you aren't able to access any CORBA servers on any other machines, so you also need to run the Naming Service, if you use it, on your web server.

The almost as big easy

If you can't get around the security system, try turning it off. In the newest versions of Java, you can *sign* your applet. Signing involves generating a certificate file that users install on their machines. When your applet runs, it is detected as a trusted, signed entity, and the normal security restrictions are lifted.

A signed applet can do anything it wants, almost. There is a hitch. As of this writing, none of the mainstream browsers correctly implements signed applets. Verify that your target browsers support signed applets before embarking on this path.

The Java 1.1.5 SDK in `Demos\Sun\Java`, on the CD-ROM that accompanies this book has detailed information and tools for signing an applet.

This old server

Some people just have to do things themselves. If you're one of those people, then you can consider the last option: You can create a set of IDL interfaces for one or more proxy classes that are used to bridge Java applet requests from the Web server to other machines.

These classes must act as both clients and servers, and they need to run on the web server machine. All they do is mimic the interfaces of the objects you really want your client to talk to. When the client calls a method in one of these servers, the server turns right around and calls a method of some other server that's not running on the same machine. This option doesn't violate sandbox security, but it has some drawbacks:

✔ You have to implement all the proxy classes.

✔ You have to write bug-free code for the proxy classes.

✔ Performance suffers, because a method call maps into several ORB requests.

> ✔ Your web server needs to run all the proxy server objects.
>
> ✔ Substitutes (like decaffeinated coffee) are never as good as the real thing.

Only consider the do-it-yourself approach if you need to access only a few remote server objects. If you're considering creating ten or more proxy server objects, it's time to consider getting a vendor-supplied product.

Playing Nice with All the Browsers

Browser compatibility with applets is more of a Java issue than a CORBA issue, but we need to mention it. Here's the standard lecture for good applet design and implementation:

> ✔ **Know your browsers.**
>
> ✔ **Don't use a version of Java that isn't supported by the industry standard browsers.**
>
> ✔ **Don't forget to install the classes your application needs in the appropriate web server directory.**
>
> ✔ **Don't forget that you also need to install classes supplied by your ORB vendor.**
>
> ✔ **Don't skimp on error-checking and user feedback.**
> Nobody likes an applet that "hangs" or crashes for no apparent reason.
>
> ✔ **Try to fail gracefully, if you do fail.**
> Notice that we don't even make the `Add Customer` button in our applet if we can't connect to the server.
>
> ✔ **Keep applets simple and focused.**
> You're using CORBA, so don't be afraid to have single-purpose applets. Sure, we can do more than just add a customer in the `AddCustomer` applet, but then again, we can always make other applets that do the other functions!

Part III
The Great Communicators

The 5th Wave   By Rich Tennant

"I'd like to thank you for this tribute to our commitment to closed standards."

In this part . . .

Part III is where we introduce some of the parts of CORBA that are designed to be used when you're creating applications with CORBA. You also see how to use CORBA with your existing legacy applications to help extend their usefulness in this modern, distributed world. We also give you plenty of great stuff on the newest CORBA features in this part, as well as a little bit of information on that other distributed object technology — DCOM.

You can impress your programmer buddies with all the cool stuff that you pick up from this part. When you're done with these chapters, you'll be a CORBA pro.

Chapter 10

Designing with CORBA in Mind

· ·

In This Chapter

▶ Being object-oriented

▶ Examining concurrency concerns

▶ Distributing objects in a variety of places

▶ Examining reuse

▶ Working with enterprise data

· ·

CORBA takes much of the drudgery out of creating large-scale distributed applications. If you do things the CORBA way, you're freed from dealing with low-level details, such as:

✔ Communication between clients and servers

✔ Differences in hardware platforms

✔ Differences in programming languages

You probably choose to use CORBA for a project when

✔ Your application is client/server.

✔ Your application is state-of-the-art.

✔ Your application is distributed.

✔ Your boss said you had to.

✔ Your application is concurrent.

✔ You need an excuse to go to an OMG conference.

✔ You need to access legacy data.

Given that so many reasons exist for using CORBA, we've decided to focus on the most significant areas, so you'll have to find another source of excuses for traveling to OMG conferences. In this chapter, we talk about analyzing and designing a CORBA-compliant application.

Taking an Object-Oriented Viewpoint

Although the object-oriented way of creating applications has been around for a while, it has only now become prevalent as *the* way to do things. You may still be using an older approach, such as breaking a program down into functions or procedures.

You can still use CORBA with a functional or procedural approach, but you can only do so at the implementation level, not at the higher analysis and design steps.

At the analysis and design levels, the object-oriented way rules for CORBA. Using the object-oriented approach with CORBA means that you

- ✔ Must use objects.
- ✔ Can use inheritance.
- ✔ Get to draw those cool object bubble diagrams.
- ✔ Can use modules.
- ✔ Can use your old ways to implement (but not analyze or design) the application.

Thinking in terms of objects

Coffee mug with handle . . . arm with hand . . . message to arm (pick up and position hand over handle) . . . message to arm (grasp handle and bring coffee mug to mouth). Mmmm, good!

Thinking in terms of objects and their operations — the object-oriented approach — can be a new way of seeing how programs work. This new way of thinking may be scary at first, but most programmers eventually find it becomes easy. Plenty of good books about the object-oriented way of creating software are available. If you aren't familiar with this approach, you should get one of these books. However, our guess is that you already know the object-oriented way, given that you're reading this book. So what we have to say next is no big surprise to you:

- ✔ The first step in CORBA is to perform object-oriented analysis and design to determine the distributed objects.
- ✔ The second step in CORBA is to use the Interface Definition Language (IDL) to describe the objects and their names, data, behavior, and distribution.
- ✔ CORBA is based on the object-oriented way of software development.

> ✔ Attempting to use another software development approach, such as the ad hoc "I'll just start coding" method, doesn't work.
>
> ✔ Objecteus, the god of objects, gets really peeved if you begin a CORBA project without making the appropriate homage to his subjects . . . oops . . . objects.

You can use any popular object-oriented analysis and design method. CORBA isn't based on any particular one. What really matters is that you think of your applications in terms of objects and their communications.

For CORBA, most of the communication is done via operation calls, so you must design your objects to make and receive calls. In other words, you can't have objects depending on low-level operating system interrupts or stream-based socket stuff in order to send and receive data.

Inheriting attributes and operations

Hazel eyes, red hair, high cheekbones — sure, today's cosmetics industry can simulate these features. But more likely, if you have them, you *inherited* them.

Families of objects

You must understand a few terms to effectively use inheritance

✔ **Inheritance:** Inheritance is the mechanism that enables the attributes and operations of one interface to be passed on to other interfaces. You define the attributes and operations once and then use inheritance to distribute them wherever you need them.

✔ **Superclass:** The superclass supplies the attributes and operations. Also known as the *parent class* or *base class*.

✔ **Subclass:** The subclass inherits the attributes and operations. In addition, the subclass can define its own attributes and

operations. Whenever you expect the superclass, you can substitute the subclass. The subclass is also known as the *child class* or *derived class*.

Looking closely at our definitions, you see we use the terms *interfaces* (objects) and *classes*. We have a good reason.

Inheritance is not done from one object to another object. Instead, it is used to pass on one class's stuff to other classes. Although an interface is technically an *object* in CORBA, you can think of an interface as a class when dealing with inheritance. That's why we use the terms *superclass* instead of *superinterface* and *subclass* instead of *subinterface*.

Inheritance allows aspects of interfaces to be reused without having to redefine them over and over again. Using inheritance gains you many other advantages, but we aren't going to get into those advantages here because this book isn't about object-oriented programming.

What you need to know is that you can use inheritance in your CORBA applications. Nothing forces you to use it, but it's available if you choose to use it.

Know this about CORBA's version of inheritance:

- Objects inherit only operations and attributes.
- Exceptions, data types, and constants cannot be inherited.
- An operation or attribute can be changed after it's inherited.
- Subclasses can define their own attributes and operations.
- *Multiple inheritance* occurs when an interface inherits from more than one interface.

Grouping objects into modules

A *module* provides a *name space* for a group of objects. Having more than one object enclosed in a module means that you can collectively refer to those objects. Within a module, all non-nested interfaces, exceptions, data types, and constant names must be unique. However, you can use the same name for an interface in two different modules.

You don't have to use modules if you don't want to, but they can make your applications easier to understand and maintain.

Deciding which objects go into which modules is part of the analysis and design phases. This decision can be a very tricky business. After all, you don't want to group objects together simply because you can. You want to group them together for a reason.

Group objects into a module for the reasons shown in Table 10-1.

Table 10-1	Reasons for Grouping Objects into a Module
Objects that . . .	*Example*
Pass data to each other via operations	An object's `PostUpdate(long in account)` operation is invoked, and it passes `account` to the object that calls it.
Access each other's constants, data types, and attributes	An object uses another object's attribute to obtain its current value.

Objects that . . .	Example
Collectively produce an output	The Sales, Production, and Marketing objects are grouped together to produce a Status Report.
Interact with an external device	Several objects that interact with a sensor in a factory control application.
Perform tasks that are logically related	Report objects that produce many different reports.
Perform tasks that must be done in the same span of time	A gas pump has one object that turns the power on to a pump and another object that opens a valve within five seconds.
Enjoy the same late-night TV shows	Two objects that watch *The Very Late Show*.
Perform tasks that must execute in a specific order	An elevator control system has an object that must play an announcement before the object that opens the elevator doors executes.
Perform many operations on the same data	Two accounting objects that operate on accounts payable data.

Implementing with non-OO language

Although CORBA requires you to use the object-oriented view of the world initially, it doesn't stick you with this view forever. After you write the interface descriptions in the Interface Definition Language (IDL), the next step is to compile the files. At this point, you specify a target language to produce the client stub and the server skeleton.

You are free to choose any language that has a mapping to CORBA as your target language. Some of these languages, such as C or COBOL, are not object-oriented. So although you must begin with an object-oriented viewpoint, you don't necessarily end up with one.

Concurrency: Programs That Do Too Much

In the past, you could follow a program's execution from one line to the next. Oh sure, the occasional goto statement or for loop interrupted the step-by-step nature of the execution. But for the most part, you could read the program from beginning to end and know what it did. Those days are long gone.

Today, programs do more than one thing at a time, so it isn't as easy to figure out what happens, when, and to what. In fact, we have a name for programs that have multiple tasks occurring in parallel — schizophrenic. No, seriously, we call it a *concurrent* program.

✔ **Concurrent Program:** A program that has more than one thread executing at the same time (that is, in parallel).

✔ **Thread:** An activity that is executed sequentially. Concurrent programs have more than one thread executing in parallel. Another term for a thread is *task*.

Here are just a few of the many advantages to having concurrent programs:

✔ **An application that is structured into concurrent threads can be faster.** However, you must take care when designing the application to avoid blocking and bottlenecks.

✔ **Concurrency is a more natural model of the real world because it reflects the parallelism found in target applications.** For example, a banking application must allow more than one customer to access account information at the same time as other customers. Otherwise, when you are in line at the ATM, you'd have to wait for all the customers at all the bank's ATMs to finish their transactions before you could make a transaction of your own.

✔ **Concurrent programs are great role models because they can "Bring home the bacon and fry it up in the pan" — all at the same time.**

✔ **A single resource can be shared by more than one thread at the same time.** This advantage is especially important for databases and other such resources that contain large amounts of data that many clients want to access.

Given all these advantages, it's no wonder that all CORBA-compliant programs are concurrent. You probably thought they were concurrent just because servers and clients always run concurrently.

When you create CORBA applications, you must make decisions regarding two areas of concern:

✔ Communication between clients and servers
✔ Access mechanisms to shared data

Getting your clients and servers talking to each other

When clients make requests of servers, they can either wait for a response or they can continue with their own processing. The decision whether to wait divides requests into two types:

- ✔ **Synchronous request:** A request in which the client waits for a reply from the server. The client is said to be *blocked* while it is waiting. Most communication between clients and servers is done via synchronous requests.

- ✔ **Asynchronous request:** A request in which the client does not wait for a reply from the server. This form of communication is called *non-blocking*.

I'm always waiting around for you

Most requests are synchronous, so you don't need to make many decisions here. What you do need to look at is how long you want a client to be blocked while it waits for a response.

The regular way of doing business in CORBA is to have clients make requests and then wait for responses from servers.

Most of the time, a server deals with clients one at a time, according to the following outline:

1. **A client makes a request of the server.**

2. **That request goes onto a queue that is processed on a first-in, first-out basis.**

3. **The server replies to the request.**

If the server is idle at the time of the request, the request is processed immediately, and the client just waits the length of time that the server takes to execute the operation and reply.

You can count on this way of communication for most of your design.

If other requests are in the queue, then a client must not only wait for its request to be received by the server, but it must also wait for its request to be processed. In this scenario, Step 2 may take a while.

If timing is an issue, you may want to

> ✔ Thread the client.
>
> ✔ Thread the server.
>
> ✔ Use the server-per-method activation policy.
>
> ✔ Make the request asynchronous.

Threading the client

Some target languages support multiple threads in a client. Multiple threads in the client solve the "blocked waiting for server" problem, because a client can make a thread and then call the server from within the thread.

The threaded client still needs to be designed so that a blocked request does not impact its main thread of execution. Consider these two scenarios:

> ✔ A client application uses a form-based interface to collect data that is sent to a server object when the user clicks the Submit button.
>
> ✔ A client application accesses an attribute of a server object for some information that is displayed in a specific area of a window.

In the first case, your client application may be able to do something useful, like display the next form and allow data entry, even if the first method call to the server (done in a different thread) hasn't returned yet.

In the second case, your client application may have a separate thread that calls the method periodically and updates the information in the window. For example, it may fetch the current temperature, using a server object that monitors an engine.

Threading the server

Some ORB implementations support multiple threads in a server. Multiple threads in a server solve the "one at a time" problem by giving each call from a client its own thread in the server.

Although this approach solves one problem, it causes another problem. You must design the server to be *thread safe,* meaning that any shared data among the threads must be accessed correctly to avoid corruption. You certainly don't want one thread changing data while another thread is trying to do the same thing.

How do you make your server thread safe? The term means different things in different implementation languages and operating systems. The general concept is that a thread safe server uses the following:

> ✔ Access locks, operating system events, semaphores, or critical regions to ensure that memory-resident data values aren't changed by two or more threads at the same time.

✔ File, database, or other locking mechanisms to ensure that external disk-resident data values aren't changed by two or more threads at the same time.

If the server keeps some memory-resident data that needs to be shared by all clients (for example, the `MyCounterValue` member variable in the counter server in Chapter 1), then that data must be kept in some shared data repository with access control. If the server is implemented under Windows 95 or Windows NT in C++, you can use *critical regions*, as shown in the following example:

```
CORBA::Long
Counter_impl::GetNextValue(CORBA::Environment &) {
    EnterCriticalSection(CounterSection);
    CORBA::Long rc = ++MyCounterValue;
    LeaveCriticalSection(CounterSection);
    return rc;
}
```

A *critical region* is just a region of code that can only be executed by one thread at a time. Other threads are blocked and forced to wait in a queue when a thread is in the critical region.

Copying a server

With the server-per-method activation policy, the object adapter runs a new copy of the server for each request that it receives. This copying allows the multiple servers to processes all requests without having clients wait in a queue. This is but one of four activation policies for servers, which are discussed in Chapter 11.

Choosing this activation policy alleviates the problem of client requests sitting in a queue. It can also generate truly impressive processor activity if the server receives a couple thousand requests at the same time.

Even when using the server-per-method activation policy, the client still needs to wait for the server to actually perform the operation and return the result.

Making the request asynchronous

If the length of time is critical, you should consider making the request asynchronous. That way, your client application doesn't have to wait for the reply.

I'm not waiting

The two ways to make requests asynchronous in CORBA are

✔ Event notification.

✔ Oneway operation.

Registering via the Event Service

A client can register with one or more event channels by using the Event Service (ES). It can then have events from that channel either

- *Pushed* onto it (asynchronously) when they occur.
- *Pulled* from it (synchronously, but optionally non-blocking) when the client is interested in them.

Event channels are part of the ES and are described in Chapter 19. They're just CORBA server objects that clients and servers use to separate their communication.

For example, a client registers with a `Portfolio` event channel to receive notifications via push when a stock's price rises over a specific value. In effect, this policy lets the client register with the ES and then say "I'm leaving, but let me know if something cool happens."

A different client may not want to miss any changes from a server, even when the client isn't running. Using an event channel, the server can generate events whether or not the client is running. Eventually, when the client is run, it can register with the event channel to receive notifications via pull. The object can then pull all the events that happened while it wasn't running, whenever it would like.

Making a request via a oneway

Servers can implement a *oneway* operation that allows a client to make a request without waiting. In this case, the client never knows exactly when (or even if) the server performs the operation.

Because the operation is one-way only, no return values can be communicated to the client, and no exceptions can be raised.

Determining the Best Distribution of Objects

CORBA applications are collections of client applications, server applications, and server objects. Part of the process of creating a CORBA application is to decide where to place these pieces. You can

- Place the parts on one machine.
- Put the parts on a table, spin it, and see which pieces fly farthest.
- Place the parts on more than one machine.

Putting all the pieces on a single machine

You don't encounter any design issues when you place all the parts on one machine. Having all the parts together is great for developing and testing small applications, but doing so isn't the intended use for CORBA.

One reason to use servers and clients on a machine is when you're mixing implementation languages, such as a server in C++ with a Java client.

Having clients all over the place

You can also place clients on a many different machines in a network. CORBA-compliant applications are intended to be used in this manner.

The only reason to place clients with servers is to accelerate communication.

Placing servers on machines

Many factors may prompt you to place server objects on separate, specific machines in a network. We give you several reasons to do so in this section.

Place servers near

- The data that they access.
- An external device that they interact with.
- Other servers whose attributes they access.
- Other servers that they collectively produce an output with.
- Other servers that they perform logically related tasks with.
- A nice warm fire on a cold winter's night.

Grouping servers on a single machine

When a single machine has many server objects, you need to ask whether grouping server objects into a server application is beneficial.

Grouping server objects into a single server application activates them as a group. Grouping server objects is the *shared server activation policy*. The persistent server activation policy is also a shared server activation policy. The difference between the two policies is that CORBA expects someone else to start the server before any requests are made.

You may want to create shared servers when

- ✔ Accessing any server in the group generally accesses the other servers.
- ✔ Servers in the group refer to, or create new instances of, other server objects.
- ✔ Initializing common information for several servers takes a long time.

If many server objects are on a single machine and activating them at the same time would be beneficial, put those objects into a server application.

Reduce, Reuse, Recycle

Let's just lay it out on the line: CORBA makes reuse happen.

Software *reuse* just means you use some software that already exists.

- ✔ **A server is reused each time it is accessed by a client.**
- ✔ **Launching multiple copies of a client reuses the client application without having to rewrite code.** Clients use the same server!
- ✔ **CORBAservices objects are reused by servers when they perform services.**
- ✔ **Wrapping legacy systems inside servers reuses their information.**
- ✔ **Servers and clients don't need to be implemented in the same language.** For CORBA systems, reuse is language-independent.
- ✔ **The IDL specification for a service lets you reuse it in several different languages without even having its source code.**

Working with Enterprise-Wide Data

Enterprise-wide data is a gold mine for applying distributed objects and reaping benefits for CORBA. In many ways, you use the same design techniques outlined elsewhere in this chapter when dealing with enterprise-wide data. However, you need to keep some specific tips in mind:

- ✔ **Server objects can open a database to the entire corporate network.** Be sure to provide access controls (either inside the client applications or by using ORB-specific extensions).
- ✔ **You can combine information from several different data sources to generate *meta* information.** For example, a single server object can combine information from Payroll, Benefits, Human Resources, and other databases to provide a single, unified view of an employee.

Chapter 11

Just What Are You Serving?

In This Chapter

▶ Playing nice with servers that know how to share

▶ Keeping it all to yourself: Servers that don't share

▶ Serving up methods and copies

▶ Being a good role model: Servers that don't give up

Someone once said that time is God's way of ensuring that everything doesn't happen at once. Well, activation policies are CORBA's way of ensuring that all requests aren't handled at the same time and that all server applications aren't activated at once.

In order for CORBA to work effectively, requests must be handled in an organized manner. This plan of action often means that requests are processed and server applications are started (or invoked) according to certain conditions. This chapter talks about these conditions, which in CORBA-speak are called activation policies.

An *activation policy* is simply the set of conditions under which a server is started (or invoked) so that it can receive method calls. An activation policy also affects the manner in which client requests are handled. For example, a server may immediately respond to a request, or it may place the request on hold.

CORBA has defined the following activation policies by which servers are activated for use by clients:

- ✔ Shared server
- ✔ Unshared server
- ✔ Server-per-method
- ✔ Persistent server

> ## How many activation policies are there?
>
> Other CORBA books (gasp) may list only three kinds of activation policies — the first three in our list. Limiting the policies to three both is and isn't true. Here's why. The persistent server policy is really the shared server policy with one additional characteristic. A persistent server, like all other servers, is just an application that instantiates one or more server objects and makes them available, using an Object Adapter. Essentially, CORBA assumes that this kind of server is started by something that is external to the ORB. If the server isn't running when a client tries to make a request, the server isn't started and the client receives an `OBJECT_NON_EXIST` exception. After the server is started, it treats message requests as if it were a shared server. Using the persistent server policy lets you start the server just once, before any clients use it.

In this chapter, we explore each of these four policies, providing a general description of each one. To help you get a better picture of how the different polices work, we provide a single example that we execute using all four activation policies, one at a time. By using a single example we can see the impact of each activation policy on the performance and behavior of an application.

Introducing the Test Subject

We need a simple server and clients to illustrate how the various activation policies really work. To keep things simple, we use Java. The server

- ✔ Is named `Hello`.
- ✔ Sits on a park bench with a box of chocolates in its lap.
- ✔ Has two operations named `SayHello()` and `SayGoodbye()`.(All it does for either operation is `sleep()` for 2.5 seconds [to simulate a lengthy operation] and then return a string with the name of the operation [`Hello` or `Goodbye`] and the current count of operations processed.)
- ✔ Has a member variable that is incremented whenever either operation is executed.

The client just calls `SayHello()` and `SayGoodbye()` twice, with a half-second `sleep()` between each call.

Obviously, this example isn't your standard CORBA application, but you'll see that even a program this simple clearly shows the impact of the different activation policies on both the server and client. Really, you will. Wait for it.

We cover implementing servers and clients in Java in Chapters 7 and 8. Refer to these chapters for a detailed description of how to implement them. The complete IDL for the `Hello` example is on the CD-ROM that accompanies this book in the `Examples\Chapter11` directory. We're only showing the relevant portions here.

Hello, IDL calling

The Hello IDL is quite easy to understand. It just declares the `Hello` interface, with the two operations:

```
module Servers {
   interface Hello {
      string SayHello();
      string SayGoodbye();
   };
};
```

Hello, how can I serve you?

We create a file named `HelloImplementation.java` that contains the server implementation. The implementation is shown below. The server implementation doesn't hold many surprises for you if you've read the section named "Implementing the Java Classes" in Chapter 7, where we discuss implementing servers in Java.

```
import Servers._HelloImplBase;

public final class HelloImplementation
      extends _HelloImplBase {
   public String SayHello() {
      ++MyCalls;
      String reply = "In SayHello(), " + MyName + "
         called " + MyCalls + " times.";
      try { Thread.currentThread().sleep(2500); }
      catch (java.lang.InterruptedException ex) {}
      return (reply);
   }
   public String SayGoodbye() {
      ++MyCalls;
      String reply = "In SayGoodbye(), " + MyName + "
         called " + MyCalls + " times.";
      try { Thread.currentThread().sleep(2500); }
```

(continued)

(continued)

```
        catch (java.lang.InterruptedException ex) {}
        return (reply);
    }
    public HelloImplementation(String name) {
        super(name);
        MyName = name;
        MyCalls = 0;
    }
    private String MyName;
    private long MyCalls;
}
```

The `HelloImplementation.java` file is on the book's CD-ROM in the `Examples\Chapter11` directory.

The two method implementations just increment the call counter in `MyCalls`, delay for 2.5 seconds, and then return information strings. The constructor for the class accepts a name for the server object and passes that name on to the base (server skeleton) class, using the `super()` method, so that the ORB knows the server's name.

This example works with VisiBroker for Java by Inprise, Corp. When you use the persistent server activation policy, you don't need to pass the server object's name on to the base class in VisiBroker or in any other ORB. When you use any of the other activation policies, however, you usually need to do something to associate a name with each server object so that the ORB can look up the activation policy (usually in the Implementation Repository) and activate the server. The way you need to name server objects for your ORB may be different. Refer to your ORB documentation to determine how to name your server objects. This is our usual disclaimer regarding variations among ORB vendors. Now back to the book, already in progress.

Hello, I'm your servant

As with any other server, we need to write a server application to actually instantiate a `Hello` server object. Otherwise, the finely crafted server object implementation just sits there, dejected and forgotten.

We create a file named `JavaServer.java` that contains the `Hello` server application. This file is much like the Java server application we create in Chapter 8, with a few new twists mandated by the use of non-persistent activation policies.

We've replaced some of the more mundane code with single-line comments to save space. Don't you wish you could really do that when writing applications? Refer to the `JavaServer.java` file on the CD-ROM (at the back of this book) in the `Examples\Chapter11` directory for the complete class.

```java
// import statements not shown
public final class JavaServer {
    public static void main(String args[]) {
        try {
            ORB orb = ORB.init(args,null);
            BOA boa = orb.BOA_init();
            HelloImplementation hello1;
            hello1 = new HelloImplementation("Hello1");
            boa.obj_is_ready(hello1);
            if (args.length == 0) {
                // register the server with NS using the name
                // Examples:Chapter11:Hello1 -- not shown
            }
            boa.impl_is_ready();
        }
        catch(SystemException se) {
            // the usual error handling omitted
        }
    }
}
```

This server application accepts one parameter on the command line. It doesn't matter what the parameter value is; if you supply any parameter, the server doesn't register with the Naming Service. If you don't supply a parameter, the server does register. Go figure!

Notice that this arrangement differs from the server application we present in Chapter 8, which registers with the Naming Service every time you run it.

Unlike the server application in Chapter 8, this time we use an explicit Basic Object Adapter (BOA) to indicate that the object and the implementation are ready. If we were to use orb.connect() like we do in Chapter 8, we'd get the default BOA behind the scenes. That BOA doesn't work for every activation policy, so we use an explicit BOA that does work for every policy.

This leads to our usual disclaimer. This example works with VisiBroker for Java. If you're using a different ORB, check its documentation to see how to use its object adapter implementation. You probably have your ORB figured out by now, but we remind you to check out the differences every time they come up.

Hello, I'm a client

The client application is complex, convoluted, and Byzantine. Not! It's easy. We create a file named `Client.java` that contains the client application.

As before, we've replaced some of the more mundane code with single-line comments to save space. Refer to the `Client.java` file on the CD-ROM for the book in the `Examples\Chapter11` directory for the complete file.

```
// import statements not shown
public final class Client {
    public static void main(String args[]) {
        ORB orb = ORB.init(args,null);
        try {
            Hello hello1;
            // Get Hello1 object reference from Naming Service
            System.out.println("\nCalling Hello1's " +
                "SayHello() twice\n");
            System.out.println(hello1.SayHello()+ "\n");
            Thread.currentThread().sleep(500);
            System.out.println(hello1.SayHello()+ "\n");
            Thread.currentThread().sleep(500);

            System.out.println("\nCalling Hello1's " +
                "SayGoodbye() twice\n");
            System.out.println(hello1.SayGoodbye()+ "\n");
            Thread.currentThread().sleep(500);
            System.out.println(hello1.SayGoodbye()+ "\n");
        }
        catch(SystemException ex) {
            // the usual error handling omitted
        }
        return;
    }
}
```

The client just does typical client stuff. It finds a server, calls some methods, and then exits. What's really interesting is how both the server object and the client applications behave differently when using the various activation policies. Those differences are outlined throughout this chapter.

Shared Server

With the shared server policy, a single server application may contain more than one server object. Also, more than one client can share the server application. These conditions translate into two issues that you must address when using this activation policy:

✔ Serving multiple client requests

✔ Activating multiple server objects

FIFO, FIFO, it's off to work we go

Sharing a server is pretty straightforward. In most ORB implementations, a single server application has a single thread, although some implementations allow a server to have multiple threads.

A *thread* is an activity that is executed sequentially. More than one thread can be run concurrently. Another term for a thread is task.

We are going to explain how requests are processed by using the terms *threads* and *queues,* but, technically, handling requests doesn't work exactly this way. We think that the concept of how the process works is easier for you to understand when you look at it in terms of threads and queues, and understanding the concepts is what is truly important. If you want to know more, see the paragraph coming up that we've tagged with a Technical Stuff icon.

The single thread gets a request from a client and places the request in a first-in-first-out (FIFO) queue. In other words, the first request that the server application receives from any client is placed in a queue. Next, the second request from any client is placed in the queue after the first request, and so on. The requests are then taken off the queue and processed in the same FIFO basis.

In fact, this whole process may not involve *any* queues. We sort of made that up. What probably happens is the server just accepts a connection on a socket, processes the request delivered by that connection, and sends the reply. Then it accepts the next connection. The operating system, rather than the server, usually gets the job of maintaining a FIFO queue of pending connections on the socket. Operating systems just love to maintain queues. It's what they live for.

Figure 11-1 shows two clients sharing a server application and the queue into which their requests go.

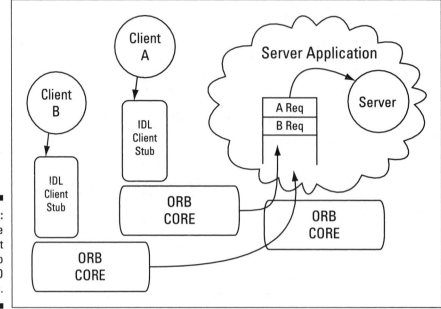

Figure 11-1:
Multiple client requests go into a FIFO queue.

When a request is in the queue, the client is in a sort of limbo — it can't continue processing. CORBA calls this waiting being *blocked*. (This blockage isn't true in some circumstances, but we don't need to get into those details here.)

Blocked is the state in which a client is stopped from executing while it waits for a reply from a server.

In Figure 11-1, you can see that Client B is blocked for however long it takes to process Client A's request.

Although the FIFO queue works well and is simple, a client can be blocked for a very long time before its request is processed, which can be a problem for time-sensitive requests. The FIFO queue can also cause bottleneck situations.

We suggest that for time-sensitive and important requests, you create a server application that has the unshared server or server-per-method activation policies.

You can start me up

The second issue concerns activating multiple server objects within a single server application. The first time any server object in the application receives a request, the object adapter activates all the server objects. These server objects travel in packs!

An *object adapter* provides the means by which a server accesses ORB operations. It is also the part of CORBA that defines how to activate a server so that it can be used.

The left side of Figure 11-2 shows a server application containing three server objects. When a request comes in to any of these servers, the other two servers are also activated. The right side of the figure shows two unshared servers.

As with most things in life, the shared-server approach comes with some good news and some bad news.

✔ The good news is that grouping server objects into a single server application means that they all activate as a unit, at the time the first request goes out to any of the server objects. Subsequent requests do not trigger reactivation. Chapter 10 discusses some design considerations for advantageously grouping server objects into a single server application.

✔ The bad news is that starting up all the servers for the first time can take a really long time.

If a request is time-sensitive, you may not want to wait while all the servers activate. In this case, you should not include the server object that processes the request with the other server objects. Instead, you should create another server application to hold this server by itself — you know, use the unshared server policy.

Shared server in action

You use several batch files (startOAD.bat, startns.bat, startserver.bat, and client.bat) to execute the example. They are on the CD-ROM at the back of this book in the Examples\Chapter11 directory.

Take a walk through the following steps to see how the shared server activation policy affects a server's behavior.

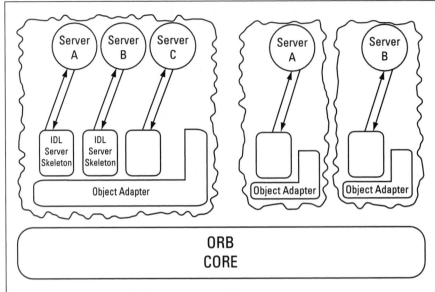

Figure 11-2:
Shared and
unshared
servers.

1. **Start the Naming Service by double-clicking** `startns.bat`.

2. **Run the server application once (to register the server with the Naming Service) by double-clicking** `startserver.bat`.

   Because you want to watch the server get activated, it can't already be running, so you must terminate the server.

3. **Terminate the server by pressing Ctrl+C in the server window.**

4. **Start the VisiBroker for Java Object Activation Daemon (OAD), using** `startOAD.bat`.

   The OAD is the thing that actually does the work of activating servers in VisiBroker for Java.

   We show what the commands look like if you run the example on your `C:` drive in a directory named `Activation`. The stuff you enter is shown in bold. Even though some commands are shown broken across several lines, you enter the whole thing on one line, only pressing Return at the end.

   ```
   C:\Activation> startOAD
   ```

   The batch file just adds the current directory to the `CLASSPATH` environment variable and then runs the VisiBroker for Java OAD. When using VisiBroker for Java, the directory in which Java server classes are stored must be in the `CLASSPATH`.

5. **Register the shared server with the VisiBroker for Java OAD by issuing the following command:**

```
C:\Activation> oadutil reg -r IDL:Servers/Hello:1.0 -java JavaServer
             -verbose -p unshared -o Hello1 -e ORBservices=CosNaming
             -e SVCnameroot=CFDExample -a noNS
```

This program works with VisiBroker for Java. If you're using a different ORB, you need to review its documentation to determine the actual command you use to register a server for the shared activation policy. The same is true for the other examples we give in this chapter.

6. **Run two clients by double-clicking the** client.bat **file twice.**

The results of all this starting and registering are that the first client activates the server, and you see a new window open (in Windows 95 or NT) for the server application. Each client makes its calls, but the server processes them one at a time. When both clients finish running, the server window remains open, indicating that the server application is still running. The output from each client follows:

Client 1:

```
Calling Hello1's SayHello() twice
In SayHello(), Hello1 called 1 times.
In SayHello(), Hello1 called 3 times.

Calling Hello1's SayGoodbye() twice
In SayGoodbye(), Hello1 called 5 times.
In SayGoodbye(), Hello1 called 7 times.
```

Client 2:

```
Calling Hello1's SayHello() twice
In SayHello(), Hello1 called 2 times.
In SayHello(), Hello1 called 4 times.

Calling Hello1's SayGoodbye() twice
In SayGoodbye(), Hello1 called 6 times.
In SayGoodbye(), Hello1 called 8 times.
```

Notice that the single Hello server (activated by the first client) processes each request, one at a time. You can tell that the processing happens one by one because the count of calls (shown in the preceding output as Hello1 called *N* times) increments by one, back and forth between the two clients.

7. **Finish up by unregistering the shared server with the VisiBroker for Java OAD.**

```
C:\Activation> oadutil unreg -r IDL:Servers/Hello:1.0  -java
         JavaServer -verbose -p shared -o Hello1 -e
         ORBservices=CosNaming -e  SVCnameroot=CFDExample -a noNS
```

8. **Terminate the shared server by pressing Ctrl+C in the server window.**

Unshared Server

With the unshared server policy, a single server application never contains more than one server object. Also, a server application is never shared by more than one client. Take a look at each of these statements to see just how the unshared server policy works.

I'm not wasting time

A single server application never contains more than one server object means that server objects are activated as individuals and not as parts in a group, like they are in the shared server policy.

The right side of Figure 11-2 shows two server objects and their associated server applications. When one of these servers receives a request, the other server is not activated. Only the requested server activates.

This activation policy has the advantage of pinpointing the activation of servers when they are needed, instead of grouping their activation with other servers. A client doesn't have to wait for the other server applications to activate. Instead, it has to wait only for its requested server to activate and reply. This difference can be important for time-sensitive requests.

The client is always first

A server application is never shared by more than one client means that a client never has to wait through any queuing, blocking, or wicked cross-checking for the server application to do its bidding. Instead, a copy of the server application is made for each client that requests it.

Figure 11-3 shows two clients, a server application, and a copy of the server application. When Client A makes a request, the server application is activated. When Client B then requests the same server application, a copy of the application is made. In this way, each client has its own copy.

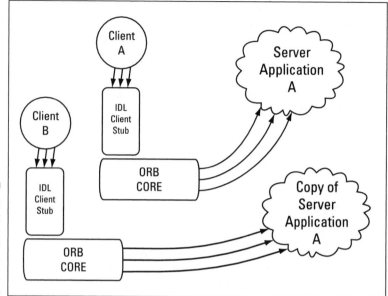

Figure 11-3:
Each client
gets its own
copy of
the server
application.

One more thing about this policy merits your attention: When a client gets associated with a particular copy of the server application, that copy takes care of all the client's subsequent requests for that server. It's like getting married: After you're associated with a particular spouse, you don't get any other spouses. Unless, of course, you become an unshared server again.

No other copies of the server application are made for that client. In Figure 11-3, notice that Client A is making three requests and that Client A's copy of the server application takes care of all these requests.

Unshared server in action

Now take a look at how the unshared server activation policy affects a server's behavior.

1. **Register the server with the VisiBroker for Java OAD by using this command:**

```
C:\Activation> oadutil reg -r IDL:Servers/Hello:1.0  -java
        JavaServer -verbose -p unshared -o Hello1 -e
        ORBservices=CosNaming -e SVCnameroot=CFDExample  -a noNS
```

2. **Run two clients by double-clicking the** client.bat **file twice.**

Each client activates its own copy of the server, and you see two new windows open (in Windows 95 or NT) for the server applications. Each client makes its calls, and because two different servers process the client calls, the calls are processed at the same time. When each client finishes, its server window closes, indicating that the server application has also terminated. Just watching the windows open and close can be quite relaxing. The output from each client is identical, so only one is shown here:

```
Calling Hello1's SayHello() twice
In SayHello(), Hello1 called 1 times.
In SayHello(), Hello1 called 2 times.


Calling Hello1's SayGoodbye() twice
In SayGoodbye(), Hello1 called 3 times.
In SayGoodbye(), Hello1 called 4 times.
```

Because each client has its own copy of the Hello server, the call count increments by one for each call. Also, notice that because separate servers handle both client requests, the two clients complete at roughly the same time and in about half the time that's required when using a shared server.

3. **To finish up, unregister the unshared server with the VisiBroker for Java OAD.**

```
C:\Activation> oadutil unreg -r IDL:Servers/Hello:1.0  -java
          JavaServer -verbose -p unshared -o Hello1 -e
          ORBservices=CosNaming -e SVCnameroot=CFDExample  -a noNS
```

Because the server always terminates when the client that activated it terminates, we don't need to shut down the server ourselves.

Server-Per-Method

With the server-per-method activation policy, a new server application is activated each time a request is made. Other than for the initial request to a server application, a new copy of the server is run for each request that it receives.

Using this policy means that

- ✔ The same client can have several active servers.
- ✔ The same method can have several active servers.
- ✔ A tennis tournament can have several active servers.
- ✔ Clients never wait in a queue.

Although this activation policy alleviates the problem of client requests sitting in a queue, it can also generate huge processor activity. So if you know that a server application is likely to receive a couple thousand requests at the same time, this policy should not be your first choice.

Figure 11-4 shows a client and its copies of a single server application. When Client A makes its first request, the server application is activated. When Client A makes another request for the same server application, a copy of the application is created, and so on.

This policy is good for time-sensitive requests but is hard on system resources and your system administrator.

To see how the server-per-method scenario behaves differently from a shared or unshared server, we run our client twice, with the Hello server registered as server-per-method.

1. **We register our server with the VisiBroker for Java ORB with this command:**

```
C:\Activation> oadutil reg -r IDL:Servers/Hello:1.0 -java
              JavaServer -verbose -p per-method -o Hello1 -e
              ORBservices=CosNaming -e SVCnameroot=CFDExample -a noNS
```

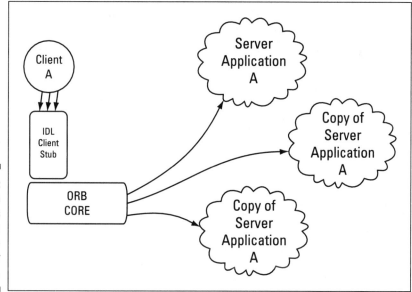

Figure 11-4: Each method gets its own copy of the server application.

2. **Run two clients by double-clicking the** `client.bat` **file twice.**

   This time, each call that either client makes to any method in the `Hello` server activates its own copy of the server, and you see new windows open (in Windows 95 or NT) for the server applications as each method is called. These windows cascade across the screen in a hypnotic dance — or at least they do on our system.

   Each client makes its calls, and because different servers process the calls, they are processed at the same time. When each call finishes, its server window closes, indicating that the server application has also terminated. The output from each client is identical, so only one is shown here:

   ```
   Calling Hello1's SayHello() twice
   In SayHello(), Hello1 called 1 times.
   In SayHello(), Hello1 called 1 times.

   Calling Hello1's SayGoodbye() twice
   In SayGoodbye(), Hello1 called 1 times.
   In SayGoodbye(), Hello1 called 1 times.
   ```

   Because each method call is processed by its own copy of the `Hello` server, the call count is always one for each call in each client. Also notice that because every client request is handled by a newly activated server, the two clients complete at roughly the same time, in a little more time than is required when using a shared server. That's because it takes a little time to activate a server, even a simple one.

3. **To finish up, we unregister our per-method server with the VisiBroker for Java ORB:**

   ```
   C:\Activation> oadutil unreg -r IDL:Servers/Hello:1.0 -java
            JavaServer -verbose -p per-method -o Hello1 -e
            ORBservices=CosNaming -e SVCnameroot=CFDExample -a noNS
   ```

   Because the server always terminates when the client that activated it terminates, we don't need to do that ourselves.

Persistent Server

This activation policy is just like the shared server policy except that CORBA assumes that the server application is always active. This policy uses an external agent, such as a scheduler or a manual process, to activate servers. After the servers have been activated, the object adapter treats all communications to these servers as if they were using the shared server policy.

Chapter 12

When Push Comes to Shove

Client/server communications generally work on the premise that clients make requests of servers when the clients need specific information. This approach is called the *pull* model because the client pulls information from the server. As you may expect, communications can go the other way, too. In the *push* model, servers send information to clients when the server deems it necessary. The server gives data to the client even when the client isn't asking for it.

In most fast-food restaurants, servers just stand around waiting for someone to ask them for whatever it is they're serving. That's the pull model — clients (customers) making requests of servers (teenagers in paper hats). It works quite well in most situations, which is why CORBA is designed around the pull model and most often works this way.

However, at times the pull model may not meet an application's needs. You may find that to solve a particular problem, you want to turn the tables on the client and server and have the server send information to the client. That's like when the kid behind the counter asks, "You want fries with that?" That's why CORBA also offers the push model.

Pulling is the modus operandi of CORBA and we talk about it throughout the book. Pushing is a different story. You can choose from two main ways to implement pushing in CORBA. In this chapter, we cover a simple, do-it-yourself way that doesn't use a CORBAservice, and in Chapter 19, we tell you all about the Event Service.

Letting the Server Get Pushy

Here are five definitions that help clarify communications and all this pushing and pulling:

- **Pull:** This term defines the normal method of client/server interaction. The server waits for client requests, and clients pull information from the server when they need it. Pull is also known as synchronous communication.

- **Push:** This word describes a rarer form of client/server interaction. A client registers with a server that has some information that the client is interested in and then goes about its business doing other things. When the server determines that it has the desired information, it pushes the information to the client. Push is also known as asynchronous communication.

- **Synchronous:** This is one of those big, impressive words. In synchronous communication, both the sender and the receiver of information agree to communicate. For CORBA, it's what happens when a client calls a server's operation and pulls information from the server.

- **Asynchronous:** This term is an even more impressive word, don't you think? In this form of communication, the receiver of information isn't specifically asking for it. Asynchronous communication is like being in the shower when the phone rings — you know you have a phone and that it may ring at any time, but you aren't expecting it to ring right now! It's probably some pushy telemarketer anyway.

- **Event:** This word means that something important has happened. Often times, *event* is used to describe the reason a server chooses to push information to a client. An event can also be a major sports playoff, a grand opening of an appliance store, or a really great sale on body piercing supplies.

Deciding when to get pushy

Some of us are naturally pushy, but the rest of us wonder how to determine when to push.

Figuring out when you need to use push is actually pretty easy. Look at the information you're serving in the server and ask yourself these questions:

- Does the information change over time?

- Do clients need to know immediately when the information changes?

- Does the server cut in lines, talk too loud, or ask personal questions?

A yes answer to any of these questions indicates that a push may be in order.

You need to use push when changes to a server's information need to be communicated to clients *when* the change happens, not when the client gets around to asking for it.

Choosing between the simple approach or the Event Service

The next set of questions helps you decide whether you need to read this chapter or Chapter 19, where we discuss the Event Service. For these questions, consider the pattern of communication between a server and its clients.

✔ Does the server need to decide which clients receive an update when information changes?

✔ Will the server have only a few (less than 100) clients registered with it at any given time?

✔ Are the clients interested in receiving pushed information only when they're running?

✔ Does the server really *listen* to its clients, or just pretend to?

✔ Did you forget to buy an Event Service package with your ORB?

Yes answers to several of these questions point to the simple push approach that we illuminate in this chapter. This method is useful in scenarios where a smallish number of clients (less than 100) register with a server to receive pushed information when the server deems it necessary.

In this approach, if a client isn't running when the server decides to push information, then that client never receives the information.

In this chapter, we describe a very simple approach to doing a bit of what you can do with the Event Service, without all the overhead. This approach is fine for basic push needs. If you answered no to most of these questions or you need to do more complicated things, you may want to check out Chapter 19 for details on the Event Service.

When you need more than a little push

So you're considering the Event Service, are you? Here's what you're getting into. The Event Service, like all CORBAservices, is a general-purpose service implemented as a suite of CORBA servers. That means it's a rather large hammer to use on small nails. It supports really cool stuff like event channels and a more general model of communication called *supplier/consumer.*

When using the Event Service, you create an event channel that acts as the conduit for one or more related events. Any event channel can have more than one supplier and more than one consumer. Event channels are independent of suppliers and consumers. If a consumer isn't actively running when an event occurs, it can receive the event later.

Basically, by using the Event Service you can do everything we talk about in this chapter as well as quite a bit more. Not surprisingly, you have to do a lot more work, even to do simple stuff, because you always have to use an event channel. So be sure that you really need the Event Service before you dig in to use it.

Implementing Push

To implement push between a server object and one or more clients, you have to use a little trick, because with CORBA, you're actually still using synchronous communication. The sneaky way of getting around synchronous communication is to create a server object (called a push server) that maintains a list of other server objects. We call these other server objects *Listeners*. Listener server objects are actually inside the client applications. When the push server needs to push information to its clients, it calls a method in the Listener server object for each client. Figure 12-1 shows the relationship between the push server and clients.

This approach to implementing push means that

- ✔ The push server contains a `Register()` method that clients call. A client passes in a Listener server object reference that the push server calls when it's time to push data.
- ✔ The Listener server object has an `Update()` method that the push server calls when it wants to push information.
- ✔ The parameters of the `Update()` method carry the pushed information to the client.
- ✔ The client code to process the push goes in the implementation of the `Update()` method.
- ✔ The client application uses threads, so that the Listener server object in the client is always running, even when the client is busy doing other things.

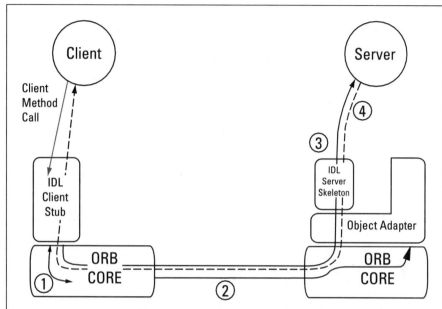

Figure 12-1:
Push server
and clients.

That last point is very important! When you're implementing push as described in this chapter, your clients must use threads so that the pushing server can call their Listener server objects whenever needed.

Threads are implemented differently by different operating systems, but threads in Java are the same on every operating system. So for the example in this chapter, we chose to use Java. That doesn't mean that you can't use this same technique in C++ or in any other language that supports threads. But if you do, you'll need to first figure out how to implement threads in your target language and operating system. The approach is the same, but the code sure is simpler in Java.

In fact, most CORBA/Java bindings already run each server object in its own thread, so you don't need to do anything related to threads to get the correct behavior when you use Java.

Threads in C++ using Windows

Threads are not all that difficult to use in C++. If you're using Windows 95 or Windows NT, your thread-specific C++ code may be quite simple. In the example below, we put in comments that represent the code you need to implement. Basic threading is written as follows:

```
DWORD WINAPI ClientListener(
    LPVOID ) {
    // Initialize the BOA
    // Allocate the client-side
    Listener server
    // Tell the BOA the object
    is ready
    // Locate a reference to
    the push server
    // Call the push server's
    Register() method,
    //    supplying a reference
    to the
    //    client Listener
    object
    // Tell the BOA the imple-
    mentation is ready
}
int main() {
    // initialize the ORB
    // create a thread for the
    Listener
    DWORD ThreadId;
    HANDLE ListenerThread =
    CreateThread(NULL,
        0, ClientListener, NULL,
    0, &ThreadId);
    // do whatever else the
    client needs to do...
}
```

In this example, we put the code that creates the Listener server object in the ClientListener() function. When the main() function executes, it creates a separate thread for that function and starts the thread. The net result is that the client application has a separate thread for its Listener server object, so the push server can connect to the Listener object even if the client is busy doing other tasks.

Looking at a Pushy Example

To show you how the do it yourself approach to implementing push works, we create an example of a server that pushes price changes in a stock to registered clients. We call this the PushStock example. When a client registers with this push server, it supplies a minimum and a maximum value for the stock, along with an object reference to a Listener server object for the push server to call. Whenever the push server gets an updated price for the stock, it pushes the new price and a status message (a string) to each client that needs it. The status message indicates whether the new price is below the minimum or above the maximum value that the client specified.

Writing push in IDL

We begin with the IDL for the push server and the Listener server. We also define a `struct` that holds the minimum and maximum values for the stock and the Listener server object reference.

The IDL for the `PushStock` example is in a file named `PushStock.idl` in the `Examples\Chapter12` directory on the CD-ROM at the back of this book.

```
module PushStock
{
    interface StockUpdate;
    interface Stock;

    struct StockUpdateRecord {
        double MinPrice;
        double MaxPrice;
        StockUpdate Callback;
    };
```

The `StockUpdateRecord struct` contains two `doubles` (for the minimum and maximum stock price) and the `StockUpdate` interface that the push server uses to push the new price to the client.

```
    interface Stock {
        readonly attribute double CurrentPrice;
        void Register(in StockUpdateRecord UpdateRecord);
        void BroadcastChange(in double NewPrice);
    };
```

The `Stock` interface, which is for the push server, has a `readonly` attribute that returns the current price of the stock. Clients use this method to pull the current value from the server.

The `Register()` operation accepts a `StockUpdate struct`. Clients call this operation to register to receive push information when a stock price falls below or rises above the supplied values. You can see in the implementation of the push server the importance of detecting when a registered client is no longer running.

The `BroadcastChange()` tells the push server that the stock has a new price. The push server pushes the new price to each client that needs it, based on each client's supplied minimum and maximum values.

```
interface StockUpdate {
   readonly attribute double CurrentPrice;
   oneway void Update(in double NewPrice,
      in string Message);
   };
};
```

The StockUpdate interface is for the Listener server in each client. It has a readonly attribute that returns the last pushed price of the stock. It also has a single operation named Update() that the push server calls when needed. The Update() operation receives the new price and the string message that indicates what event triggered the push.

In your face Stock server

The Stock server implementation follows the general form of other Java CORBA server objects. (In this chapter, we focus only on the parts of the implementation that are important for a push server. See Chapter 7 for a detailed description of implementing interfaces in Java.)

The complete source code for the Stock server object implementation is in a file named StockImplementation.java on the CD-ROM that accompanies this book, in the Examples\Chapter12 directory.

Getting class preliminaries out of the way

The server implementation starts with the necessary import statements, which we've omitted here and replaced them with a single comment. These statements are followed by the method that implements the readonly attribute.

```
// import necessary classes
public final class StockImplementation
   extends _StockImplBase {

   public double CurrentPrice() {
      return MyPrice;
   }
```

Using the Register() method

The Register() function is a bit more interesting. It uses a Java Vector stored in the member variable ListenerVector to hold the StockUpdateRecords it receives from clients.

```
public void Register(StockUpdateRecord UpdateRecord) {
   int i;
```

```
StockUpdateRecord RegisteredListener;
for (i = 0; i < ListenerVector.size(); i++) {
    RegisteredListener =
        (StockUpdateRecord)ListenerVector.elementAt(i);
    if (UpdateRecord.Callback._is_equivalent(
            RegisteredListener.Callback)) {
        System.out.println("Duplicate Listener " +
            "removed at position " + i);
        ListenerVector.removeElementAt(i);
        break;
    }
}
ListenerVector.addElement(UpdateRecord);
}
```

Before the `Register()` method saves a `StockUpdateRecord`, it checks to make sure that no current elements in the `Vector` refer to the same client Listener object reference. It performs the check by comparing the object reference in each `StockUpdateRecord` in the `Vector` against the object reference in the new `StockUpdateRecord`.

When you want to compare two server object references, use the `_is_equivalent()` member function of one server object and pass in the object reference of the other. If the two references refer to the same server, the method returns `true`.

If the `Register()` method finds that it already has an entry for the same client, it removes the old entry from the `Vector`. This practice allows a client to update the minimum and maximum values for the stock simply by calling the `Register()` function again. It also insures that a client is only called once, even if it mistakenly registers multiple times.

Finally, the new `StockUpdateRecord` is added to the `Vector`. At this point, the `Stock` server can push information to the client whenever it needs to or whenever Jupiter aligns with Mars.

Pushing with BroadcastChange()

The `BroadcastChange()` method does the actual pushing of information to registered clients. This method looks a bit complicated, but it's actually pretty simple. We talk about it in several chunks. Here's the first chunk:

```
public void BroadcastChange(double NewPrice) {
    NumberFormat nf = NumberFormat.getInstance();
    nf.setMinimumFractionDigits(2);
    nf.setMaximumFractionDigits(2);
    nf.setMinimumIntegerDigits(1);
    MyPrice = NewPrice;
```

The first bit of the method creates a number format object so that we can hand clients a nicely formatted dollar amount for the string. Then it sets the member variable holding the stock price to the new value.

```
int i;
for (i = 0; i < ListenerVector.size(); i++) {
    StockUpdateRecord Listener =
        (StockUpdateRecord)ListenerVector.elementAt(i);
    if ((NewPrice >= Listener.MinPrice) &&
        (NewPrice <= Listener.MaxPrice))
    continue;
```

Next, the method enters a for loop, where it tests the new stock value against the minimum and maximum values supplied by each registered client. If the new value is greater than the minimum and less than the maximum value, then that client is skipped. If it's not, then the client needs to have the new value pushed to it, which happens next.

```
if (Listener.Callback._non_existent()) {
    System.out.println("Detected a nonexistent " +
        "Listener at position " +
        i + ", removing.");
    ListenerVector.removeElementAt(i);
}
```

Before trying to push the data, test to make sure the object reference to the Listener server in the client is still available. Use the _non_existent() method of the object reference to do the check. If that method returns true, the client has exited. Remove the client's StockUpdateRecord instead of pushing data to it.

If the client checks out okay, the next block of code pushes the data to it.

```
else {
    try {
        if (NewPrice < Listener.MinPrice)
            Listener.Callback.Update(NewPrice,
                "Stock price under $" +
                nf.format(Listener.MinPrice));
        else if (NewPrice > Listener.MaxPrice)
            Listener.Callback.Update(NewPrice,
                "Stock price over $" +
                nf.format(Listener.MaxPrice));
    }
    catch(Exception ex) {
```

```
              System.out.println("Exception pushing to "
                 + Listener at position " +
                 i + ", removing.");
             ListenerVector.removeElementAt(i);
          }
       }
     }
   }
```

Inside of a try/catch block, we compare the new price to the minimum and maximum values supplied by the client. If the value is out of the specified range, we call the Update() method in the client Listener server object to push the current stock price and the string value that specifies the reason for the push.

Be paranoid here. Wrap the call to the client Listener server object in a try/catch block. If an exception is raised, assume that the client has exited and remove the client's StockUpdateRecord instead of pushing data to it.

Wrapping up the class

All that's left to do is write the constructor and declare the member variables. Take a look:

```
public StockImplementation() {
   ListenerVector = new Vector();
   MyPrice = 0.0;
}
private Vector ListenerVector;
private double MyPrice;
}
```

The class constructor allocates the Vector used to hold the StockUpdateRecords of the clients, and it initializes the stock price to 0.0. The last step is to declare the two member variables that hold the Vector and the stock price.

The client side of the street

The client Listener server contains the code that we want to execute when the client receives pushed data. This code may specify an action as complex as updating a database, updating a GUI, drawing a chart, or juggling a bowling ball, a knife, and a peanut. Or it can be as simple as printing a message to standard output. We're going to print a message, because we've never gotten the hang of that juggling thing.

We don't show the whole class in this section. The complete source code for the StockUpdate server object implementation is in a file named StockUpdateImplementation.java on the book's CD-ROM in the Examples\Chapter12 directory.

The real action happens in the Update() method.

```
public void
Update(double NewPrice, String Message) {
    NumberFormat nf = NumberFormat.getInstance();
    nf.setMinimumFractionDigits(2);
    nf.setMaximumFractionDigits(2);
    nf.setMinimumIntegerDigits(1);
    SimpleDateFormat formatter
        = new SimpleDateFormat ("hh:mm:ss a");
    Date currentTime = new Date();
    String dateString = formatter.format(currentTime);
    System.out.println(dateString + " - Price: $" +
        nf.format(NewPrice) + " Note: " + Message);
    MyPrice = NewPrice;
}
```

The Update() method does quite a bit of standard Java stuff so that it can print the current time along with the new price and the message pushed in from the server.

The important thing to remember is that we could have done anything we wanted in this code. This code executes in the client, so it can access other client objects that are passed in via its constructor. If you want to update a window, field, or whatever, just add the necessary member variables to the Listener server implementation and pass in references to the desired items in its constructor. You could even pass in references to other (non-CORBA) client-side objects and call their methods from within the Update() method. Go wild!

Serving the server application

We still need to write the server application. We stick with the tried-and-true persistent server activation policy, Naming Service, and SimpleNames class approach that we present in Chapter 8. Refer to that chapter for the details of implementing a server application in Java.

Our server contains a slight twist. We're going to use the main application thread to generate random stock prices every 5 seconds — much simpler than connecting to the New York Stock Exchange just to run an example.

The complete source code for the server application is in a file named JavaServer.java in the `Examples\Chapter12` directory on the CD-ROM at the back of this book. Also in that directory is the `SimpleNames.java` file containing the SimpleNames class. The SimpleNames class is described in Chapters 8 and 18.

```
// import necessary classes
public final class JavaServer {
   public static void main(String args[]) {
      try {
         ORB orb = ORB.init(args,null);
         StockImplementation pusher;
         pusher = new StockImplementation();
         orb.connect(pusher);
```

The server application begins by creating an instance of the `Stock` server object and then uses the `connect()` method of the ORB object to indicate that the object is ready.

In many Java-based ORBs, each server object runs in a separate thread. So we don't need to do anything specific to get a thread for the Listener server object if this is the case for our ORB. VisiBroker for Java runs each server object in its own thread, so you won't see any threads in our code.

Next, register the server object with the Naming Service.

```
         NameComponent myName[] = new NameComponent[3];
         // Set myName to "Examples/Chapter12/StockPusher"
         if (!SimpleNames.bindToName(orb,
               (Object)pusher, myName)) {
            return;
         }
```

The main thread doesn't have anything else to do, so we use it to create random stock prices (between 50 and 70 dollars) every 5 seconds. Note that in the code below, we use a `for (;;)` statement. This is faster than the `while (true)` statement.

```
         // Set NumberFormat nf to format dollar amounts
         double NewPrice;
         Random StockPrice = new Random();
         for (;;) {
```

(continued)

(continued)

```
        SimpleDateFormat formatter
            = new SimpleDateFormat ("hh:mm:ss a");
        Date currentTime = new Date();
        String timeString = formatter.format(
            currentTime);
        NewPrice = 50.0 +
            (20.0 * StockPrice.nextDouble());
        System.out.println(timeString +
            " - New price for Stock: $" +
            nf.format(NewPrice));
        pusher.BroadcastChange(NewPrice);
        try {
            Thread.currentThread().sleep(5000);
        }
        catch (java.lang.InterruptedException ex) {
        }
      }
    }
    catch(SystemException se) {
        System.exit(1);
    }
  }
}
```

Watching stocks in the client application

We create a single client application that registers with the Stock push server object. The client prompts for the stock prices to watch and prints a message when the Stock push server sends new stock price information. Because it's a standard Java client application, we've omitted some of the more mundane code from the example in this chapter. Refer to Chapter 8 for a complete description of a client application in Java.

The complete source code for the WatchStock client application is in a file named WatchStock.java on the CD-ROM in the Examples\Chapter12 directory. Also in that directory is the FindStockPusherFn.java file, containing the FindStockPusherFn class. That class is very similar to the FindPortfolioBrokerFn class in Chapter 8.

The WatchStock client begins by locating the Stock push server.

```
// import necessary classes
public final class WatchStock {
   public static void main(String args[]) {
   ORB orb = ORB.init(args,null);
   try {
      Stock Pusher =
         FindStockPusherFn.FindStockPusher(orb);
      if (Pusher == null)
         return;
```

Next, the client prompts for the minimum and maximum price. It stores the entered values in variables named Min and Max. We've omitted the code from this example, but it's just like the client examples in Chapter 8.

```
      StockUpdateRecord UpdateRecord =
         new StockUpdateRecord();
      StockUpdateImplementation Callback;
      Callback = new StockUpdateImplementation();
      orb.connect(Callback);
      UpdateRecord.MinPrice = Min;
      UpdateRecord.MaxPrice = Max;
      UpdateRecord.Callback = Callback;
      Pusher.Register(UpdateRecord);
```

This is the interesting part. The client creates a StockUpdateRecord and a Listener server object. It then uses the ORB connect() method to indicate that the Listener server object is ready to receive requests.

In many Java ORBs, each server object runs in a separate thread, so the client application has a separate thread for the Listener server object.

Next, we set the MinPrice and MaxPrice values of the StockUpdateRecord to the entered Min and Max values, and we set the Callback value to the Listener server object. Finally, we use the Register() method of the Stock push server to tell the server to push information to our Listener server object when needed.

This client doesn't do anything else, so we join the main() thread to the thread for the Listener server object.

```
      System.out.println("Watching Stock value...");
      try {
         Thread.currentThread().join();
      }
      catch(InterruptedException e) {
         System.exit(1);
      }
```

You don't need to join the `main()` thread to the thread for the Listener server object if your client application is GUI-based or does other work in addition to waiting for a push server to call it.

Putting Push in Action

To put the push method in action, you compile all the classes that make up the server and client applications and then run the server application.

We compiled all the classes for you on the book's CD-ROM in the `Examples\Chapter12` directory. We also include a Windows batch file named `vbmake.bat` that compiles all the classes with VisiBroker for Java. The CD also has three batch files to run the Java applications:

- ✔ `startns.bat` **starts the VisiBroker Naming Service.**
- ✔ `startserver.bat` **starts the** `Stock` **persistent push server.**
- ✔ `WatchStock.bat` **runs the client that registers with the push server.**

Before running the server, you need to install your ORB and start any ORB servers (including the Naming Service) that you need in order to run CORBA applications. Your ORB may also require that your `Stock` and `StockUpdate` servers be registered with the Implementation Repository before you run the example. If you must, register the push server with the name `Stock` and make it a persistent server. Use the name `StockUpdate` (also persistent) for the `StockUpdate` Listener server. VisiBroker for Java doesn't need this step.

To run the applications, follow these steps. Your entries are shown in bold.

1. Run the server first in one window.

```
C:\StockPushJava\> startserver
```

The server starts printing new stock prices every 5 seconds:

```
-- Server ready
10:49:44 AM - New price for Stock: $50.20
10:49:49 AM - New price for Stock: $50.57
10:49:54 AM - New price for Stock: $69.43
10:49:59 AM - New price for Stock: $57.11
10:50:04 AM - New price for Stock: $62.62
```

2. **Run a** WatchStock **client in another window and enter a minimum and maximum price**:

```
C:\StockPushJava \> WatchStock
Located the Stock Pusher

Minimum Value for Stock: 52
Maximum Value for Stock: 67
Watching Stock value...
```

3. **Run several more** WatchStock **clients in other windows and enter different minimum and maximum prices**:

```
C:\StockPushJava \> WatchStock
Located the Stock Pusher

Minimum Value for Stock: 54
Maximum Value for Stock: 66
Watching Stock value...
```

4. **Watch as the** WatchStock **clients receive push information!**

   Whenever a price change in the server window causes a push to a client, the client prints a message. For example, suppose that the server sets a price at $51.57. The client started in Step 2 prints the following:

```
10:54:41 AM - Price: $51.57 Note: Stock price under $52.00
```

5. **Terminate a client by entering Ctrl+C in the client window.**

   The next time the server generates a price that would be pushed to that client, the server prints the following message instead:

```
10:57:46 AM - New price for Stock: $67.49
Detected a nonexistent Listener at position 0, removing.
```

Note that the actual position number (0 in this example) may vary if you've started several clients.

Chapter 13

Legacy Applications Are Now Assets

. . . .

In This Chapter

▶ Rediscovering valuable assets in your legacy systems

▶ Creating a cozy IDL wrapper for legacy applications

▶ Wrapping a very old MS-DOS legacy application

. . . .

*L*egacy systems are the new repository of reusable information. They've always held lots of useful information, but they've been largely ignored because they're implemented in languages such as COBOL, or because no one understands exactly what they do. Before CORBA, the few ways of accessing the data that legacy systems contain were complicated. Now, with CORBA as the key, you can unlock the data trapped within these forgotten applications, and mine the rich deposit of information that has lain dormant inside. My, that sounds like a brochure for CORBA, doesn't it?

This chapter covers the kinds of legacy systems that CORBA can wrap in server objects and gives a simple example, using an MS-DOS executable as the legacy application.

Mining That Legacy Gold

Picture this: Your boss decides that the ancient machine in the basement has some really valuable data on it, and it's your job to make that information available on your organization's network. Your choices are to

✔ Update your resumé and look for another job.

✔ Take a discreet poll of your office mates to find out who is naive enough to think that this is an easy job and give it to them.

✔ Wrap the applications in CORBA.

We aren't the best resources for polishing your resumé or for scamming an office mate, so you're left with us talking about how to wrap your company's legacy systems in CORBA.

A *legacy system* is a system or an application that has been around since the Paleozoic era. It usually runs on a hardware platform that is rarely used in day-to-day operations. It often contains data or produces output that the company still finds valuable enough to keep but not valuable enough to upgrade to a new platform or new application.

Legacy systems and CORBA: The golden duo

Why would you want to deal with CORBA and a legacy system? Isn't using CORBA to access a legacy system like trying to hit an insect with a baseball bat instead of a swatter? Well, yes and no.

The disadvantage of using CORBA is that it increases the overhead involved in performing all the steps necessary to create CORBA applications.

However, wrapping legacy systems as CORBA-compliant applications has several advantages:

- ✔ You can encapsulate a resource, thus making visible only what others need to know. Encapsulation allows the resource, such as a printer, to manage its own information with very little or no involvement from others. Just the way it should be!

- ✔ You can reuse applications, thus making application development faster. In other words, you don't have to reinvent the wheel every time you want to do something. If your company created a really good parts and inventory report ten years ago, you have no reason to throw it out. Just wrap it as a CORBA application and go merrily on your way to developing your new, full-fledged inventory system.

- ✔ You can take advantage of all the processing power on your corporate LAN or the Internet that may not have been available when the application was first created.

- ✔ After an application is wrapped and made CORBA-compliant, it can talk to any other CORBA-compliant applications. This compatibility can extend the application's usefulness to the organization and may change its role from that of a small corporate application to a more active resource.

- ✔ CORBA lets you distribute the parts of the legacy application across the corporate network without regard for the operating systems or the hardware of the machines themselves. This distribution can greatly expand the opportunities for use of this legacy system.

Oh, those golden nuggets

You now know why you want to encapsulate legacy systems in CORBA wrappers. Another issue is deciding which systems are good candidates. We suggest that you wrap applications that

- ✔ **Take in a small number of parameters on the command line and spit out a known output.** In other words, you run the application and get an answer from it. A simple example is an inventory report. You run the application with a part number included on the command line, and the report states the number of units on hand for that item.

- ✔ **Are difficult or too costly to modify.** Instead of changing them, you can just encapsulate them.

- ✔ **More than one corporate department uses.** This way, you get more bang for the buck. Go to your accounting and human resource departments to see which systems they want made available as CORBA-compliant. It never hurts to ask!

When selecting applications to wrap, choose those that receive their input via standard input and produce their output via standard output or to a file, not ones that use a complicated interface, such as a graphical user interface (GUI). Usually, you look for applications that have command-line interfaces, which often accept a single option or a small set of options. An example is an application that is run by batch. Note that the output can go to a file; the CORBA server object can then access that file.

Wrapping Legacy Applications in IDL

To wrap a legacy system, your first task is to write the IDL for the server object or objects that implement the wrapper. This task is similar to creating a server object from scratch with IDL. Chapter 4 discusses IDL in detail, but here's a recap of the steps you take to create the IDL, with legacy systems in mind.

Before you write the IDL, you need to know

- ✔ **What the objects are.** For a legacy system, you may use a single object to wrap a legacy application if it performs a single function, or you may create several objects that deal with different functions for a large legacy application.

- ✔ **What each object is named.** You can make up your own names, but naming a legacy system object something specific, such as `EastCoastPayroll`, may not be a bad idea.

✔ **When the boss wants the IDL finished.** You can tell your boss that wrapping a legacy application solves the year 2000 problem (which it doesn't, of course!), so it gets done by December 31, 1999.

✔ **What data each object deals with.** The data is determined by the command-line interface of the application (inputs) and the output it produces. Often, the output is in the form of a textual report that your wrapper needs to read in, break up into chunks, and return as a struct, sequence, or other more complex data structure. This is a vital spot to carefully consider what information clients need and how best to give it to them.

✔ **What each object is supposed to do.** At last, an easy one! You already know exactly what the legacy system does.

After you answer these questions, you set about the usual process for writing the server objects. We cover that process in Chapter 5, and nothing special about making a legacy system wrapper prevents you from using the same process in this case.

MS-DOS: An Unusual Example

MS-DOS is a legacy system. Just ask Microsoft! At any rate, plenty of MS-DOS commands live on in the bowels of Windows 95 and Windows NT, years or even decades after they were state of the art.

One such dinosaur is the MS-DOS Extract.exe program. Its sole job is to deal with Cabinet — or CAB — files. What's a CAB file, you ask? A CAB file is a single file that contains a bunch of other compressed files in it. It's no different than a UNIX TAR file or a Windows Zip file. The Extract.exe program lets you accomplish several tasks with a CAB file. We single out two functions that look promising as operations for a CORBA server wrapper:

✔ List to standard output the contents of the CAB file, including each file modification date, file attributes, size, and name.

✔ Extract one file from the CAB file to a selected directory.

You tell Extract.exe to do one or the other of these tasks by using command-line parameters. It's a perfect candidate for wrapping!

IDL wrapper

We've already decided on the operations we want our wrapper to include. In other words, we know what the operations do. Now, all we need to know is what data the operations require.

The source code of this example is on the book's CD-ROM in the
`Examples\Chapter13` directory. The `SourceCab.idl` file contains the IDL
for the wrapper object.

The IDL wrapper defines just the interface we need:

```
typedef sequence<string> DirList;

interface SourceCab
{
    readonly attribute DirList Directory;
    string FetchFile(in string FileName);
};
```

We take the simple approach here. We decide that the List action of
`Extract.exe` is best represented as a read-only attribute, named `Direc-`
`tory()`. That attribute returns a `DirList`, which is just a sequence of
`strings`. Each entry in `DirList` is just the name of one of the files in the
CAB.

Although the List action returns the modification date, file attributes, and
size in addition to the name, we're not worrying about any of this information in our example. Because we're the ones creating the wrapper, we get to
decide what we want to include and exclude. If we wanted to, we could
define a struct in the IDL file with values for name, modification date,
attribute, and size.

The Extract action of `Extract.exe` is represented by the `FetchFile()`
operation. It needs to know the name of the file to extract, so that's the
`FileName` parameter. It returns the file contents as a `string`. If the supplied
value for the filename isn't contained in the CAB file, it throws the
`CORBA::BAD_PARAM` exception. You can't see that these exceptions are
thrown by reading the IDL file, but throwing a `CORBA::BAD_PARAM` exception
is a pretty standard behavior for CORBA servers, and we follow it here.

Returning the file contents as a `string` is probably not a good idea for
anything but text files. But then again, this is just a simple example. We
could have defined a sequence of `octet` type and used that. However,
`string` works well enough for small text files.

Even with some simplifying assumptions, the `SourceCab` CORBA object
presents a nice interface to the `Extract.exe` application. After implementation, we can serve up a CAB file to any client on the network, and it can list
its contents and fetch files out of it simply by calling these operations.

Server implementation

With only one attribute and one operation, implementing the SourceCab server is straightforward.

IDL to C++ class

In this chapter, we focus on those aspects of the server implementation that deal with wrapping the legacy application. We cover implementing server objects in detail in Chapter 5. Refer to that chapter for general guidelines of server object implementation.

The SourceCab_impl.h file in the Examples\Chapter13 directory of the CD-ROM at the back of this book contains the C++ header file for the wrapper object implementation.

```
#ifndef SOURCECAB_IMPL_H
#define SOURCECAB_IMPL_H
#include <SourceCab.h>

class SourceCab_impl : public virtual SourceCabBOAImpl {
public:
    virtual DirList * Directory(CORBA::Environment&);
    virtual char * FetchFile ( const char *  FileName,
        CORBA::Environment&);
    SourceCab_impl(const char * CabFilePath);
private:
    int RunCmd(const char * cmd);
    CORBA::String_var MyCabFile;

;

#endif
```

The server implementation header contains few surprises. We declare a method for the Directory attribute and one for the FetchFile() operation. The constructor accepts one parameter that specifies the full path to the CAB file to serve.

We also declare a private method named RunCmd() that is, oddly enough, used to run the Extract.exe command. We talk more about this method in a minute. Finally, we declare a member variable named MyCabFile that holds the name of the CAB file passed in to the constructor.

Implementing the C++ class

The SourceCab server object implementation is where the real action is. Its job is to wrap the Extract.exe file in a warm, safe CORBA blanket.

The `SourceCab_impl.cpp` file on the book's CD-ROM in the `Examples\Chapter13` directory contains the C++ source file for the wrapper object implementation.

Driving the legacy application

The `RunCmd()` method's job is to execute the `Extract.exe` legacy application, supplying the correct parameters on the command line to get it to do the correct action. It also redirects standard output from the `Extract.exe` file to a file pointer so that the `SourceCab` server object can capture the output from the legacy application.

```
int
SourceCab_impl::RunCmd(const char * cmd) {
    int hpipe[2];
    if (_pipe( hpipe, 512, _O_TEXT | _O_NOINHERIT) != 0)
        throw CORBA::NO_RESOURCES(0, CORBA::COMPLETED_NO);
    int origStdout = _dup(_fileno(stdout));
    if(_dup2(hpipe[1], _fileno(stdout)) != 0)
        throw CORBA::NO_RESOURCES(1, CORBA::COMPLETED_NO);
    close(hpipe[1]);
    system(cmd);
    if(_dup2(origStdout, _fileno(stdout)) != 0)
        throw CORBA::NO_RESOURCES(2, CORBA::COMPLETED_NO);
    close(origStdout);
    return hpipe[0];
}
```

This method is like a plumber — it does most of its work with a pipe. We need to capture the output from the `Extract.exe` command, so we redirect its output into a pipe that the `SourceCab` server object can read.

We begin by creating a pipe, which is just a pair of file descriptors. One file descriptor is for reading, the other for writing. We then save a copy of the current standard output file descriptor and duplicate the write side of the pipe onto the current standard output. That connects the pipe to standard output. We then close the original write side of the pipe so that anything written to standard output goes into the pipe, rather than being displayed in the command window.

After the pipe is connected, we execute the supplied command by using the `system()` function call. Anything the command outputs can be read from the pipe, which is just what we want. We then restore standard output for the `SourceCab` server to the saved standard output file descriptor and then return the read side of the pipe. If anything bad happens, we throw the CORBA standard `CORBA::NO_RESOURCES` exception.

By calling RunCmd() and supplying a command line that specifies Extract.exe and the desired parameters, we get back a file descriptor that we can read to retrieve anything it prints while it runs.

You can also redirect standard input to another pipe before running the command. In that way, your server object can supply input to the running legacy application simply by writing to the pipe. This capability is handy if the legacy application has a simple menu-driven interface, rather than a command-line interface.

Directory service

The Directory() method uses Extract.exe to create and return a DirList sequence containing the names of the files stored in the CAB. We explain this method in several chunks. Here's the first chunk:

```
DirList *
SourceCab_impl::Directory(CORBA::Environment&) {
    CORBA::Long size = 0;
    DirList * cabDir = new DirList();
    char extractCmd[MAXCMD];
    sprintf(extractCmd, "Extract /D %s", MyCabFile);
    int readFd = RunCmd(extractCmd);
    ifstream extractOutput(readFd);
    char readBuf[MAXCMD+80];
    char cabContentFile[MAXCMD];
```

We begin by allocating an empty DirList sequence. Then we build a command line that supplies the /D option, as well as the CAB filename, to the Extract.exe program. The /D option tells Extract.exe to list a directory of the CAB file to standard output.

We then run the command, using RunCmd(), and save the returned file pointer into readFd. Next, we create an input stream with that file descriptor and declare a couple of buffers that we use to read the output from Extract.exe.

```
    while (!extractOutput.eof()) {
        extractOutput.getline(readBuf,MAXCMD+80);
        if (isdigit(readBuf[0])) break;
    }
```

We read the output from Extract.exe a line at a time until we get to a line that starts with a digit. That skips over the header information output by Extract.exe and gets to the first line of the directory listing.

```
while (!extractOutput.eof()) {
    sscanf(readBuf,"%*s %*s %*s %*s %s", cabContentFile);
    cabDir->length(size+1);
    (*cabDir)[size++] = CORBA::string_dup(cabContentFile);
    extractOutput.getline(readBuf,MAXCMD+80);
    if (!isdigit(readBuf[0])) break;
}
```

For each line we read, we use `sscanf()` to extract just the filename from all
the information `Extract.exe` prints. We extend the `DirList` sequence by
one and use `CORBA::string_dup()` to copy the filename into the new
sequence element. Then we read the next line of output from `Extract.exe`.
If it doesn't start with a digit, we know we're done.

```
    extractOutput.close();
    return cabDir;
}
```

All that's left to do is close the pipe to `Extract.exe` and return the
`DirList`. You can see that the legacy application (`Extract.exe`) is doing all
the work, while the CORBA server just wraps it all up nice and tidy and
serves up the information!

Fetching files

The `FetchFile()` method uses `Extract.exe` to extract and return a single
file stored in the CAB. We explain this method in several chunks, too. It's the
explanation that's so chunky, you can eat it with a fork.

```
char *
SourceCab_impl::FetchFile (const char * FileName,
      CORBA::Environment&) {
   char extractCmd[MAXCMD+80];
   sprintf(extractCmd,"Extract /Y /L \\tmp %s %s",
      MyCabFile, FileName);
   int readFd = RunCmd(extractCmd);
   ifstream extractOutput(readFd);
   char readBuf[MAXCMD+80];
```

We build a command line that supplies the `/Y` and `/L` options, extraction
directory, CAB filename, and filename to extract to the `Extract.exe` program. The `/Y` option tells `Extract.exe` to not prompt before overwriting a
file, and the `/L \\tmp` option tells it to extract the file to the `\tmp` directory.

We then run the command, using `RunCmd()`, and save the returned file
pointer into `readFd`. Next, we create an input stream with that file descriptor and declare a buffer that we use to read the output from `Extract.exe`.

```
const char * msg = "Extracting \\tmp\\";
   int msglen = strlen(msg);
   while (!extractOutput.eof()) {
       extractOutput.getline(readBuf,MAXCMD+80);
       if (strncmp(msg, readBuf, msglen) == 0) {
          break;
       }
   }
   if (extractOutput.eof())
       throw CORBA::BAD_PARAM(0, CORBA::COMPLETED_NO);
   extractOutput.close();
```

Next, we read the output from `Extract.exe` to verify that the file was extracted. If it wasn't, we throw the `CORBA::BAD_PARAM` exception.

```
CORBA::String_var openName =  CORBA::string_dup(FileName);
char * dot = strchr(openName, '.');
if (dot == NULL) {
   if (strlen(openName) > 8)
       openName[(CORBA::ULong)8] = '\0';
}
else {
   if (strlen(dot) > 4) dot[4] = '\0';
   if ((dot - openName) > 8) strcpy(openName+8, dot);
}
char extractedFile[MAXCMD];
sprintf(extractedFile, "\\tmp\\%s", openName);
```

We then convert the filename to the 8.3 format. `Extract.exe` is really an MS-DOS legacy program, and it truncates long names into 8.3 names.

```
int fd;
if ((fd = _open(extractedFile, _
      O_RDONLY |_O_BINARY)) == -1)
    throw CORBA::NO_RESOURCES(0, CORBA::COMPLETED_NO);
struct _stat theStat;
if (_fstat(fd, &theStat) != 0)
    throw CORBA::NO_RESOURCES(0, CORBA::COMPLETED_NO);
char *fileBuf = new char[theStat.st_size+1];
int numRead = _read(fd, fileBuf, theStat.st_size);
fileBuf[numRead] = 0;
_close(fd);
_unlink(extractedFile);
return fileBuf;
}
```

All that's left to do is determine the new file's size, allocate a buffer to hold its contents, and read it in. The resulting string is returned.

Implementing the C++ application

The server application is just like other server applications we present elsewhere in the book.

The Server.cpp file on the CD-ROM in the Examples\Chapter13 directory contains the C++ source file for the wrapper object server application.

We need to allow the user to specify which CAB file to use on the command line as an argument. This value passes into the constructor for the SourceCab_impl object so it knows which CAB file to use.

Client implementation

The client is also just like any other C++ client application. This client accesses the SourceCab server object, gets a directory of the available files in the CAB file, and presents the directory as a menu. It then accepts the user selection from the menu, retrieves the file from the server, and prints it.

The Client.cpp file in the Examples\Chapter13 directory of the CD-ROM at the back of this book contains the C++ source file for the client application. Refer to the file on the CD-ROM for the full listing. We present detailed information on creating client applications in C++ in Chapter 6.

The client uses the Directory() attribute to obtain a DirList sequence of filenames from the SourceCab server. It then prints those names as a menu and accepts the user's choice of menu item. Using the selected name, it calls the FetchFile() method to retrieve the string containing the contents of the file. It then prints the string.

Compile and run

Take a look at Extract.exe transformed into a CORBA server!

The Makefile that builds the entire example is on the CD-ROM that accompanies this book, in the Examples\Chapter13 directory.

Before running the servers, you must have installed your ORB and started any ORB servers that you need in order to run CORBA applications. Your ORB may require that your servers be registered with the Implementation Repository. If so, register the server using the name SourceCab and say that it is a persistent server. For Orbix, we use this command:

```
C:\Legacy\> putit SourceCab -persistent
```

To run the applications, follow these steps:

1. Run the SourceCab **server first in one window.**

```
C:\Legacy\> server Ch1src.cab
```

An example CAB file named Ch1src.cab is on the book's CD-ROM in the Examples\Chapter13 directory. It contains the source files to the example presented in Chapter 1.

2. Run the client.

```
C:\Legacy\> client
Located the SourceCab
```

3. When prompted, select a file from the menu.

```
Select file to display from Source CAB server
1) Client.cpp
2) Counter.h
3) Counter.idl
4) Counter_impl.cpp
5) Counter_impl.h
6) Server.cpp
Enter 1-6, x to exit: 5
```

The selected file is retrieved from the server and printed to standard output:

```
Source file Counter_impl.h:
/*
 Counter_impl class header for server object
 Orbix version
 */
#ifndef COUNTER_IMPL_H
#define COUNTER_IMPL_H
#include <Counter.h>
class Counter_impl : public virtual CounterBOAImpl
{
public:
        // class constructor
    Counter_impl();
        // method for GetNextCounter operation
    virtual CORBA::Long GetNextValue(CORBA::Environment &);
private:
        CORBA::Long MyCounterValue;
};
#endif
```

Chapter 14

Getting Dynamic in Your Interface

● ●

In This Chapter

▶ Introducing yourself to the CORBA Dynamic Invocation Interface (DII) and the Interface Repository (IFR)

▶ Locating desired server objects

▶ Using the IFR to determine each object's interface

▶ Using the DII and the IFR in a client to build and make a request

▶ Invoking a request and retrieving the returned values

▶ Putting all the parts together

● ●

*C*ORBA uses IDL to define an interface to a server object. When the IDL is compiled, the client stub and server skeleton code that is generated hide the complexity of the low-level communication between a client and a server. This setup is quite wonderful, and we strongly recommend that you stick with the stub/skeleton approach for 99.99 percent of your projects. However, 0.01 percent of the time you may find that having the client (or even the server) use a predefined interface just isn't quite what you're looking for.

Suppose that you want to create a client application that uses any server object that has a Print() operation, so long as that operation takes one parameter of either a string or long type. You can't do that with the static client stub approach, because you'd need to recompile and relink the client every time you wanted to access a new server interface. Think this example is far-fetched or useless? Maybe you know this approach by another name. Having a client gain new capabilities automatically also goes by the following buzz phrases:

✔ Plug and Play

✔ Beans

✔ Gratuitous use of technology

✔ Components

All these buzzwords refer to a common idea — designing and implementing a system that you can extend, even while it's actively in use, simply by adding or replacing server objects.

Client applications discover new servers based on the services that the servers offer and make use of the new services to extend, enhance, or upgrade the client's capabilities. If you find yourself in that position, you're going to need to use the CORBA Dynamic Invocation Interface (DII) and the Interface Repository (IFR).

The IFR and DII are joined at the hip. Using one without the other is pretty difficult, so we define them together:

- **Dynamic Invocation Interface (DII):** This is the actual low-level interface to the ORB. DII is the methods that the client stub calls, behind the scenes, when you call a method in a server object. It's pretty icky, which is why you're generally better off using the client stubs.

- **Interface Repository (IFR):** This is a database that contains the IDL description, in an internal form, for server interfaces. The description is sometimes called *metadata,* because it's data that describes data. All this abstraction can make your head spin, but the bottom line is that the IFR contains the information you need to figure out how to call operations in an interface without using the client stub.

The normal way you invoke an operation on a server in CORBA is by calling a method of an object. That process only works when you use the client stub, however, because the invocation of the method in the client is actually processed and turned into a request in the client stub. We talk about this procedure in Chapter 3.

When you use the DII, you must build the request yourself. In order to build a request that the server can understand, you use the IFR to determine

- The name of the operation.
- The number of parameters it accepts.
- Its astrological sign.
- Each parameter's type.
- Each parameter's mode (that is, in, out, or inout).
- The operation's return value type.

After you have all the information outlined in the preceding list, you use the DII to build the request and send it to the server object. If the operation returns a value, you can then extract the value from the request.

Servers can be dynamic, too

In this chapter we focus on the client side of the DII because that's the way it's most commonly used. A server can also create a new interface (not specified in IDL) and place it into the Interface Repository while the server is running. This interface is known as the Dynamic Server Interface (DSI). Trying to come up with a good reason for a server object to construct a DSI is challenging, but we're sure that someone out there needs this capability. We don't discuss it in this book, but the techniques you use with a DSI are similar to those you use for the DII.

When you're using the DII and the IFR in a client to make a request, you perform the following steps:

1. **Locate the desired server object(s).**

2. **Determine each object's interface by using the IFR.**

3. **Build a request.**

4. **Invoke (send) the request.**

5. **Retrieve the returned values.**

We spend the rest of this chapter showing you how to perform these steps, We conclude the chapter with an example and an exuberant pat on the back.

Finding Servers

Even when using the DII, you still need to have a reference to a server object before you can make requests. Some things never change. Step 1 in our step-by-step process is to locate the desired server object(s). Your options for obtaining a reference are the same as when you use client stubs:

- ✔ Use a string reference and the `string_to_object()` ORB function.
- ✔ Use the Naming Service.
- ✔ Discreetly try to catch the waiter's eye in a restaurant.

You can find examples of using a string reference to get a server object reference in Chapters 1 and 9. Chapters 6 and 8 include examples of using the Naming Service to get an object reference, and Chapter 18 covers the Naming Service in detail.

When you use `string_to_object()` or the Naming Service to get an object reference, you end up with a somewhat generic CORBA object reference. If you're using stubs, the next step is to use the `_narrow()` method of a specific server implementation to turn the generic reference into a reference to that server's implementation. When you use the DII, you don't take this step because you aren't going to use the client stub at all. Instead, you use the IFR to determine how to make requests to the server, and you use the DII to build and invoke (send) the request. You may think that omitting a step makes things easier, but in this case, it just means that you get to do all the heavy lifting yourself!

When using string references, you can design your client application to look in a specific file or directory of files to find string references for server objects. As you add new server objects, you simply add the string reference to the end of the file or create a new file in the directory. The next time the client runs, it finds the new reference and can use the new server.

When using the Naming Service, you can design your client application to look in a specific Naming Context for server objects. As you add new server objects, they register themselves in the specific Naming Context with unique names. The next time the client runs, it finds the new servers and can use them. We show an example that uses this technique in the section "Plugging Our Example," later in this chapter.

Determining the Interface Repository

After you obtain a generic CORBA object reference, the next step is to figure out exactly what operations that object supports. You do so by using the Interface Repository (IFR).

A single method opens the door to the IFR entries for an object. The `CORBA::object` class contains a method named `_get_interface()`. That method returns a reference to a server object that implements the `InterfaceDef` interface. The IDL for `InterfaceDef` is part of the CORBA standard. If it weren't, we wouldn't be talking about it, would we?

An `InterfaceDef` has all the information about a particular interface in it, contained as a number of attributes. It also includes a few operations that make creating requests much easier. When you have an `InterfaceDef` and you want to generate a request for an operation, you use the following techniques:

✔ Use the `lookup_name()` operation of `InterfaceDef` to find the information about a specific operation by name. We call this technique "plug and play with the IFR."

✔ Use the Dragnet approach, which involves using the `describe_interface()` operation of `InterfaceDef` to provide a structure containing all the details about the interface, including a sequence of all the operations it contains.

✔ Go for broke and ignore the `InterfaceDef` by hard-coding the request in your client, with the hope that everything works out okay. Think of this method as "plug and play without the IFR."

In the following sections, we take a look at each technique.

Plug and play

Generally speaking, your client application is most likely to expect to find a specific operation in an interface. That's what plug and play is all about. You design a client application in such a way that it can use the DII to determine how to call any server object that includes an operation with a specific name, parameters, and return value.

Here's one way to use the DII to implement plug and play:

1. **Write the client application so that, when it's run, it first locates all the server objects that are available to it by using either string references or the Naming Service.**

2. **In a loop, use the `_get_interface()` method of each server object located in step 1 server object to get the `InterfaceDef`.**

3. **Call the `lookup_name()` method in the `InterfaceDef` to find the desired operation by name.**

4. **If no operation with the desired name is found, the server object is not used. Loop back to Step 2 and try the next server.**

5. **If an operation with the desired name is found, the value that `lookup_name()` returns is not null. Use `_narrow()` to turn the value into an `OperationDef` server object.**

6. **Determine all the details about the parameters and return value of the operation by using the methods of the `OperationDef` server object.**

When you have an `OperationDef` object, you can determine everything you need to know to build a request for the operation. For the following example, we assume that you've followed the preceding steps and that you have a reference to an `OperationDef` server object in a variable named `opdef`.

To build the request, you get the type of the return value and the parameters of the operation. The next two sections tell you how.

The operation's return value type

To determine the return value's type, use

```
IDLType_var retdef = opdef->result_def();
```

The `result_def()` method returns a server object implementation for the `IDLType` interface. The `IDLType` interface in the IFR describes the type definition used in the IDL for the operation. It can describe both primitive types and user-defined types.

Primitive types aren't less sophisticated than user-defined types; they're just the types that are part of the IDL itself. Examples include `string`, `long`, `double`, and so on. User-defined types are any types (including `interface`, `struct`, and anything defined with `typedef`) that are not part of the IDL.

You can determine whether an `IDLType` refers to a primitive type by asking it to solve a simple math problem. Because it's not really going to solve a math problem in either case, just check the value of its `def_kind()` attribute instead. If the value is `dk_Primitive`, then the `IDLType` is a primitive type.

```
if (retdef->def_kind() == dk_Primitive)
```

To find out exactly which primitive type it is, you need to narrow the `IDLType` server object reference to an interface named `PrimitiveDef`, like this:

```
PrimitiveDef_var primdef= PrimitiveDef::_narrow(retdef);
```

Then you can discover the actual primitive type by using the `kind()` attribute of the `PrimitiveDef` server object:

```
switch (primdef ->kind()) {
    case pk_null:
    case pk_void:
    case pk_short:
    // etc.
}
```

Think of using the `result_def()`, then `def_kind()`, and finally `kind()` methods as your basic one-two-three punch for determining the return type value.

The complete list of PrimitiveDef values returned by the kind() attribute are listed in the CORBA specification.

What about non-primitive types? The other values for def_kind() are:

- ✔ dk_Alias
- ✔ dk_Struct
- ✔ dk_Union
- ✔ dk_Enum
- ✔ dk_String
- ✔ dk_Sequence
- ✔ dk_Array
- ✔ dk_Wstring
- ✔ dk_Fixed

Interfaces in the IFR, such as AliasDef, StructDef, and so on, correspond to each of these types. If the IDLType is one of these types, you can narrow it down to the corresponding Def interface and then use the attributes and operations of that interface to gather the relevant details.

For example, a StringDef interface represents a bounded string and includes the single attribute bound(), which returns an unsigned integer representing the size of the string.

Determining the return value type of an operation may seem like a lot of work, but these same interfaces are also used to determine the types of the operation's parameters. So you don't have to memorize a whole new set of interfaces!

Generally, when you examine an interface with the IFR, you just try to verify that an operation fits the expected profile for your plug. You don't need to cover every possible permutation of IDLTypes or even of PrimitiveDefs. Instead, you check for specific types and just ignore the rest.

The operation's parameters

You determine the number, type, and mode (in, out, or inout) of the parameters of the operation by using the OperationDef server object. The params() attribute returns a sequence of ParameterDescription server objects, each of which describes one parameter:

```
ParDescriptionSeq_var params = opdef->params();
```

Because the returned value is a sequence, you use params->length() to determine the number of parameters for the operation. Then you access each element in the sequence to find out more about the parameter.

Use params[i].mode to determine the mode (PARAM_IN, PARAM_OUT, or PARAM_INOUT) of the parameter. In this and the following examples, i is a CORBA::ULong variable, with a value between 0 and params->length()-1.

Use params[i].name to get the name (as a string) of the parameter, as defined in the IDL for the operation.

Use params[i].type_def to get the IDLType of the parameter. You can then use the same techniques described in the section called "The operation's return value type," earlier in this chapter, to find out all about the type definition for the parameter.

Just the facts, IFR

If you don't know a specific operation or you want more information than the plug and play technique provides, the describe_interface() operation of the IFR may be what you're looking for.

This technique is handy if you're writing a tool that lets you browse and display all the interfaces in an IFR, or if you have a long afternoon to kill at work one day.

The steps you need to take when writing a client application to use the describe_interface() operation of the IFR are right this way:

1. **Write the client application so that, when it's run, it first locates all the server objects that are available to it by using either string references or the Naming Service.**

2. **In a loop, use the _get_interface() method of each server object located in Step 1 server object to get the InterfaceDef.**

3. **Call the describe_interface() operation in the InterfaceDef to get a CORBA struct named FullInterfaceDescription.**

4. **Use the fields of the FullInterfaceDescription struct to determines everything about the server object interface, because it contains all the details.**

The IDL for the FullInterfaceDescription struct is

```
struct FullInterfaceDescription {
    Identifier name;
    RepositoryId id;
    RepositoryId defined_in;
    VersionSpec version;
    OpDescriptionSeq operations;
    AttrDescriptionSeq attributes;
```

```
    RepositoryIdSeq base_interfaces;
    TypeCode type;
};
```

Go for broke

Last but not least is the technique that lets you go for broke and ignore the Interface Repository by hard-coding the request in your client. If you decide that the client should call an operation only with a specific name, parameters, and types, then you can just hard-code this information into the request. In this way, you can actually implement the plug and play technique without using the IFR. Your decision to use this technique saddens the IFR, but you may make your deadline.

Here's how hard-coding the request works:

1. **Write the client application so that, when it's run, it first locates all the server objects that are available to it by using either string references or the Naming Service.**

2. **In a loop, build a request for each server object located in Step 1 using the expected operation name, parameter modes and types, and return type.**

3. **Attempt to send the request inside a** `try/catch` **block.**

4. **If the request succeeds, then you are lucky, and it is actually implemented in the server object, so process the results.**

5. **If the request fails because of the CORBA exception** `NO_IMPLEMENT`, **you find out that the server doesn't actually have the operation that you thought it has, so don't attempt to process the results.**

Building Requests

Whether you use the IFR or not, if you don't use client stubs, you need to use the DII to build and invoke every request that a client makes on server objects. As with everything else in life, some requests are easy and some are hard.

Easy requests invoke operations that use primitive-type parameters and which return either no value (in other words, `void` operations) or return values that are primitive types. They're easy because CORBA includes a class named `Any`, which is designed to hold a value of any type. Using the `Any` class with primitive types is a cinch, but it isn't so easy with user-defined types.

Hard requests, as you probably can guess, include user-defined types for either parameters or the return value. They also tend to work out at the gym at least 30 minutes a day.

You're at the mercy of the server interface designer when you use the DII. If you happen to be the server interface designer, you can make your job easier by sticking with primitive types, or at least simple user-defined types, when defining the operations of servers that you know you'll be invoking with the DII.

Building a request is actually simple — and a bit tedious. Follow these steps, and you'll be requesting services like a hungry patron in a busy restaurant:

1. **Use the ORB** `create_list()` **method to allocate a** `CORBA::NVList` **with the same number of elements as parameters to the operation.**

2. **Use the** `add()` **method of the** `NVList` **object to allocate and add** `NamedValue` **objects to the** `NVList`.

   Specify the mode (`CORBA::ARG_IN`, `CORBA::ARG_OUT`, or `CORBA::INOUT`) as the parameter in the `add()` method.

   You add one `NamedValue` object for each parameter in the operation. These objects hold the parameter name, value (for `in` parameters), or a pointer to a buffer to hold the returned value (for `out` and `inout` parameters).

   The `add()` method returns a `NamedValue` object, but it still owns the object. That means you don't need to, and should not, delete the object.

3. **Insert values into each** `NamedValue` **object's** `value()` **attribute.**

   These are the values for the parameters of the operation, and they're stored in an instance of the `Any` class, accessed via the `value()` attribute.

   If you're using C++, the `<<=` operator is overloaded for the `Any` class. That means there is a separate `<<=` operator defined for each primitive type. Just use `<<= <value>` to insert a value of any of the primitive types.

   If you're using Java, you need to use the corresponding `insert_<IDL typename>` method of the `Any` class. For example, `insert_long()`, `insert_string()`, and so on.

   Insert the values into the elements of the `NVList` in the same order as the parameters are defined in the sequence returned by `opdef->params()`.

4. **Allocate a** `NamedValue` **object to hold the result of the operation.**

5. **Use the** `_create_request()` **method of the generic CORBA object you want to call.**

   Specify the name of the operation you want to call and pass in the `NVList` you created in Step 1 and the `NamedValue` object you created in Step 4. You get back a `Request` object.

6. **Set the return result type of the request to the proper** `TypeCode` **by using the** `set_return_type()` **method of the** `Result` **object.**

   The primitive types have predefined `TypeCode`s, named `CORBA::TC_void`, `CORBA::TC_long`, and so on.

When you're all done with these steps, you're ready for a couple of jokes. You're also ready to invoke the request.

Invoking Requests

Actually making a request is simple, compared to dealing with the IFR and building the request. When you're using the client stubs, your request is hidden inside the client stub that is called when your client invokes a method in a server object. You aren't using the stubs when you use the DII, so you get to decide whether you want to make a blocking or non-blocking request. A non-blocking request is called a *Deferred Synchronous Operation* (DSO) in the CORBA specification.

✔ **Blocking Request:** This type of request is similar to the normal CORBA behavior for a client. The client calls a method in a server using a client stub. The client waits until the server processes the request and returns a reply or until an exception is thrown. During the wait, the client is said to be *blocked* because it isn't doing anything else. The only difference with the DII is you don't use the client stub, but rather call a method of the request object.

✔ **Deferred Synchronous Operation (DSO):** This type of request is the CORBA way to say that the client makes the request but does not wait for a reply. It is also called a non-blocking request.

Without using the DII, a client has no way to make a request and not wait for the reply, unless the server operation is declared `oneway`. With the DII, the client can choose not to wait for the reply for any invocation. The client can make multiple requests with one call and can even check back later to get the replies.

A `Request` object can be used only once. You cannot invoke the same request object multiple times. The behavior is undefined if you do, which is a nice way of saying bad things happen. Just don't do it.

I'm blocked

A blocking request is just like a regular method invocation using the client stub, except of course you don't use the client stub. Your client is blocked — that is, loitering around the malt shop not doing anything — until the server processes the request and returns a reply. This type of request is the sort of stuff that we talk about throughout the book.

You cannot use a blocking request on an operation that is declared `oneway` in the IDL. Not only does doing so not make sense, but it also raises an exception and generally annoys the ORB.

Let's say that you have a variable named `request`, which holds a `Request` object. You use the `request` variable to initiate a blocking request by using the following statement:

```
request->invoke();
```

The client blocks until the server processes the request and returns.

Even though the CORBA 2.2 specification shows that the `invoke()` operation returns a `Status` value and accepts a `Flag` argument, neither of these items is actually used in the C++ or Java language mappings. If the `invoke()` method fails, then either a CORBA-standard or application-defined exception is raised.

Always wrap request invocations inside `try/catch` blocks. That way, you can tell whether an invocation fails.

My way, the highway, or oneway

You can use the DII to get really fancy when you finally get around to making invocations, by using a Deferred Synchronous Operation (DSO). DSOs come in three varieties:

- ✔ The first type is exactly the same as when a client invokes a server operation declared `oneway`, in that you send the request and never check back to see what the reply was.

- ✔ The second type is not like anything possible when using the client stubs. Your client sends the request, and then some time later (any time it gets around to it!), it checks to see whether the request has been processed. If it has, your client retrieves the return value and any `out/inout` parameter values. If not, the client can choose to wait for the reply, or just check back later.

The DSO and error handling

When using DSOs, error handling becomes very dicey at best. Unlike both plain old client stub method invocations and the DII invoke() method, you may not receive an exception even if one is raised by the server. The two times when you may receive an exception are

✔ When you send the request.

✔ When you check the reply status.

Be sure to include exception-handling code both when sending the request and when checking the reply status.

✔ In the third type, your client builds several different requests and then sends them all at the same time. It then checks on each request at its leisure to find out whether the request has been processed and then extracts values, if desired.

Only oneway

You must use a DSO request for operations that are declared as oneway in IDL. A surprising and often useful feature of the DII is that you can also make oneway requests to operations that are not defined that way in IDL. Pretty nifty, especially when you're using somebody else's server and you can't change the server code.

If you're invoking a oneway operation using the DII, just keep in mind that the same two rules apply as when using client stubs:

✔ A oneway request is not guaranteed to be delivered, although it usually is.

✔ You cannot receive any values back from a oneway request.

Suppose that you have a variable named request, which holds a Request object. Hey, it could happen! You use the request variable to initiate a DSO oneway request by using the following statement:

```
request->send_oneway();
```

The send_oneway() method indicates that you want a DSO and that you won't be checking for a response, so the server object needn't bother sending one.

I'll get back to you

One of the coolest reasons to use the DII is that you can send a request without blocking and still check back for the reply and retrieve the returned values at a more convenient time.

Say that you have a variable named `request`, which holds a `Request` object. See, it happened again! You use the `request` variable to initiate a DSO request by using the following statement:

```
request->send_deferred();
```

You need to keep the `Request` object around until you receive and process the reply. That means you can't delete it until you get the response for the request.

To check whether the request has been processed and the results are available without blocking, use these lines:

```
if (request->poll_response()) {
    request->get_response();
    // process returned values
}
```

The `poll_response()` call returns `true` if the reply is available. You still need to actually get the reply by using `get_response()`.

If you just call `get_response()` and the reply isn't available yet, your client blocks until it is available.

The party line

If your client needs to send out a large number of requests, essentially at the same time, you can either call the `send_deferred()` method of each request object, or you can send them all at once by using the ORB methods `send_multiple_requests_oneway()` or `send_multiple_requests_deferred()`. Each acts exactly the same as its single-sending brethren, except that they both take a sequence of type `RequestSeq` as a parameter. The sequence is a list of request objects, and these methods send the requests all at the same time.

Assuming that the `Request` objects you build ahead of time are in variables named `request1`, `request2`, and `request3`, a multiple request send looks like this:

```
CORBA::RequestSeq multi;
multi.length(3);
multi[0] = request1;
multi[1] = request2;
multi[2] = request3;
// orb is a CORBA::ORB object
orb-> send_multiple_requests_deferred(multi);
```

When you use `send_multiple_requests_deferred()`, you still need to check for and process each of the replies.

Getting Results

Suppose that you've survived all the work involved in setting up and invoking (or sending) a request, and you want to actually retrieve the results. What a concept!

Even when using the DII, you can retrieve the return value for the operation as well as the values returned in any `out` or `inout` parameters.

At this point, you may be expecting a long process that includes microsurgery and trained seals, but in fact, getting the request's return value, as well as the `out` and `inout` values after the request has been processed, is relatively easy.

The first step in retrieving results is to get the return value, which you accomplish via the following steps:

1. **Declare a `CORBA::NamedValue_ptr` variable to hold the result.**

2. **Fetch the result value, using `request->result()`, and store it into the `NamedValue` variable declared in Step 1.**

   Alternately, you can just use the original `NamedValue_ptr` variable you passed into the `create_request()` call.

   The `result()` method returns a `NamedValue_ptr` object, but it still owns the object. That means you don't need to, and should not, delete the object.

3. **Use the information from the IFR to determine the type of the return value.**

4. **Extract the value out of the `NamedValue` variable and into a variable of the appropriate type.**

   The value is stored in an instance of the `Any` class, accessed via the `value()` attribute.

   If you're using C++, the `>>=` operator is overloaded for the `Any` class. Just use `>>= <variable>` to extract a value of any of the primitive types. The operator returns `true` if the extraction succeeds (in other words, if the type of the variable you're storing into matches the type of the value in the `Any` instance).

If you're using Java, you need to use the corresponding extract_<IDL typename> method of the Any class — for example, extract_long(), extract_string(), and so on. These methods throw the CORBA.BAD_OPERATION exception if the type of the value stored in the Any object doesn't match the type specified by the method.

Getting the values of out and inout parameters is very similar and does not require any seals at all:

1. **Declare a** CORBA::NVList_ptr **variable to hold the list of parameters.**

2. **Fetch the parameters, using** request->arguments(), **and store them into the** NVList **variable declared in Step 1.**

3. **Use the information from the IFR to determine which of the parameters are** out **or** inout **parameters.**

4. **Extract the desired values out of the** NamedValue **elements stored in the** NVList **into a variable of the appropriate type.**

   To access a particular NamedValue element, use the item() operation of the NVList. The item() operation returns a NamedValue object reference. Getting the value out of that reference is performed exactly the same as for the return value.

The arguments () method returns a NVList_ptr object, but it still owns the object. That means you don't need to, and should not, delete the object.

As is the case with the return value, you can keep around the NamedValue objects you used to build the Request in the first place instead of retrieving the NamedValue objects from the Request object. The objects will contain updated information after the request is processed.

Plugging Our Example

To prove to you that we know what we're talking about in this chapter, we use the IFR and the DII to create a simple plug and play example. We write a client application that can use any server object that includes a Print() operation. It can handle Print() operations that return either string or long values. It expects the Print() operation to accept a single parameter, again either a string or a long. It's a simple application, but it does use just about all the basic IFR and DII features discussed in this chapter.

The client comes first

In other chapters, we begin with the IDL, then implement the server object, and then implement the server and client applications. This time, we begin with the client. With the DII, the client is where the action is. Because the client doesn't use client stubs, IDL and the server implementations don't really come into play, at least not right away.

Our client application follows the steps outlined at the beginning of this chapter:

1. **Locate the desired server object(s).**

   We use the Naming Service. The client searches within a Naming Service context named `Examples\Chapter14\Printers` to locate all the server objects that have `Print()` operations.

2. **Determine each object's interface by using the IFR.**

   We're not taking any chances with these servers. Just because they claim to have a `Print()` operation doesn't mean we have to take their word for it. We use the IFR to verify that each server we find in the Naming Service context has a `Print()` operation and that it accepts either an `in long` or `in string` parameter. We're not too picky about what it returns, however.

3. **Build a request.**

   We build a request for the `Print()` operation by prompting the user to enter either a `long` or a `string` value, based on the type of the parameter, as determined in Step 3.

4. **Invoke the request and retrieve the return values.**

   We then invoke (send) the request. We print out the reply if it's a `string` or a `long`.

Finding Print() servers by using the Naming Service

Chapter 18 discusses the Naming Service in detail. We use the search capability of the Naming Service to find every server object registered in a particular Naming Context. Using the service is like finding all the files in a particular directory or that sock that the dryer ate.

We cover implementing clients in C++ in Chapter 6. Refer to that chapter for a detailed description of how to implement clients. The complete C++ source file for the `PrintClient.cpp` client application is on the CD-ROM (inside the back cover of this book) in the `Examples\Chapter14` directory. We only show the relevant portions here.

The client begins like every other CORBA client, by getting an ORB object.

```
// #include lines omitted
int
main(int argc, char* argv[], char*[]){
    try {
        CORBA::ORB_var orb = CORBA::ORB_init(argc,
            argv, "Orbix");
        // Orbix specific -- turn off Diagnostics
        orb->setDiagnostics(0);
```

It then gets a reference to the root context in the Naming Service.

```
CosNaming::NamingContext_var rootContext;
try {
    CORBA::Object_var initServ;
    initServ =
        orb->resolve_initial_references("NameService");
    rootContext =
        CosNaming::NamingContext::_narrow(initServ);
    if (!rootContext || CORBA::is_nil(rootContext)) {
        cerr << "Name Service does not exist." << endl;
        return 1;
    }
}
catch(CORBA::ORB::InvalidName& ex) {
    cerr << "Name Service does not exist." << endl;
    return 1;
}
```

From the root context, we locate the Naming Context, where all the server objects that support `Print()` operations are registered.

```
CosNaming::NamingContext_var listContext;
CORBA::Object_ptr obj;
CosNaming::Name name;
name.length(3);
name[0].id   = (const char*) "Examples";
name[0].kind = (const char*) "CORBA_for_dummies";
name[1].id   = (const char*) "Chapter14";
name[1].kind = (const char*) "CORBA_for_dummies";
name[2].id   = (const char*) "Printers";
name[2].kind = (const char*) "CORBA_for_dummies";
try {
    obj = rootContext->resolve(name);
}
catch(CosNaming::NamingContext::NotFound& ex){
```

```
        cerr << "No Print servers found." << endl;
        return 1;
    }
    catch (CORBA::COMM_FAILURE& ex) {
        cerr << "Unable to contact the naming service." << endl;
        return 1;
    }
    listContext = CosNaming::NamingContext::_narrow(obj);
```

We extend the list used to specify the `Print()` Naming Context by one,
because we're going to reuse it to retrieve the object references from the
Naming Service. Then we set up a `bindList`, `bindIterator`, and
`foundBinding` object so that we can iterate through all the contexts within
the `Printers` context. Finally, we retrieve up to ten of the contexts with the
initial `list()` call. Using the Naming Service search facility in this way is
detailed in Chapter 18.

```
    name.length(4);
    const CORBA::ULong numList = 10;
    CosNaming::BindingList_var bindList;
    CosNaming::BindingIterator_var bindIterator;
    CosNaming::Binding foundBinding;
    listContext->list(numList, bindList, bindIterator);
```

For each context we find, we check to see whether it's an object registration
by using the `binding_type` attribute. If it isn't, we just skip to the next one.
If it is, we update the `CosNaming::Name` sequence by tacking on the found
item `id` and `kind` as the fourth context and then attempt to resolve the new
name to retrieve a generic CORBA server object. If the retrieve fails, we just
skip to the next one. If it succeeds, then we proceed to the next step.

```
    CORBA::ULong i;
    do {
        for (i = 0; i < bindList->length(); i++) {
            if (bindList[i].binding_type !=
                CosNaming ::nobject) continue;
            name[3].id   = CORBA::string_dup(
                bindList[i].binding_name[0].id);
            name[3].kind = CORBA::string_dup(
                bindList[i].binding_name[0].kind);
            obj = rootContext->resolve(name);
            if (CORBA::is_nil(obj)) continue;
```

Checking out a server interface with the IFR

Step 2 is where we use the IFR to discover the server object interface. We
need to verify that the server object has a `Print()` operation and that it has
the expected parameters. First, we get the `InterfaceDef` from the IFR for
the server object.

```
InterfaceDef_var objInf =
    obj->_get_interface();
```

The `InterfaceDef` contains the interface for the server. Next, we use the `lookup_name()` operation of the `InterfaceDef` to locate all the `Print()` operations defined in the interface.

```
ContainedSeq_var ops =
    objInf->lookup_name("Print", 1,
        dk_Operation, TRUE);
if (ops->length() != 1) continue;
```

If we don't find exactly one, we skip further processing of this server and move on to the next one. We then retrieve the `OperationDef` for the `Print()` operation, which is the first (and only, in this case) value returned by `lookup_name()`. We retrieve the type definition of the result by using `result_def()` and verify that it returns a primitive type. If it does, we fetch and store the `PrimitiveDef` for the return type, so that we can use it later to extract the return value of the invocation.

```
OperationDef_var opdef =
    OperationDef::_narrow(ops[(CORBA::ULong)0]);
IDLType_var retdef = opdef->result_def();
if (retdef->def_kind() != dk_Primitive)
    continue;
PrimitiveDef_var retPrimdef =
    PrimitiveDef::_narrow(retdef);
```

We then turn our attention to the parameters of the `Print()` operation. We make sure that only one parameter is specified, that it's an `in` parameter, and that its type is either `long` or `string`.

```
ParDescriptionSeq_var params = opdef->params();
if (params->length() > 1) continue;
ParameterDescription param =
    params[(CORBA::ULong)0];
if (param.mode != PARAM_IN) continue;
IDLType_var paramdef = param.type_def;
if (paramdef->def_kind() != dk_Primitive)
    continue;
PrimitiveDef_var paramPrimdef =
    PrimitiveDef::_narrow(paramdef);
if ((paramPrimdef->kind() != pk_long) &&
    (paramPrimdef->kind() != pk_string))
        continue;
```

If the server passes through this gauntlet of tests, we're fairly confident that we can call it with the DII.

Building the Print ( ) request

Step 3 is building the Print() request itself.

```
CORBA::NVList opArgs;
CORBA::NamedValue_var opVal;
orb->create_list(1, opArgs);
opVal = opArgs->add(CORBA::ARG_IN);
```

We create the NVList pointer that holds the parameter list. Note that we use the _ptr instead of the _var type here. That's because we don't want the automatic deletion of the object pointer in this case.

Our example has just one parameter. We use the ORB method named create_list() to build the list and then use the add() operation to allocate and insert the one NamedValue variable into the list.

```
char stringVal[31];
CORBA::Long longVal;
switch (paramPrimdef->kind()) {
case pk_long:
    cout << "Enter a long: ";
    cin >> longVal;
    *(opVal->value()) <<= longVal;
    break;
case pk_string:
    cout << "Enter a string: ";
    cin.getline(stringVal,30);
    *(opVal->value()) <<= stringVal;
    break;
}
```

We then prompt the user for either a string or long value, based on the parameter IDL type we got from the IFR. The kind() method of the PrimitiveDef class returns an enumeration value indicating which primitive type was used. We just use a case statement to select either the pk_long or the pk_string value. For either one, we prompt the user to enter the value and then read it into a variable of the correct type.

The somewhat bizarre expression *(opVal->value()) <<= stringVal; is how we insert the value into the parameter variable for the request. Then we use the overloaded <<= operator to insert the value entered by the user.

```
CORBA::Request_var printReq;
CORBA::NamedValue_var result =
    CORBA::NamedValue::IT_create();
if (obj->_create_request(
    CORBA::Context::_nil(), "Print",
    opArgs, result, printReq, 0)) {
```

(continued)

(continued)

```
switch (retPrimdef->kind()) {
case pk_long:
   printReq->set_return_type(
       CORBA::TC_long);
   break;
case pk_string:
   printReq->set_return_type(
       CORBA::TC_string);
   break;
default:
   cout << "Unsupported return type!\n";
}
```

All we need to do now is create the `Request` object itself. We declare a `Request` object and another `NamedValue_ptr` for the result. Notice that we allocate the `NamedValue` object by using `CORBA::NamedValue::IT_Create()`. That's because we want to reuse the `result` variable to retrieve the returned value after the request is processed.

We use the CORBA object's `create_request()` method to create the request, passing in a `nil` context, the operation name, parameter list, result object, and the `Request` pointer. If the call succeeds, it returns `true` and we set the type of the return value. We use the `IDLType` object we got from the IFR and set the type using one of the predefined CORBA `TypeCode` objects. After we finish this step, we're ready to invoke the request. If the `create_request()` method fails, we just print an error message and skip this server. The code that prints the error message is shown later in the chapter.

Invoking the request

Step 4 is to invoke the request and extract the return value.

```
try {
   printReq->invoke();
   cout << endl << objInf->name() <<
       "'s Print() called\n\n";
   CORBA::Long longReturn;
   CORBA::String_var stringReturn;
   switch (retPrimdef->kind()) {
   case pk_long:
      if (*(result->value()) >>=
             longReturn)
         cout << "Returned Long: " <<
             longReturn << endl;
      else
         cout << "Expected a Long, " <<
             "but didn't get one!\n";
```

```
            break;
        case pk_string:
          if (*(result->value()) >>=
                stringReturn)
            cout << "Returned String: \"" <<
                stringReturn << "\"\n";
          else
            cout << "Expected a String, " <<
                "but didn't get one!\n";
          break;
        default:
          cout <<
            "Returned an unsupported " <<
            "type!\n";
        }
      }
    catch (CORBA::SystemException &ex) {
      cout << "Call failed\n";
      cout << "Exception: " << ex;
    }
  }
  else {
    cout << "create_request failed!\n";
  }
```

Inside a `try/catch` block, we use the `invoke()` method of the `Request` object to call the `Print()` operation in the server. If the call fails, a CORBA exception is raised and we just print an error message. If it doesn't, we use the `IDLType` object we got from the IFR to retrieve the return value. When we attempt to extract the value, using `*(result->value()) >>=`, we enclose it in an `if` statement. If the extraction is of the correct type (and it is, because we use the `IDLType` from the IFR to choose which variable to extract into), then the expression returns `true` and we print the value we got back. If not, we print an error message.

Continuing the Naming Context search

We're all done with the current object that we located in the Naming Context. Now we need to get the next object and repeat the process of examining its interface, building a request, invoking it, and then extracting the returned value.

```
      }
      if (CORBA::is_nil(bindIterator)) break;
    }
  while (bindIterator->next_n(numList, bindList));
}
```

(continued)

(continued)

```
    catch(CORBA::SystemException& ex)
    {
      cerr << "CORBA Exception!" << ex << endl;
      return 1;
    }

    return 0;
}
```

If the `bindIterator` has returned all the Naming Contexts, our search is over. If not, we retrieve the next set of contexts, and we loop back to the `for` loop that processes the found contexts. The last chunk of code is our `catch` block for the opening `try` statement.

Plugable servers

We cover implementing servers in C++ in Chapter 6. Refer to that chapter for a detailed description of how to implement servers. The complete C++ source files for the two server applications, including their IDL files, server object implementations, and server applications, are on the book's CD-ROM in the `Examples\Chapter14` directory.

Server IDL

For this example, we create two servers that can be "plugged into" the client application. The IDL for each contains just a single operation, named `Print()`:

```
interface LongPrinter
{
    string Print(in long itemLong);
};

interface StringPrinter
{
    long Print(in string itemString);
};
```

We could include any number of additional operations and attributes, and these two servers would still "plug in" to our client correctly.

Server object implementation

The implementation of the server objects is straightforward. Basically, the `LongPrinter` server prints the `long` that was passed in and returns a string that says "Printed <value>". The StringPrinter prints the supplied string and returns a long value that is the length of the supplied string.

Server application implementation

The implementation of the server applications is also pretty simple. Refer to the files on the CD-ROM if you want to see them. The only thing specific to using the DII is that each server application registers its server in the Naming Service, in the Examples\Chapter14\Printers context. For our LongPrinter server, the Naming Service registration code looks like this:

```
CosNaming::Name name;
name.length(4);
name[0].id   = (const char*) "Examples";
name[0].kind = (const char*) "CORBA_for_dummies";
name[1].id   = (const char*) "Chapter14";
name[1].kind = (const char*) "CORBA_for_dummies";
name[2].id   = (const char*) "Printers";
name[2].kind = (const char*) "CORBA_for_dummies";
name[3].id   = (const char*) "LongPrinter";
name[3].kind = (const char*) "Object";
if (!SimpleNames::bindToName(orb, longPrinter, name))
{
    cerr << "Could not bind LongPrinter to name."
       << endl;
    return 1;
}
```

The StringPrinter code is very similar, except it uses the name "StringPrinter" for the Naming Service entry.

Compile and run

Bet you're ready to see it work, aren't you?

The Makefile that builds the entire example is on the CD-ROM that accompanies this book, in the Examples\Chapter14 directory.

Before running the servers, you need to have installed your ORB and any ORB servers (including the Naming Service and Interface Repository) that you need in order to run CORBA applications. Your ORB may require that your servers be registered with the Implementation Repository; register the servers using the names LongPrinter and StringPrinter and say that they are persistent servers. For Orbix, we use these commands:

```
C:\DII\> putit LongPrinter -persistent
C:\DII\> putit StringPrinter -persistent
```

Next, load the IDL for the two servers into the Interface Repository. The way you load the IDL depends on your ORB. For Orbix, we use these commands:

```
C:\DII\> putidl LongPrinter
C:\DII\> putidl StringPrinter
```

To run the applications, follow these steps. You enter the bold code.

1. **Run the** LongPrinter **server first in one window.**

```
C:\DII\> lpserver
```

2. **Next, run the client and, when prompted, enter a long value:**

```
C:\DII\> pclient
Server object LongPrinter has operation string Print(in long itemLong)
Checking to see if server application LongPrinter is running...
Server is available.
Enter a long: 12345
LongPrinter's Print() called
Returned String: "Printed 12345"
```

3. **Leave the** LongPrinter **Server running and begin running the** StringPrinter **server in another window.**

```
C:\DII\> spserver
```

4. **Run the client again and, when prompted, enter a** string **value and a** long **value:**

```
C:\DII\> pclient
Server object StringPrinter has operation long Print(in string itemString)
Checking to see if server application StringPrinter is running...
Server is available.
Enter a string: Hey, it works!
StringPrinter's Print() called
Returned Long: 14
Server object LongPrinter has operation string Print(in long itemLong)
Checking to see if server application LongPrinter is running...
Server is available.
Enter a long: 54321
LongPrinter's Print() called
Returned String: "Printed 54321"
```

The client is able to call both the LongPrinter and StringPrinter server objects. It calls any server it finds via the Naming Service, as long as that server has a Print() operation the client understands.

Chapter 15

Mr. Bean, JavaBeans, CORBAbeans

• •

In This Chapter

▶ Exploring the relationship between an English character and CORBAbeans

▶ Looking at the existing JavaBeans

▶ Considering what CORBAbeans may be

• •

*I*n a perfect world, the technology you're trying to use is fully developed and readily available. Unless you're very lucky, this isn't a perfect world. So it is with the whole subject of Beans. Yes, that's *Beans* with a capital *B,* to distinguish it from the little *b* in *beans* that go in your soup, salad, or up your nose, if you happen to be a toddler.

The day just wouldn't be complete without some definitions, so here's your quota for the chapter:

> ✔ **Bean:** A reusable component. A Bean is really just a Java class that is created applying special rules.
>
> ✔ **Property:** An editable data value for a Bean. It's just like a member variable in a class.
>
> ✔ **Event:** An event occurs when something important happens. For Beans, that "something important" usually means that a data value changes. When this change occurs, a Bean sends an event.

Beans, in the Java world, is the name given to reusable components that can be easily composed in a visual editing environment. A *visual editing environment* is one in which a developer simply draws or lays out an interface, using some visual editor, by dragging and dropping Beans into a window. The developer then customizes the individual Beans by setting their Properties. The developer can connect Beans to each other by dragging links associated with the Events that they generate to other Beans.

You don't have to use a visual editing environment to use a Bean, but the visual editing environment is a big part of what makes Beans fun and interesting! We're always up for a whopping good time, so we use a visual editing environment (specifically, the Java BeanBox supplied with the Bean Development Kit) in this chapter.

A reusable component is little more than an object or class. What makes it a Bean is that "little more" part. Unlike traditional reusable components, Beans are smart. They know how they can be used, and they can interact with other Beans and with a Bean-based visual editor. This interaction makes using and reusing Beans much simpler than reusing classes. Stay tuned for more on this topic because we talk about it in the JavaBeans section of this chapter.

Unlike the lesser legumes, the three-bean salad we discuss in this chapter has a little — or a lot — to do with rapidly creating both client and server applications. Actually, Mr. Bean has almost nothing to do with creating client and server applications, but if you do a search on the Web for *Bean,* you get hundreds of sites relating to him, so we prepare you for that barrage of silly stuff by taking a quick peek in on him before we get started.

Mr. Bean

If you're blissfully unaware of Mr. Bean, feel free to skip this section. If you're the world's biggest Mr. Bean fan, you probably know more than we do about the character. Mr. Bean is a fictional TV and screen character whose daily affairs turn into farces at every available opportunity. Sometimes he comes out on top, and sometimes he doesn't.

Mr. Bean is a fairly noncommunicative sort. He gets by mostly on body language or short, mumbled words. He gets into and out of predicaments. He can be childlike as well as ingenious. He's certainly not a person to be intimidated by, and he often triumphs despite of (or is it because of?) his limitations.

JavaBeans

Okay, so CORBAbeans currently don't exist. What's a developer to do? Play racquetball all day? No such luck. We think that a more productive thing for you to do is spend some time playing with JavaBeans.

A fully functional JavaBeans toolkit is included with the current Java Development Kit (JDK) on the CD-ROM at the back of this book. Also on the CD-ROM is the Beans Development Toolkit (BDK), which is a free visual editor for creating Beans-based applications. The CD-ROM doesn't contain any other beans, so if your CD drive sounds like it's grinding, it's not our fault!

We can't tell you everything you need to know about JavaBeans in just a few pages. Instead, we give you a brief guided tour of the current JavaBeans approach and show you what it looks like to develop an application that Mr. Bean would be proud of, by using Beans and the Beans Development Toolkit.

What makes a Bean a Bean?

JavaBeans are really just plain old Java classes, with a little zing to them. Specifically, any Java class can be a Bean, so long as it supports these zingy qualities:

- ✔ **Introspection:** The knowledge of its own interface, so that it can tell a visual editor how it can be used.
- ✔ **Customization:** The ability to have both its appearance and behavior changed by setting Property values in a visual editor.
- ✔ **Events:** The way it talks to other Beans.
- ✔ **Properties:** The chunks of data that are used for customization, as well as for storing information.
- ✔ **Persistence:** The ability to save its internal state (basically, its Properties) so that, after it is customized within the visual editing environment, its customized state can be saved. The saved state can then be restored using the customized state at a later time.

Take a look at a simple Bean to see how these characteristics are reflected in the implementation of the class.

The following class is for a very simple Bean that can count:

```
import java.beans.*;
public class Counter implements java.io.Serializable {
  public Counter() { reset(); }
  private void reset() { count = 0; }
  public int getCount() { return count; }
  public int getCountBy() { return countBy; }
  public void setCountBy(int delta) { countBy = delta; }
  public void Count() {
    int oldCount = count;
```

(continued)

(continued)

```
        count += countBy;
        changes.firePropertyChange("count",
            new Integer(oldCount),
            new Integer(count));
    }
    public void Zero() {
        int oldCount = count;
        count = 0;
        changes.firePropertyChange("count",
            new Integer(oldCount),
            new Integer(count));
    }
    public void addPropertyChangeListener(
            PropertyChangeListener l) {
        changes.addPropertyChangeListener(l);
    }
    public void removePropertyChangeListener(
            PropertyChangeListener l) {
        changes.removePropertyChangeListener(l);
    }
    private void readObject(java.io.ObjectInputStream s)
            throws java.lang.ClassNotFoundException,
            java.io.IOException {
        s.defaultReadObject();
        reset();
    }
    private PropertyChangeSupport changes =
        new PropertyChangeSupport(this);
    private int countBy = 1;
    private int count = 0;
}
```

We review this class in its full Bean-ness. JavaBeans need to include the "ness" of Introspection. This quality can be incorporated either by providing an additional `BeanInfo` class or by examining the classes interface, using a few simple rules. These rules are called *design patterns,* simply because you, the designer, need to follow a specific pattern when designing a Bean in order for the Bean to work. The three patterns followed are

- ✔ A pair of `get` and `set` methods for the `countBy` Property.
- ✔ A pair of `add` and `remove` methods for a `PropertyChangeListener`.
- ✔ Several public methods in the class.

When a visual editor that uses Beans finds a pair of `get` and `set` methods, it considers the Property that they refer to as a Property that can be edited within the environment.

Because our class has such a pair only for `getCountBy()` and `setCountBy()`, `CountBy` is considered a Property of the Bean.

Whenever a pair of `add` and `remove` methods exists, the thing that they add and remove is considered an Event.

When the `Counter` Bean is selected in a visual editor, you have the option to connect the `PropertyChange` Event to some other Bean.

All public methods are considered to be valid *targets,* or external methods, when linking one Bean to another. In our case, this idea means that when linking an Event in a different Bean to the `Counter` Bean, you can choose from `Count()`, `Zero()`, or any of the other public methods for the target.

Other rules govern the design pattern, too, but you get the idea. Basically, you just need to do things the expected way, so that the visual editor can figure out what to do with your Bean.

If you don't like rules because you're a rebel, you can use the option of adding a `BeanInfo` class that tells the visual editor what methods are associated with Properties, Events, External Methods, and so on.

What about those other "nesses"?

- ✔ *Customization* is reflected in the `CountBy` Property. Changing the value of this Property in a visual editor makes our Bean count differently.
- ✔ *Events* is reflected in our use of a `count` Event that's sent whenever the value of the `Counter` changes.
- ✔ *Properties* is reflected again in the `CountBy` Property.
- ✔ *Persistence* is reflected in the use of the `Serializable` base class and the `readObject()` method, which is used to restore an object from serialized data.

Building a Bean

Building a Bean is a simple process. You knew we were going to say that, didn't you?

1. **Because a Bean is just a Java class file, you compile it into a** `.class` **file, using the usual Java compiler.**
2. **You put the Bean — and any other number of Beans — into a Java** `.jar` **file.**
3. **You add a manifest to the** `.jar` **file.**

   The *manifest* is just a text file that lists the Bean class filename and a flag that indicates that it is, indeed, a Bean.

4. **You drop the** .jar **file into the appropriate directory for your Bean visual editor.**

The next time you run it, the Bean is available for use. Nifty.

We're going to do just that, using the BeanBox visual editor supplied with the BDK.

The complete Java source file for the Counter.java Bean is on the book's CD-ROM in the Examples\Chapter15 directory. Also in that directory is a batch file named Makefile.bat that compiles the Bean and then adds it and the file named manifest.tmp into a .jar file named counter.jar.

Install the BDK onto your system. Make the Bean by running Makefile.bat. Copy the resulting counter.jar into the jars folder of the BDK.

Building a Bean example

Here's a step-by-step approach to making a working application with Beans — with no coding at all. If the prospect of no code doesn't get you hooked on JavaBeans, nothing will!

Laying them out

Laying out Beans with the BeanBox visual editor just like drawing a picture. You select a Bean from a palette of installed Beans, then click in the desired location of the container window. The new Bean appears there.

1. **Run the BeanBox visual editor by double-clicking the** run.bat **batch file in the** beanbox **subdirectory of the BDK.**

An empty container appears, along with a ToolBox window containing all the example Beans of the BDK, as well as the new Counter Bean you added in the preceding section. Figure 15-1 shows this initial display.

2. **Click the ChangeReporter Bean in the ToolBox window and then click in the upper middle portion of the BeanBox window.**

3. **Click the Counter Bean in the ToolBox window and then click a little below the new text box in the BeanBox window.**

4. **Click the ExplicitButton Bean in the ToolBox window and then click a little below and to the left of the new Counter word in the BeanBox window.**

5. **Change the label Property in the Properties window to Count.**

6. **Click the ExplicitButton Bean in the ToolBox window and then click a little to the right of the Count button in the BeanBox window.**

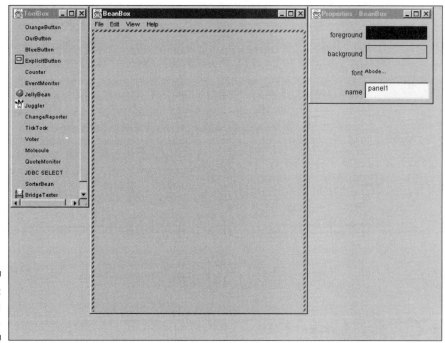

Figure 15-1:
The
BeanBox.

7. **Change the label Property in the Properties window to Reset.**

   Notice that the button label in the BeanBox window changes to
   Reset, too.

Linking them up

Turning the four Beans in the BeanBox into a working application is just a
matter of linking them!

1. **Click the Count Button in the BeanBox window.**

2. **Choose Edit⇨Events.**

3. **In the menu that pops up, choose button push⇨actionPerformed.**

4. **Click the word Counter in the BeanBox window.**

5. **Choose Count and then click the OK button.**

6. **Repeat the same steps for the Reset button: Choose Edit⇨Events⇨
   button push⇨actionPerformed, and then click on the word Counter
   in the BeanBox window. This time, select Zero from the list and then
   click OK.**

7. **Click the word Counter in the BeanBox window and then choose
   Edit⇨Events⇨propertyChange⇨propertyChange.**

Look into my crystal CORBAbean

CORBAbeans are an emerging technology. The specification for them is due to be completed in 1998, but even so, it takes some time for ORB vendors to implement and release products based on new specifications.

The current wisdom is that CORBA's Beans will be very similar to Java's Beans. Because JavaBeans are often concerned with user interfaces and CORBA server objects are usually not associated with user interfaces, it's a little unclear exactly how it's all going to work out. But it is pretty clear that CORBA will include Bean-like things and that you'll be able to create some or all of a client application by dragging and dropping CORBAbeans into some visual editor and then somehow connecting them to each other and your client objects to make an application.

8. **Click the text box, and when the EventTargetDialog dialog box opens, select reportChange and click OK.**

CORBAbeans

So where are the CORBAbeans? Right now, they're just a glimmer in the eyes of the OMG folks. It's not hard to imagine what they're going to be like, based on the fact that JavaBeans are already out and they actually work.

We expect that CORBAbeans will do what JavaBeans do:

✔ Support the creation of CORBA client applications in a visual editor by simply adding CORBAbeans to a window and then connecting them to each other and to user-interface Beans.

✔ Provide everything a client developer needs to use the CORBAbean immediately, without messing with IDL or Interface Repositories.

We can also guess how the OMG will implement CORBAbeans:

✔ Plenty of technology within CORBA, specifically in the Interface Repository (IFR), can let a CORBA server object support introspection. In CORBA, clients use the IFR to determine every aspect of a server object's interface. This capability, along with design patterns like those used in JavaBeans, can be used by a CORBAbeans visual editing environment to determine the Bean interface.

✔ CORBA objects already are specified in IDL, where both attributes (*Properties* in JavaBeans) and interfaces (*Methods* in JavaBeans) are clearly defined.

The future is your oyster — or in this case, your Bean.

Chapter 16

Think Components When You Think Beans

● ●

In This Chapter

▶ Designing CORBA servers and JavaBean wrappers to create CORBAbeans

▶ Implementing a CORBAbean

▶ Using a CORBAbean in a visual editing environment

● ●

*B*eans are just another way to design and deliver reusable components. What makes them different is that they make it easier for application developers to actually use reusable components. Developers can use a visual editing environment to compose a client application by simply dragging and dropping Beans into a window and then connecting the Beans to each other and to application objects.

It all sounds wonderful in theory, but for CORBAbeans, you do have some issues that you need to consider:

✔ CORBAbeans don't actually exist just yet.

✔ Cream tastes much better than skim milk in coffee, but it's way more fattening.

✔ Designing a server object as a Bean requires you to jump through some hoops.

✔ Using a server object Bean in a client application requires you to jump through more hoops.

The first point is the whopper. How can we talk about CORBAbeans when they're not yet available? Well, we do have JavaBeans, which are the working model for CORBAbeans. We call JavaBeans a *working model* because they're actually working — they exist and are being used. Chapter 15 discusses JavaBeans and even gives an example of one. We use JavaBeans again in this chapter as a model of what CORBAbeans may be like.

Even if CORBAbeans don't end up being exactly like JavaBeans, you can be sure that the issues we raise here and the approaches we show are relevant. It's the *concept* of components that's central to JavaBeans and to whatever CORBAbeans end up being.

When you're considering Beans, you have to consider

- What you need to do when you develop a Bean.
- How many beans are in the "guess the bean count and win a prize" jar at the barber shop.
- What you need to do when you use a Bean.

Because CORBAbeans haven't come to a theater near you yet, in this chapter we show you a way to use JavaBeans to wrap CORBA server objects. We use the Java language binding to create a Java client stub for a server object, and then we write a plain old JavaBean class that uses the client stub class to access the server. This little caper results in something that resembles our futuristic guess of how CORBAbeans will look. We call these faux CORBAbeans, because they're like faux diamonds — they look real, except to an expert.

Developing Beans

Take a look at some of the issues that crop up when you develop a Bean.

As any South American coffee bean grower knows, the richness of the coffee depends on the quality of the bean. Much the same is true of our Beans. If you have a well-designed Bean, you get the richest, most aromatic client applications when you use it.

Use the following tips when designing a Bean wrapper for a CORBA server:

- Create JavaBean Properties for all non-`readonly` attributes of the CORBA server object.
- Create JavaBean Events for all CORBA server object methods that return values.
- Create JavaBean External Methods for all CORBA server object methods that don't return values.

You're just creating a nice storefront for the CORBA client stub class that's usable in a JavaBeans visual editing environment! This yields a faux CORBAbean. That's something that looks and acts like a CORBAbean should, but isn't as real as you might think.

Follow these steps to make a faux CORBAbean:

1. **Define a CORBA server interface in IDL.**

2. **Implement the server and server application.**

3. **Implement a JavaBean wrapper class.**

An example you can count on

In Chapter 15, we create a simple Bean counter — we create a `Counter` class that is a Bean. In this chapter, we turn that Bean counter into something that accesses a `Counter` CORBA server object. Then it will almost be a CORBAbean.

The IDL for the `CounterBean` example is in a file named `Counter.idl` on the CD-ROM at the back of the book, in the `Examples\Chapter16` directory.

We follow the steps outlined in the preceding section. The first step is to write some IDL.

```
module CounterBean {
    interface Counter {
        readonly attribute long Value;
        long GetNextValue(in long Increment);
        void Reset();
    };
};
```

The `Counter` interface is very similar to the one we present in Chapter 1, except that this one has a new twist. The `GetNextValue()` operation now accepts a parameter specifying the increment value. We also added a new `Reset()` operation that sets the counter back to zero.

Step 2 is to implement the `Counter` server object and server application, which we do in Java. We show how to implement server objects and server applications in Chapters 7 and 8, respectively. You don't do anything special in these implementations, so we don't show the code here. The only thing you need to know about the implementation is that we write a string reference to the server object in a file named `Counter.ior`.

The complete source code for the `Counter` server object implementation is in a file named `CounterImplementation.java`. The server application is in a file named `JavaServer.java`. Both files are in the `Examples\Chapter16` directory on the CD-ROM that accompanies this book.

Clients need some way to find CORBA server objects. The two most common ways are by using the Naming Service or by using a string reference. You can use either technique when you create a JavaBeans wrapper for a CORBA server. Chapter 8 includes an example of using the Naming Service in Java, and Chapters 9 and 19 present examples using a string reference with Java.

A tiny CORBA client stub hides inside

Next, we create a JavaBeans class that wraps the Counter server client stub. This is Step 3 in our process, where we see some interesting stuff. We create a class named Counter that acts as our Bean wrapper. It's similar to the Counter Bean we create in Chapter 15, with the necessary changes to access the CORBA server to actually do the counting.

The complete source code for the Counter Java Bean is in a file named Counter.java in the Examples\Chapter16 directory on the book's CD-ROM.

```
import java.beans.*;
import org.omg.CORBA.ORB;
import org.omg.CORBA.Object;
import org.omg.CORBA.SystemException;
import java.io.*;
public class Counter implements java.io.Serializable {
```

The Bean begins like any other, by importing what it needs and declaring a class based on the Serializable class. Our constructor looks a little different from your average Bean.

```
public Counter() {
    try {
        BufferedReader s =
            new BufferedReader(new InputStreamReader(
            new BufferedInputStream(
            new FileInputStream("Counter.ior") )));
        ior = s.readLine();
        s.close();
    }
    catch (FileNotFoundException fe) {
        System.out.println("Start the Counter Server!");
        return;
    }
    catch (IOException ie) {
        System.out.println("Start the Counter Server!");
        return;
    }
    build();
}
private void build() {
```

```
    ORB orb = ORB.init();
    counterServer = CounterBean.CounterHelper.narrow(
      orb.string_to_object(ior));
  }
```

The `Counter()` constructor reads in the string version of the Counter CORBA server object reference from the file `Counter.ior`. It then calls the `build()` method to do the actual job of converting the string into an object reference.

You should split up your Bean constructors in a similar way, because a JavaBean can be saved in a serialized state. After the Bean is reconstructed, its constructor can't be called. So you need another private method that you can call, one that acts like the constructor. You see this call in action a little later.

Beans use the new Object Serialization features of Java 1.1:

- ✔ **Serialized:** This is the act of encoding all the information stored in a class into a byte stream that can be saved to disk. When this happens, an object is said to be Serialized. Basically, all the data in a class's member variables are encoded into a stream of data. If any of those member variables point to another class, the data in that class is also added to the stream.

- ✔ **Reconstructed:** This is the act of rebuilding an object, given its serialized data. When this happens, an object is said to be Reconstructed.

In the `build()` method, we get a reference to the ORB and then use the ORB method `string_to_object()` to convert the string reference into an object reference to the `Counter` server object.

If you're using the Naming Service, this is where you'd use it. See Chapter 8 for an example of using the Naming Service in a Java client.

The next pair of methods just defines a JavaBean Property named `CountBy`.

```
public int getCountBy() { return countBy; }
public void setCountBy(int delta) { countBy = delta; }
```

You can have Properties in the Bean wrapper that aren't specifically part of the CORBA server. In this case, we use the JavaBean `CountBy` Property as a parameter to the `Counter` server object's `GetNextValue()` method.

```
public void Count() {
   if (counterServer != null) {
     int oldCount = counterServer.Value();
     int newCount =
```

(continued)

(continued)

```
            counterServer.GetNextValue(countBy);
        changes.firePropertyChange("count",
            new Integer(oldCount),
            new Integer(newCount));
    }
}
public void Zero() {
    if (counterServer != null) {
        int oldCount = counterServer.Value();
        counterServer.Reset();
        changes.firePropertyChange("count",
            new Integer(oldCount),
            new Integer(0));
    }
}
```

The Count() and Zero() methods are External Methods for the JavaBean. They allow other Beans to call the Counter CORBA server's GetNextValue() and Reset() methods.

The Count() method uses the firePropertyChange() method to send the count Event, so other Beans can see the new value for the Counter. The Zero() method also uses the firePropertyChange() method, even though the Counter's Reset() method doesn't return a value. That's because the value does change to 0, although it's not returned from the CORBA server object.

```
public void
 addPropertyChangeListener(PropertyChangeListener l) {
    changes.addPropertyChangeListener(l);
}
public void
 removePropertyChangeListener(PropertyChangeListener l){
    changes.removePropertyChangeListener(l);
}
```

This pair of methods indicates that the Bean supports a PropertyChange Event. We need them so that other Beans can "see" the count property when it changes values.

```
private void readObject(java.io.ObjectInputStream s)
    throws java.lang.ClassNotFoundException,
    java.io.IOException {
    s.defaultReadObject();
    build();
}
```

This method makes serialization work. The readObject() method is called to restore the state of the Bean from a saved file. We perform the default read action, which restores the saved string object reference. Then we call the build() private method that acts as our real constructor, and it converts the string reference into a valid Counter server object reference.

```
private PropertyChangeSupport changes =
    new PropertyChangeSupport(this);
private int countBy = 1;
private transient CounterBean.Counter counterServer = null;
private String ior;
}
```

All that's left is our member variables. Because the Counter CORBA client stub isn't serializable, we mark the member variable holding a reference to it as transient. This notation lets Java know not to try to save its state when the Counter Bean is serialized.

Using Faux CORBAbeans

Follow these steps to use a faux CORBAbean:

1. **Compile the classes and create the** .jar **file for the wrapper class.**

2. **Install the** .jar **file in your JavaBeans visual editing environment.**

3. **Carefully adjust your** CLASSPATH **so that everything works in your visual editing environment.**

4. **Start the server that the Bean wraps, and, if necessary, copy the resulting string reference file to the same directory as the Bean visual editor.**

5. **Start the Bean visual editor, and drag and drop at will!**

Grinding the Beans

We compiled all the classes for you on the book's CD-ROM, in the Examples\Chapter16 directory. We've also included a Windows batch file named vbmake.bat that compiles all the classes with VisiBroker for Java (by Inprise Corporation) and creates the Counter.jar file. A batch file named startserver.bat starts the Counter persistent server.

Use vbmake.bat to compile the classes and create the .jar file. Next, copy the .jar file into your Bean editor directory. If you're using the BDK from Sun off the CD-ROM, it's the folder named jars in the main BDK directory.

Getting the CLASSPATH just right is an exercise in perseverance. If you're using the BDK, it wants a directory named classes in the CLASSPATH. You also need to add the full path to the directory where you compiled the example, so that the BDK can find the various CORBA classes used by the Bean. Assuming that you're using Windows 95 or NT, as well as the BDK, and that you copied the example from the CD-ROM into a directory named C:\CounterBean, you can set your CLASSPATH as follows:

```
C:\> CLASSPATH=%CLASSPATH%;classes;C:\CounterBean
```

Start the server by double-clicking the startserver.bat file. Copy the file named Counter.ior that's created into the beanbox directory of the BDK.

Before running the server, we're counting on you to install your ORB and start any ORB servers that you need in order to run CORBA applications. Your ORB may also require that your Counter and server be registered with the Implementation Repository before you run the example.

Finally, start your visual editing environment. To use the BDK with VisiBroker for Java, you need to open a command window. Change directories to the BDK's beanbox directory and enter this command:

```
C:\BDK\beanbox> vbj sun.beanbox.BeanBoxFrame
```

The BDK opens, and the Counter Bean is available in the ToolBox window.

Making applications with faux CORBAbeans

We can build the same JavaBean application that we build in Chapter 15, so the steps are the same. Rather than repeat them here, turn to Chapter 15 and follow the steps listed there for building a JavaBean application.

Did you do it? If you did, you probably noticed that nothing looked any different while you were building the application in the BDK. Ah, but here's the difference: The Counter Bean really does access a CORBA server. To see that it does, you need to run two copies of the BDK.

1. **Save the application in the BDK.**

2. **Open another command window and start another copy of the BDK.**

3. **Load the saved application into the new copy of the BeanBox window by choosing File⇨Load.**

4. **Now click the Count button in each of the two BeanBox windows, alternating back and forth.**

Chapter 17

DCOM and CORBA 3

*Y*ou're probably wondering what this chapter is doing in this book. After all, this isn't a book about DCOM; it's a book about CORBA. CORBA 3 doesn't exist now (the *now* when we're writing this book). It may or may not exist now (the *now* when you're reading it). What will eventually exist sometime in 1998 is the next major revision of the CORBA specification from the OMG. This will be either CORBA 2.3 or CORBA 3.0 — in either case, a *3* will be in there somewhere!

DCOM, Microsoft's Distributed Component Object Model, is how Microsoft does what CORBA does. Until very recently, DCOM only ran on the Microsoft Windows operating systems. What's changing is that most major UNIX vendors are announcing their support of DCOM. Even if you don't "do Windows" for your operating system, you can expect to be able to use DCOM some day.

Meanwhile, those wacky kids over at the OMG have been busy coming up with the next big thing for CORBA. They've got big plans for our favorite distributed object technology.

What both DCOM and CORBA 3 have in common is that both are changing the distributed object landscape. This chapter has two simple goals:

✔ To give you a bird's-eye view of the DCOM landscape so that you know what it's all about, how it's both similar to and different from CORBA, and how to access DCOM objects from CORBA.

✔ To give you a glimpse into the crystal ORB and view the future of CORBA — or at least to see what the OMG is considering for the future.

DCOM

The first thing you need to know about DCOM is that it's not really new. In fact, DCOM is just Distributed COM. Component Object Model (COM) objects have also had many names, including ActiveX and Object Linking and Embedding (OLE). If you've ever used any Microsoft Office products (Word, Excel, and so on), you've used COM. The new part in DCOM is the Distributed part. It adds capabilities for clients to access COM objects over a network. The way you access and use those objects is the same as it was for COM.

Comparing DCOM to CORBA

At first blush, DCOM and CORBA are quite similar:

- ✔ Both use an Interface Definition Language (MIDL for DCOM; IDL for CORBA) to define interfaces for objects. The two IDLs are even pretty similar.

- ✔ Both allow for a client to access operations of a remote server by invoking methods in local stub objects.

- ✔ Both are implementation language- and platform-independent.

They also differ in several key ways:

- ✔ DCOM objects can provide multiple interfaces but do not support inheritance.

- ✔ CORBA interfaces can inherit from other interfaces, but a single CORBA server implementation can only provide one interface.

- ✔ CORBA includes a rich set of services including Naming, Event, Transaction, and Persistence.

- ✔ DCOM interfaces have unique identifiers that are included in their IDL.

Neither system is better; they're just different. Although DCOM has always been viewed as a Microsoft-proprietary technology, it has actually been turned loose from the Microsoft mother ship. The Active Group (see www.activex.org/) now oversees the ActiveX standard. Because DCOM is part of that standard, it's technically out of the direct control of Microsoft. This group consists of 12 members versus the more than 800 OMG members, but it's a start.

Living with DCOM

Suppose that you've decided to stick with CORBA — after all, you're reading this book. And maybe you have a team of DCOM-crazed developers creating really wonderful DCOM objects. You are no doubt hoping to access those objects from a CORBA client or server. Lucky for you, you have several ways to do just that:

- The OMG COM mapping
- The wrapping mapping
- Holiday gift wrapping
- Vendor-specific products

In the current and future CORBA specification, the OMG provides detailed mappings between CORBA IDL and DCOM MIDL. It also describes how the low-level protocols of each technology can be mapped to the other. That means that some ORB vendors can implement the mappings as described by the CORBA specification. For example, Orbix, from IONA Technologies PLC, includes ActiveX Integration, which implements the interworking standard.

Another way to access DCOM objects is to treat them as legacy applications. Chapter 13 discusses how to wrap a legacy application in a CORBA server object. With DCOM objects, wrapping is just a matter of writing the CORBA IDL necessary to expose the desired DCOM interface. When implementing the wrapper class, you just call the DCOM object's corresponding method and supply the parameters. Then you return whatever the DCOM object returns.

Because you do have to write and maintain a wrapper server object, this approach is only recommended if you need to access just a few DCOM objects and you don't have or can't buy a commercial DCOM/CORBA bridge product.

Speaking of bridges, we're not selling you the Brooklyn Bridge. Instead, we're selling you on the idea of buying a commercial DCOM/CORBA bridge product. One such product is COMet, from IONA Technologies PLC. This product, and others like it, support bi-directional access between COM/DCOM objects and CORBA server objects, without requiring wrapper classes. A bridge product really is the way to go if you're planning on mixing and matching multiple CORBA and DCOM objects.

CORBA: The Next Generation

In Chapters 15 and 16, we take a sneak peek at one new thing that's coming in CORBA 3: CORBAbeans. CORBAbeans actually represent one facet of a larger shift in the OMG's goals for CORBA. Now that it has the basics pretty well nailed down in the standards, the next step is to start specifying things at the application, versus the object, level.

To get higher-level abstractions, the OMG is dappling in that old black magic — metamodels.

Literally, a *metamodel* is a model of a model. IDL basically builds a model of how a server object works. Being able to model how an application works is another layer of abstraction on top of IDL.

The OMG has adopted the Unified Modeling Language (UML) as its way of describing all metamodels in future CORBA specifications. You'll probably be hearing more about UML in the future, too. The OMG has even added a new facility called the *Metaobject Facility,* or MOF, which is fun to say but hard to grasp. The MOF is a metamodel for metamodels. Any more layers of abstraction, and the OMG is in danger of attaining full enlightenment!

All this abstraction is supposed to enable CORBA to do three things:

- ✓ **Get totally abstract.** Use UML to describe an application and have it translated to IDL.

- ✓ **Add the missing semantic capabilities (that is, meaning) to IDL.** IDL just describes an interface; it doesn't tell you what the operations *do*.

- ✓ **Establish a component model (that is, CORBAbeans) that supports Business Object development and use.**

New lamps for old

Some of the stuff that's changing in CORBA 3 is just a reworking of what's already here. The OMG throws out these specifications, and if something doesn't work out, the OMG kids go back and fix it. Or at least they take another shot at it.

Three areas that are getting a second look are

- ✓ **The Persistent State Service (PSS).** This service is replacing the Persistent Object Service (POS) that we describe in Chapter 21. The POS isn't well-liked in the industry, and the PSS is an attempt to make a more "vendor-friendly" persistence service.

What's a Business Object?

The OMG actually has a definition for a Business Object, which is never called a BO, for obvious reasons. It's a "representation of a thing active in the business domain, including at least its business name and definition, attributes, behavior, relationships, rules, policies, and constraints." That was helpful, wasn't it?

Think of it this way: Every business application tends to deal with the same stuff — employees, payments, invoices, customers, products, and so forth. How many times do you think

these things have been implemented as CORBA objects? Don't you think that's enough? The OMG does, too — so it wants to standardize a whole bunch of them so that you don't have to re-implement them over and over. Standardization would also make it possible to buy larger components, like accounting and payroll applications, that would work with your own custom applications. That's because they would use the same Business Objects that your own applications use — the standard OMG Business Objects.

✔ **Pass by value.** Right now, all server objects returned via operations are references. That's generally a good thing, but some folks really want to get an actual local copy of a server (in other words, its value) returned. The pass by value specification addresses this issue.

✔ **Java to IDL mapping.** Some folks just live in Java land. They want to write Java classes and then generate IDL from them. Go figure.

Beans, scripts, and screenplays

We talk about Beans in Chapters 15 and 16. CORBAbeans are the way the OMG hopes to evolve CORBA servers into Components. Components are good, because they work together in a pre-agreed-upon way. That's called a component model. Great, another model!

You get good things from this component model, including the ability to

✔ Use visual editing environments, just like you can with JavaBeans

✔ Use higher-level scripting languages to do basic application development with CORBAbeans

✔ Create server objects with multiple interfaces, just like DCOM

✔ Leap tall buildings after downing a really strong cup of joe

✔ Create server objects that combine several interfaces

Some new stuff

The Workflow Management Facility is a brand-spanking-new Facility in CORBA 3. It defines interfaces that deal with workflow creation, mainte-nance, and execution. A *workflow* defines a sequence of steps that have to be performed just so for everything to work. They can be simple, like

1. **Put on shoes.**

2. **Tie shoe laces.**

They can also be very complex, like

1. **Write a book about the meaning of life.**

2. **Get a spot on *Oprah* so you can make millions.**

In the CORBA world, workflows can make using a set of related CORBA server objects more "safe," in that you needn't worry if the client has done Step 21B before she does Step 21C.

Masters of their domains

Keeping the spirit of metamodels and higher-level abstractions alive and kicking, the OMG is also working on domain-specific objects, services, and facilities. These fall into several broad areas, including Electronic Com-merce, Finance, Health Care, Manufacturing, Telecommunications, Transpor-tation, and Utilities.

Like Business Objects, the goal is to standardize much of the mundane work that must be done over and over. The OMG hopes that by viewing these things in a manner specific to a more focused business area (that is, a domain), their specifications will be more readily accepted.

The knee bone's connected to the thigh bone

All the changes described in this chapter are interconnected. IDL is one of the most fundamental elements of CORBA, and it's likely to get a little (or a lot) of tweaking in the next major revision. That doesn't mean that the OMG is expected to toss the baby out with the bath water. It's most likely to make additions to IDL.

You can also expect tweaks to the various language bindings, including C++ and Java, to support some of the new features. But not to worry. What you know about CORBA 2 is usable with CORBA 3.

Part IV
Services Are Always Welcome

The 5th Wave   By Rich Tennant

"WHAT DO YOU MEAN IT SORT OF IS AND ISN'T COMPATIBLE?"

In this part . . .

*P*art IV is where we make your life simpler. The Object Management Group went to a great deal of trouble to define plenty of very useful services for CORBA. These CORBAservices are the key to creating powerful CORBA applications quickly and easily. In these chapters, you find discussions of the most commonly used CORBAservices with practical advice on how and when to use them.

This part contains everything you need to round out your CORBA knowledge. You can use the CORBAservices instead of reinventing them from scratch or relying on ORB vendor-specific extensions.

Chapter 18

Name That Object

Server objects exist in a vast, unknowable space. In other words, they can be anywhere — on your local workstation, on one of your company's servers, on any other machine on the network, or on the Internet.

It makes sense, then, that a client needs a reference to a server object before it can call any of the server's methods. After all, without a reference, an object can spend all its time searching space without much success. In fact, although some people may disagree with us, this seems to be the fate of the Starship *Enterprise* in its many incarnations.

This chapter talks about creating a server object reference and searching for a server object reference by using the Naming Service. It also gives you a freebie service called `SimpleNames` that you can use to make and get object references without going through a bunch of steps. Instead, you just call our pre-made service, and voilà — all is taken care of for you. Chapter 3 outlines four ways in which a client can get a reference to a server object. The most desirable way is by using the Naming Service.

General facts to know about the Naming Service include the following:

✔ It enables server objects to be added and located by name.

✔ After a server has registered itself with this service, clients can find the server object's reference and use it to call methods on the server.

✔ The OMG has provided this service as a means by which object references to servers can be found.

✔ It never returns the name *fuddy-duddy*.

> ✔ Like all other CORBAservices, it is specified as a standard CORBA server object, which means that its interface is defined in IDL.
>
> ✔ You use the appropriate language binding to access the methods of the Naming Service server object. We show the C++ binding in this chapter.

The Naming Service is usually an add-on product that you buy in addition to your ORB. Such a package includes programmer's reference documentation that details the IDL Specification for the Naming Service. For example, the OrbixNames evaluation Naming Service (which is on the CD-ROM that accompanies this book, in the `Eval\Iona\Naming` directory) includes this information.

Naming Service Basics

At its heart, the Naming Service is just a general directory system for references to server objects. It's very much like the folders and files on a computer's disks. The Naming Contexts provide the structure for storing and retrieving unique object references. The Name Component is a single server object's Name.

Naming Contexts are like folders and Name Components are like files.

> ✔ **Naming Context:** This is a single namespace (much like a disk drive directory). Everything inside a Naming Context has a unique Name.
>
> ✔ **Name Component:** This is a single object Name (much like a file in a directory).

Key points to know about Naming Contexts are that

> ✔ They have an `identifier` field (a `CORBA::String`) that represents the server object's Name.
>
> ✔ They have a `kind` field (a `CORBA::String`) that represents application-specific information.
>
> ✔ Like disk directories, they contain subdirectories, other Naming Contexts, and, of course, Name Components.
>
> ✔ They often Name Names and snitch like the proverbial jailbird.
>
> ✔ They have a root context that is unnamed.

Key points to know about Name Components are that they

> ✔ Have an `identifier` and a `kind` field, just like Naming Context.
>
> ✔ Contain an object reference to a server object.
>
> ✔ Are like loyal members of a crime ring in that they never snitch or name names.

Not exactly a directory

The Naming Service isn't limited to using a hierarchical organization of Naming Contexts. It's quite legal to have a single Naming Context appear inside several other Naming Contexts, as well as to have circular paths (Naming Contexts that include other Naming Contexts, which include the original Naming Context) and other somewhat bizarre organizations — any organization is possible.

The same is true for Name Components. The same Name Component can appear in several Naming Contexts, and a single server object can belong in any number of Naming Contexts.

Supporting any organization for Naming Contexts, and allowing the same Naming Component within multiple Naming Contexts allows for a flexible system for naming servers. You don't need to make weird hyper-cube paths with your Naming Contexts, even though you can. For most folks, using plain old hierarchies works just fine. Figure 18-1 shows two legal organizations for Naming Contexts.

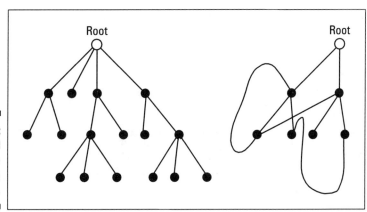

Figure 18-1:
Hierarchical and bizarre naming organizations.

Not exactly a file

The Naming Service does all its magic using a data structure called `COS::Naming`. This structure consists of a CORBA sequence of `Name` structures. Each `Name` contains an `identifier` string and a `kind` string.

Use the `identifier` portion to hold the Name of the Context or Component, and use the `kind` portion to hold its type or application-specific indicator. For example, you might have a number of server objects that deal with a payroll system. In this case, the `kind` field is always set to `"Payroll"`. Because the `identifier` and `kind` are both used to determine whether a

`Name` is unique, you may have a `Name` consisting of the `identifier` `"Accounts Payable"` and the `kind` `"Payroll"` and another `Name` using the `identifier` `"Accounts Payable"` and the `kind` `"Personnel"` in the same Naming Context.

Using the Naming Service

You perform two basic activities with the Naming Service:

- ✔ Create an entry in the service (called *registering*) for a server object that contains the object's Name and its reference.
- ✔ Find and return the object reference for a server object, given its Name.

Making a Name for yourself

To create or register a Name with the Naming Service, head down this path:

1. **Locate the Naming Service root context server object by using the ORB function** `resolve_initial_references("NameService")`.

2. **Narrow the returned object into a Naming Context object.**

3. **Do some error-checking!**

   The Naming Service may not be running, in which case you get a nil object.

4. **Create a** `Name` **for the Naming Context.**

5. **Try to create the Naming Context within the root context.**

   If the Naming Context already exists within the root context, just retrieve the existing context.

6. **Repeat Step 5 as many times as needed.**

   For example, you may want to use a number of nested Naming Contexts to represent a directory tree like `"\Examples\Chapter5"`.

7. **Add the Name Component with the** `bind()` **operation.**

   If the `bind()` operation throws the exception indicating that the Name Component is already bound to an object, use `rebind()` to change the binding to the new object. Binding and rebinding associate a server's Name with its reference.

Although these steps seem like a lot to remember, you follow exactly the same procedure any time you want to make a Name in the Naming Service. The only things that change are the Naming Contexts and the Name Components. Everything else is the same to register any server.

In C++, these steps look like this:

```
// 1. Locate the Naming Service root context server
CosNaming::NamingContext_var rootContext;
try {
   CORBA::Object_var initServ =
   orb->resolve_initial_references("NameService");

// 2. Use _narrow()
   rootContext =
       CosNaming::NamingContext::_narrow(initServ);

// 3. Do some error checking!
   if (CORBA::is_nil(lastContext)) return false;
}
catch(CORBA::ORB::InvalidName& ex) {
   return false;
}


// 4. Create a Name for the Naming Context
CosNaming::Name contextName;
contextName.length(1);
contextName[0].id   = (const char *) "Some Name";
contextName[0].kind = (const char *) "Some Kind";

// 5. Try to create the Naming Context in the root context.
CosNaming::NamingContext_var subContext
try {
   subContext =
       rootContext -> bind_new_context(contextName);
}

// 6. If it already exists just retrieve the context
catch(CosNaming::NamingContext::AlreadyBound& ex) {
   CORBA::Object_var tmpobj =
       rootContext ->resolve(contextName);
   subContext =
       CosNaming::NamingContext::_narrow(tmpobj);
   if (CORBA::is_nil(subContext)) return false;
}

// 7. Repeat steps five and six as many times as needed

// 8. Add the Name Component
CosNaming::Name objectName;
```

(continued)

(continued)

```
objectName.length(1);
objectName[0].id   = (const char *) "Object Name";
objectName[0].kind = (const char *) "Object Kind";
try {
    subContext ->bind(objectName,obj);
}
catch(CosNaming::NamingContext::AlreadyBound& ex) {
    subContext ->rebind(objectName,obj);
}
```

Finding a Name

The procedure for trying to look up a Name using the Naming Service is pretty easy:

1. **Follow Steps 1 through 3 in the section called "Making a Name for yourself" earlier in this chapter.**

2. **Create a `Name` for the Naming Context(s) and the Name Component.**

3. **Try to find the `Name` within the root context.**

4. **Do some error checking!**

   The Naming Service may not be running or the object you're looking for isn't there. In either case, you get a nil object.

You follow exactly the same routine any time you want to look up a Name in the Naming Service. The only things that change are the Naming Contexts and the Name Components. Everything else is the same to locate any server.

Here's what Steps 2 through 4 look like in C++:

```
// 2. Create a Name for the Naming Contexts/Name Component
CosNaming::Name name;
name.length(2);
name[0].id   = (const char *) "Some Name";
name[0].kind = (const char *) "Some Kind";
name[1].id   = (const char *) "Object Name";
name[1].kind = (const char *) "Object Kind";

// 3. Try to find the Name within the root context
try {
    obj = rootContext->resolve(name);
}
```

```
// 4. Do some error checking!
catch(...){
    return CORBA::Object::_nil();
}
```

Wrapping the Naming Service

When you create entries in the Naming Service, you always follow exactly the same routine. In fact, the only thing that changes is the actual number and names of the Naming Contexts and Name Component. The same is true when you look up a Name. This repetition cries out for a general solution!

We have created a general-purpose class that you can use to simplify these two tasks immensely. We call it SimpleNames. It uses the general techniques outlined in the preceding sections to name objects and to retrieve objects by Name. We do the work, and you get all the credit!

The complete source code for SimpleNames is on the book's CD-ROM in the Examples\Chapter18 directory. A C++ version is in the files named SimpleNames.h and SimpleNames.cpp. A Java version is in the file named SimpleNames.java.

The SimpleNames.h header file defines the SimpleNames class:

```
#ifndef SIMPLENAMES_H
#define SIMPLENAMES_H

#include "NamingService.h"
class SimpleNames {
public:
    static bool bindToName(CORBA::ORB_ptr,
        CORBA::Object_ptr, CosNaming::Name&);
    static CORBA::Object_ptr getReference(CORBA::ORB_ptr
        orb, CosNaming::Name&);
};
```

Making a Name using SimpleNames

The bindToName() method of the SimpleNames class makes a new Name using the Naming Service. To complete its task, it needs

✔ An ORB pointer.
✔ A pointer to the server object that you are naming.

✔ Some time to get in touch with its inner child.

✔ A CosNaming::Name unbounded sequence that represents each Naming Context in a path leading up to the final Name Component.

The bindToName() method takes all these ingredients and, by following the steps outlined in the section "Making a Name for yourself," earlier in this chapter, it creates or opens each of the Naming Contexts. Then it creates or rebinds the Name Component, as specified in the supplied CosNaming::Name unbounded sequence.

Take a look at how the bindToName() method makes a Name by using the Naming Service. We're assuming that you already have an ORB pointer via the CORBA::ORB_init() method and a server object that you want to name. After you have these items, using the bindToName() method takes just two steps:

1. **Create the** CosNaming::Name **unbounded sequence for the desired Name by entering the following code:**

```
CosNaming::Name name;
name.length(3);
name[0].id   = (const char*) "Examples";
name[0].kind = (const char*) "CORBA_for_dummies";
name[1].id   = (const char*) "Chapter18";
name[1].kind = (const char*) "CORBA_for_dummies";
name[2].id   = (const char*) "MyObject";
name[2].kind = (const char*) "Object";
```

This Name specifies two levels of Naming Context from the root context (\Examples\Chapter18), followed by the object Name itself (MyObject).

2. **Call** SimpleNames::bindToName() **and pass in the ORB pointer, the object to be named, and the** CosNaming::Name **unbounded sequence.**

```
SimpleNames::bindToName(orb, broker, name));
```

The bindToName() method returns true if the operation succeeds and false if it fails. You need to check the return value and take evasive action if it's false. Binding and rebinding associate a server's Name with its reference.

Finding a Name using SimpleNames

You can do more that just create a Name with the SimpleNames class. You can also find a Name. This is done by calling the getReference() method in the SimpleNames class. The getReference() method needs

> ✔ An ORB pointer.
>
> ✔ A friendly boss who doesn't mind giving a reference.
>
> ✔ A `CosNaming::Name` unbounded sequence that represents each Naming Context in a path leading up to the final Name Component.

The `getReference()` method follows the steps outlined in the section "Finding a Name," earlier in this chapter, and returns the located `CORBA::Object`.

After you have an ORB pointer, using the `getReference()` method takes just three steps:

1. **Create the `CosNaming::Name` unbounded sequence for the desired Name by entering the following code:**

```
CosNaming::Name name;
name.length(3);
name[0].id   = (const char*) "Examples";
name[0].kind = (const char*) "CORBA_for_dummies";
name[1].id   = (const char*) "Chapter5";
name[1].kind = (const char*) "CORBA_for_dummies";
name[2].id   = (const char*) "Broker";
name[2].kind = (const char*) "Object";
```

2. **Call `SimpleNames::getReference()` and pass in the ORB pointer and the `CosNaming::Name` unbounded sequence:**

```
obj = SimpleNames::getReference(orb, name);
```

3. **Narrow the returned object and test it to make sure that it's valid:**

```
Broker = PortfolioBroker::_narrow(obj);
if (!CORBA::is_nil(Broker) &&
    Broker->_non_existent())
    Broker = PortfolioBroker::_nil();
}
catch(CORBA::SystemException& ex) {
    Broker = PortfolioBroker::_nil();
}
```

The `getReference()` method returns a `CORBA::Object` reference that may be a nil reference. You must use the `_narrow()` method of the desired server object class to convert the returned object to the correct type. Next, you must test to see whether the resulting object is not nil and verify that it does actually exist. If it is nil or nonexistent and you don't test it before using it, the method call throws a CORBA exception the first time you attempt to call a method on the object. Chapter 6 discusses narrowing and using the `_non_existent()` method to test whether a server object really exists.

General Searching

The Naming Service also provides a way to retrieve the contents of any given Naming Context. This capability is handy if you want to snoop around the Naming Service and see what is in it.

More commonly, you use the Naming Service along with the kind field to locate all the names of objects of a given type. Doing so is helpful when a client application needs to locate a server object of a particular kind, regardless of what its actual identifier is. For example, consider a client that can interact with any server of kind "Payroll". A corporation may have several "Payroll" server objects. The client can find all of them by searching the Naming Service and can then access each of them.

General searching is supported within a Naming Context. To search a Naming Context, walk this way:

1. **Follow Steps 1 through 3 in the section "Making a Name for yourself," earlier in this chapter.**

2. **Create a Name for the Naming Context to search with.**

3. **Try to find the Name within the root context.**

4. **Do some error-checking!**

5. **Retrieve a** BindingIterator **for the context.**

   The BindingIterator is an object that you use to retrieve every entry in the Naming Context. Every time you call the list() or next_n() methods in this object, you get back a sequence of Binding structures for the next entries in the Naming Context. The method itself returns true if it finds more entries, or false if no more entries appear in the Naming Context.

6. **Use the list() and** next_n() **methods of the** CosNaming::BindingIterator **to retrieve all the entries in the Naming Context.**

   When next_one() returns false, you've retrieved every entry from the Naming Context.

Chapter 19

Excuse Me and Other Events

● ●

In This Chapter

▶ Pushing and pulling event models

▶ Implementing the push event model

▶ Comparing events to those other pushes and pulls

● ●

*I*f a server generates data and no clients are there to receive it, does it generate an event? That question, in one form or another, has bedeviled programmers since the dawn of time, or at least since the dawn of networks.

When designing a distributed application, most developers use what is commonly called *tightly coupled communication* between clients and servers. It's called tightly coupled because the server and the client are connected, in some way, before they can exchange information.

Not surprisingly, CORBA uses tightly coupled communication as the basic form of exchanging information between a client and a server. The client:

1. Locates the server object

2. Makes a request

3. Waits for the server to receive, processes, and return information

4. Retrieves the information and does something with it

What if you could wave a magic wand and separate the client and the server? What if a server could just generate information and shove it into a big fire hose, without concern for the existence of clients? Looking at it from the client side of the street, wouldn't it be useful for a client to simply get a hold of the end of a fire hose from which data may someday gush out?

As you may guess, this form of communication is called *loosely coupled communication*. The OMG calls it *event-based communication*. It's also known as

- ✔ Asynchronous communication
- ✔ Telephone tag
- ✔ Decoupled communication
- ✔ Something we think you may need

The Event Service is the CORBA way to do decoupled, asynchronous, event-based communication. Go ahead, say that three times fast. The Event Service supports both the push model and the pull model of communication.

The push model is what we just described, where servers push data into a big fire hose. Because *big fire hose* doesn't sound very technical, the kids at the OMG decided to call it an *Event Channel*. We call it that, too, but you can still think of it as a big fire hose.

The pull model is more like the normal way that clients and servers interact in CORBA. Clients still request information, but in this case, they request it from the Event Channel. It's a bit like sucking on the end of a straw to pull soda from a glass. Clients and servers are still decoupled, because the client has no way of knowing which server, if any, is at the other end of the straw!

A Model Communicator

We're not talking about supermodel talk shows here; we're talking about a model of how clients and servers interact.

When you use the Event Service, you have several choices

- ✔ Pure push model
- ✔ Pure pull model
- ✔ Pure supermodel
- ✔ Mixed push/pull or pull/push model

Other than the supermodel, they all have to do with the way clients and servers deal with the Event Channel.

Pure 100-percent push

Thinking again of the Event Channel as either a fire hose or a straw, servers are on one end and clients are on the other. In the pure push model, zero or more servers shove data into their end of the channel. On the other end, the data gushes out onto zero or more clients. It sounds messy, but it's the traditional way that event-based communications work.

A single Event Channel usually transmits events (data) relating to some specific thing. Servers that produce those kinds of events locate the desired Event Channel (which is just another CORBA server object) and then start pushing event data into it. Clients interested in receiving that kind of event data locate the desired Event Channel and register to receive the event data whenever it is available.

Pure 100-percent pull

If the Event Channel is a straw or a fire hose, why can't a client suck on its end to draw out event data whenever it wants it? Why not, indeed! The pure pull model has zero or more servers waiting around by their end of the straw. On the other side, zero or more clients hang around their end, and occasionally one of them gets the urge for some data. It lets whatever servers are on the other end know that it's interested in some data — right now, please — by sucking on the end of the straw.

When that happens, servers on the other side are asked whether they have any data available, in a random (or at least undocumented) order. If one responds that it does have some data, that data is pulled from it and supplied to the client. If no servers have data available or no servers are available at all, the client blocks until data is available. A client can even take a tentative "sip" on the straw, using a method that returns `false` if no data is available instead of blocking.

Pushing and pulling like a room full of toddlers

Because the Event Channel, like a straw, really doesn't care whether data is pushed or pulled through it, you can use a mix of push and pull on both ends. You can have some push servers and some pull servers. You can have some pull clients and some push clients. It all works.

When push clients and pull servers are on either side of an Event Channel, the pull servers are asked to supply information constantly because a push client is ready for new events all the time. This situation is just like a pull client that pulls all the time, as far as the Event Channel is concerned.

Pushing Ahead

We focus on the push model in this book, but the pull model is very similar. In fact, you use the same techniques as you do with push — you just use slightly different interfaces.

So how does this push thing work, you ask? We're glad you did, because we're about to tell you.

Push producer

What we usually call *push servers* are usually called *push producers,* at least in the Event Service specification.

To make a working push producer and Event Channel, follow these steps:

1. **Run a server application that creates a CORBA server object named** EventChannel.

   That server object comes, ready to use, with your Event Service. Often times, so does a server application that creates EventChannel servers. If one does not, then you'll need to write one yourself. This would be just like writing a server application, as is shown in Chapter 6 (C++) or Chapter 7 (Java).

2. **Save a string reference to the** EventChannel **to a file.**

3. **For the push producer (push server), implement the Event Service standard** PushSupplier **interface, shown here in IDL:**

```
interface PushSupplier {
    void disconnect_push_supplier();
};
```

   See Chapter 5 (C++) or Chapter 7 (Java) for examples of implementing IDL interfaces in a target language.

4. **Write a client application for the push producer.**

   Yes, we said a client application! See Chapter 6 (C++) or Chapter 8 (Java) for examples of writing client applications.

We tell you to make a client application for the push producer because, technically, even push producers are clients of the Event Channel server. You can also have a server object that's a push producer! In that case, you do Steps 3 through 9 within the server object.

5. **Have the push producer read the string reference to the** Event Channel **and use** string_to_object() **and** EventChannel:: _narrow() **to turn it into a reference to the** EventChannel **server that you created in Step 1.**

6. **Use the** EventChannel**'s** for_suppliers() **method to get a** SupplierAdmin **object.**

7. **Use the** SupplierAdmin**'s** obtain_push_consumer() **method to get a** ProxyPushConsumer **object.**

8. **Create and activate the** PushSupplier **server object that you implemented in Step 3.**

9. **Use the** ProxyPushConsumer**'s** connect_push_supplier() **method and pass in the** PushSupplier **server object that you created in Step 8.**

   When the push supplier wants to push data, it calls the ProxyPushConsumer's push() method and passes in an Any object with the data it wants to push.

That's a bunch of steps, isn't it? And they look a bit tricky. You can see some of that old CORBA magic at work here — the push producer hands the EventChannel a server object, and it also receives a server object (in the form of the ProxyPushConsumer object reference returned in Step 6) from the EventChannel. This arrangement allows for two-way, asynchronous communication between the push supplier and the EventChannel, because each server can receive and process requests as needed.

Any? Any what?

The Any class, a special CORBA class that can hold any value, is one of the most aptly named classes in CORBA. Out of the box, you can use the Any class to hold any of the primitive types in IDL. With a little hard work and some study of your OBR vendor documentation, you can also use Any classes to hold user-defined types. We stick with primitive types in this chapter.

All you need to know about Any classes right now is that you create instances of them with the ORB create_any() method. To insert a primitive value when coding in Java, use the insert_<type>() method, where <type> is long, double, string, and so on. To get a primitive value out of an any object when coding in Java, use the extract_<type>() method. You can find a bit more on the Any class in Chapter 14.

Push consumer

What we've been calling *push clients* are usually called *push consumers,* at least in the Event Service specification.

To make a working push consumer, follow these steps:

1. **Make sure that you've run a server application that creates an** EventChannel **server so that the consumer has an** EventChannel **server to talk to.**

2. **For the push consumer (client), implement the Event Service standard** PushConsumer **interface.**

```
interface PushConsumer {
    void push (in any data) raises(Disconnected);
    void disconnect_push_consumer();
};
```

Put your client-specific code in the push() method implementation, because that's what gets called when new event data comes out of the EventChannel. See Chapter 5 (C++) or Chapter 7 (Java) for examples of implementing IDL interfaces in a target language.

3. **Write a client application for the push consumer.**

See Chapter 6 (C++) or Chapter 8 (Java) for examples of writing client applications.

We tell you to make a client application for the push consumer because push consumers are clients of the Event Channel server. You can also have a server object that's a push consumer! In that case, you do Steps 2 through 9 within the server object.

4. **Have the push consumer read the string reference to the** Event Channel **and use** string_to_object() **and** EventChannel:: _narrow() **to turn it into a reference to the** EventChannel **server that you created in Step 1.**

5. **Use the** EventChannel**'s** for_consumers() **method to get a** SupplierAdmin **object.**

6. **Use the** SupplierAdmin**'s** obtain_push_producer() **method to get a** ProxyPushProducer **object.**

7. **Create and activate the** PushConsumer **server object that you implemented in Step 2.**

8. **Use the** ProxyPushProducer**'s** connect_push_consumer() **method and pass in the** PushConsumer **server object that you created in Step 7.**

When the push consumer receives push data, its push() method is called. The push() method is called with an Any object with the data that was pushed.

A consumer looks a lot like a producer, but it's just sitting on the other end of the `EventChannel`. Like the producer, it exchanges sever objects with the `EventChannel` server, so two-way asynchronous communication is possible.

Because both the producer and the consumer are clients of the `EventChannel`, you can have zero or more of each. As long as the `EventChannel` server object exists, both producers and consumers can come and go as they please, which is why this way of doing things is called decoupled communication. The producer and consumer are not directly connected to each other. They deal directly with the `EventChannel`, using proxy versions of each other's interfaces.

An example in Java

In Chapter 12, we implement server push using a do-it-yourself approach. In that example, we create a stock price server that pushes new stock prices to clients every five seconds. Clients establish a minimum and maximum price for the stock and then sit back and wait for the server to push them prices that are below or above that range. We re-implement that same example in this chapter, using the Event Service. The first step is getting an `EventChannel` server running.

The exact way you get an `EventChannel` server running varies depends on the implementation of the Event Service you're using. We're using VisiBroker for Java, so the command to create a new `EventChannel` named `"Stocks"` is shown here in bold

```
C:\EventService> vbj com.visigenic.vbroker.services.CosEvent.Channel Stocks >
                 Stocks.ior
```

This command starts a new server for the `EventChannel` and prints its string reference. We redirect the output of the command to a file named `Stocks.ior` so that our producer and consumer client applications can find the `EventChannel`.

Making the producer

To make a producer, follow the steps described in the section called "Push producer," earlier in this chapter. Step 1 is to run the server application that creates the Event Channel, and Step 2 is to save a string reference to the newly created Event Channel server object. Step 3 in making the producer client application is to write the `PushProducer` server implementation.

The Java source file for the `StockPusher.java` PushProducer server implementation is on the CD-ROM that accompanies this book, in the `Examples\Chapter19` directory.

```
import org.omg.CosEventComm.*;
import org.omg.CORBA.ORB;
public final class StockPusher extends
    _PushSupplierImplBase {
  public StockPusher(ORB myOrb) {
    _orb = myOrb;
  }
  public final void disconnect_push_supplier() {
    System.out.println("StockPusher was disconnected!");
    _orb.disconnect(this);
    System.exit(0);
  }
  private ORB _orb;
}
```

The `disconnect_push_supplier()` method is called when the `EventChannel` is deleted, so it just prints a message, disconnects this server object via the ORB `disconnect()` method, and then exits the application. Because we need an ORB object reference to disconnect the server, we create a private member variable for it and initialize the private member variable in the constructor.

For Step 4, we write the push producer client application. The remaining steps are done inside the client application, so we explain them in several chunks in the next few pages.

We cover implementing clients in Java in Chapter 8. Refer to that chapter for a detailed description of what to do. The complete Java source file for the `JavaServer.java` client application is on the book's CD-ROM in the `Examples\Chapter19` directory. We only show the relevant portions here.

We begin with the usual client stuff you do with Java. We initialize the ORB:

```
// import statements omitted
public final class JavaServer {
  public static void main(String args[]) {
    try {
      ORB orb = ORB.init(args,null);
      EventChannel stockChannel;
      ProxyPushConsumer consumerProxy;
      String ior;
```

Step 5 is to read in the string reference for `Stocks.ior` and convert it into an `EventChannel` server object reference:

```
// inside a try/catch block, open Stocks.ior
// and read the string into the ior variable
stockChannel = EventChannelHelper.narrow(
  orb.string_to_object(ior));
```

Steps 6 and 7 are actually accomplished with just one statement. We get the `SupplierAdmin` object from the `EventChannel`, using the `for_suppliers()` method call, and then immediately call its `obtain_push_consumer()` method to get the `ProxyPushConsumer` server object:

```
consumerProxy = stockChannel.for_suppliers().
  obtain_push_consumer();
```

Step 8 is to start our `PushProducer` server object. We pass in our ORB object to the `StockPusher` constructor and then use the `connect()` ORB method to enable the server:

```
StockPusher pusher = new StockPusher(orb);
orb.connect(pusher);
```

Step 9 is to use the `connect_push_supplier()` method to connect our `StockPusher` server to the `ProxyPushConsumer`. That method raises the `AlreadyConnected` exception if we happen to connect the same `PushSupplier` to the same `EventChannel` twice, so we make the call inside a `try/catch` block:

```
try {
    consumerProxy.connect_push_supplier(pusher);
}
catch (AlreadyConnected ae) {
    System.out.println("StockPusher already connected.");
    return;
}
```

At this point, we're ready for Step 9, where we push the data into the `EventChannel`. The push supplier application generates random double values between `50.0` and `70.0` every 5 seconds. When a new number is generated, it's pushed, using this block of code:

```
// the double NewPrice holds the new value
try {
    Any priceChange = orb.create_any();
    priceChange.insert_double(NewPrice);
    consumerProxy.push(priceChange);
}
```

(continued)

(continued)

```
        catch(Disconnected e) {
        System.out.println("Disconnected!");
    }
        catch(SystemException e) {
        System.out.println("Event channel closed!");
          pusher.disconnect_push_supplier();
    }
```

We use an `Any` object to hold the value. We use the `ORB create_any()` method to allocate it and then use its `insert_double()` method to copy in the new value. Then we push it using the `ProxyPushConsumer`'s `push()` method. If an exception is raised, it means that the `EventChannel` itself exited, so we clean up as well.

Making the consumer

To make a producer, follow the steps described in the section called "Push consumer," earlier in this chapter. Step 1 is to run the server application that creates the Event Channel. Step 2 in making the consumer client application is to write the `PushConsumer` server implementation.

The Java source file for the `StockConsumer.java PushConsumer` server implementation is on the book's CD-ROM in the `Examples\Chapter19` directory. We only show the relevant portions here.

The constructor needs to save the supplied ORB object, as well as the minimum and maximum values to look for, into member variables:

```
// import statements omitted
public final class StockConsumer extends
    _PushConsumerImplBase {
  public StockConsumer(ORB myOrb, double min, double max){
    _orb = myOrb;
    _min = min;
    _max = max;
  }
```

The `push()` method is called when new event data is received from the `EventChannel`. It's a bit long, and we don't show the less interesting parts, so we look at several pieces in this section.

First, we try to extract a double value from the `Any` object. If that fails, the `BAD_OPERATION`exception is thrown, and we just return from the `push()` method. In other words, we ignore stuff we can't deal with!

```
public void push(Any data) {
   double NewPrice;
   try {
      NewPrice = data.extract_double();
   }
   catch (BAD_OPERATION oe) {
      System.out.println("I wasn't pushed a double!");
      return;
   }
```

Next, we filter out only those stock prices we care about. If the price is below the minimum or above the maximum, we set up a String with the appropriate message. Otherwise, we return from the push() method and ignore the event data. The rest of the push() method just prints out the current time, price, and Message:

```
String Message;
if (NewPrice <= _min)
   Message = "Price below minimum";
else if (NewPrice >= _max)
   Message = "Price above maximum";
else return;
```

The disconnect_push_consumer() method is called when the EventChannel is deleted, so it just prints a message, disconnects this server object with the ORB disconnect() method, and then exits the application:

```
public void disconnect_push_consumer() {
      System.out.println(
         "StockConsumer was disconnected!");
      _orb.disconnect(this);
      System.exit(0);
   }
   private ORB _orb;
   private double _min, _max;
}
```

For Step 3, we write the push consumer client application. The remaining steps are done inside the client application, so we explain it in several chunks over the next page or two, as usual.

The complete Java source file for the WatchStock.java client application is on the CD-ROM. We only show the relevant portions here.

We begin with the usual client stuff you do with Java. We initialize the ORB:

```
// import statements omitted
public final class WatchStock {
    public static void main(String args[]) {
        try {
            ORB orb = ORB.init(args,null);
            EventChannel stockChannel;
            ProxyPushSupplier supplierProxy;
            String ior;
```

Step 4 is to read in the string reference for `Stocks.ior` and convert it into an `EventChannel` server object reference:

```
// inside a try/catch block, open Stocks.ior
// and read the string into the ior variable
stockChannel = EventChannelHelper.narrow(
    orb.string_to_object(ior));
```

Steps 5 and 6 are accomplished with just the following statement. We get the `SupplierAdmin` object from the `EventChannel`, using the `for_consumers()` method call, and then immediately call its `obtain_push_supplier()` method to get the `ProxyPushSupplier` server object:

```
supplierProxy = stockChannel.for_consumers().
    obtain_push_supplier();
```

Step 7 is to start our `PushConsumer` server object. We pass in our ORB object, along with the minimum and maximum price values, to the `StockConsumer` constructor and then use the `connect()` ORB method to enable the server:

```
// Accept user input for minimum (Min)
// and maximum (Max) stock value
StockConsumer consumer =
    new StockConsumer(orb, Min, Max);
orb.connect(consumer);
```

Step 8 is to use the `connect_push_consumer ()` method to connect our `StockConsumer` server to the `ProxyPushSupplier`. That method raises the `AlreadyConnected` exception if we happen to connect the same `PushConsumer` to the same `EventChannel` twice, so we make the call inside a `try/catch` block:

```
    try {
        supplierProxy.connect_push_consumer(consumer);
    }
    catch (AlreadyConnected ae) {
        System.out.println(
            "WatchStock already connected.");
        return;
    }
```

At this point, we're ready for Step 9, where we receive pushed data in the push() method of the StockConsumer server object.

Events in Action

Compile all the classes that make up the server and client applications and then run the server application.

We compile all the classes for you on the CD-ROM at the back of this book, in the Examples\Chapter19 directory. We also include a Windows batch file named vbmake.bat that compiles all the classes with VisiBroker for Java. Three batch files that are used to run the Java applications are also on the CD:

- ✔ startEventChannel.bat starts the VisiBroker EventChannel server and saves the string reference for it into the file named Stocks.ior
- ✔ startProducer.bat runs a push producer
- ✔ WatchStock.bat runs a push consumer

Before running the server, we expect you to have installed your ORB, because it's hard to run a CORBA application without an ORB. You should have started any ORB servers that you need in order to run CORBA applications, too.

To run the applications, follow these steps. The stuff you enter is shown in bold.

1. **Start the** EventChannel **first in one window.**

```
C:\EventService\> startEventChannel
```

2. **Run a** WatchStock **consumer in another window and enter a minimum and maximum price.**

```
C:\EventService\> WatchStock
Minimum Value for Stock: 55
Maximum Value for Stock: 63
Watching Stock value...
```

3. Run a push producer in another window.

```
C:\EventService\> startProducer
```

The push producer starts printing new stock prices every five seconds:

```
-- StockPusher ready
11:29:44 AM - New price for Stock: $50.20
11:29:49 AM - New price for Stock: $50.57
11:29:54 AM - New price for Stock: $69.43
11:29:59 AM - New price for Stock: $57.11
11:30:04 AM - New price for Stock: $62.62
```

You can run several more WatchStock consumers in other windows, entering different minimum and maximum prices in each one.

4. Watch in awe and delight as the WatchStock consumers receive push information!

Whenever a price change pushed to a consumer is outside its price range, the consumer prints a message. For example, suppose that the producer sets a price at $51.40. The consumer started in Step 2 prints the following:

```
11:34:41 AM - Price: $51.40 Note: price below minimum
```

5. Terminate the push producer by entering Ctrl+C in its window.

Notice that nothing happens to the push consumers. That's because they're not directly connected to the stock pusher. You can terminate one or all of the push consumers; doing so has no effect on the push producer.

6. Run two or more push producers.

Notice that they all merrily push new stock prices into their end of the EventChannel and that the push consumers receive these price changes, too.

7. Terminate the EventChannel by entering Ctrl+C in its window.

Any active push producers detect that the EventChannel has exited, and they also exit. You need to terminate any push consumers yourself.

Chapter 20

Transactions and Concurrency Control

*T*oday it is widely accepted that transactions and the control of concurent access to resources are the keys to constructing reliable distributed applications. The OMG has specified two services to meet these needs: the Transaction Service and the Concurrency Control Service.

The Transaction Service lets you group one or more operations on objects into a transaction. It also allows you to cancel the transaction, undoing all the changes made to the objects up to that point. The Concurrency Control Service is the traffic cop of a CORBA application. It supports access to shared resources by multiple clients.

In this chapter, we first talk about why these services are needed. Then we spend time on each topic.

As with all CORBAservices, getting up to speed takes a little time. We suggest that you begin here and then head for the specification. This advice isn't heresy. The specifications aren't that hard to read, and they have some really neat pictures, too. If you aren't ready to go that far, plenty of other resources are out there for you to go to. We send you out with our blessings.

Finding Out Why You Need These Services

CORBA applications are distributed and concurrent — a fact which comes as no surprise to you if you've read any portion of this book. The reason we point out this fact here is that these two characteristics are the driving forces behind the need for the Transaction and Concurrency Control services.

The distributed nature of a CORBA application means that resources (such as servers) are scattered all over the place and can, therefore, be called by multiple clients who are also scattered all over the place. If something goes wrong in the middle of an operation, having the ability to go back to all the resources and clients that were visited and changed and undo those changes allows only completed operations to be supported, not half-done (or half-baked) operations. Being able to undo half-done operations is one of the major reasons why CORBA has the Transactions Service.

The concurrent nature of a CORBA application means that more than one thread of execution is active at the same time. The result is that a resource such as a server object can, potentially, be accessed by more than one client at the same time — or that a set of related servers that manipulate related information may be accessed by more that one client at the same time. Things could get pretty messy in a hurry if you didn't have a way to control access to these resources. That's why the OMG specified the Concurrency Control Service.

Exploring the Transaction Service

Multistep tasks in a distributed environment usually involve more than one object. If an error occurs midway through completing a task, the system can be left in an inconsistent state. Consider the following scenario to see an example of why a system in an inconsistent state can be a problem.

Say that you're depositing your paycheck into your checking account via an Automatic Teller Machine (ATM). The first thing the ATM does after identifying you as the current customer is ask for the amount that you're depositing. Now suppose that at that moment the system locks up. You got it — it's deader than a doorknob. After minutes and minutes of banging on it, you still can't get your card out, and it still thinks that you're the current customer. What do you do? Set up camp in front of the stupid machine? You probably should, because otherwise someone could come along and clean out your account if the system eventually wakes up and still considers you to be the current user.

Now, take a deep breath. You don't need to cut up your ATM card. Today's banking systems use transactions to prevent scenarios such as this one.

But if banking systems didn't use transactions, there would be a few basic questions about this scenario:

✔ What is the state of the data in the system?

✔ If multiple objects were affected, such as a login object and security objects, do they show accurate information such as the date and time that you logged in and that you entered a valid PIN on your first try?

✔ What kind of lawyer do you need in order to sue the bank?

✔ Which object's persistent data was affected? Maybe some of the objects' methods were called and some data items changed, but others were not called before the system went down.

As you can see, without the Transaction Service to undo any changes and take the system back to where it was before the transaction started, this situation could be quite a mess.

Defining a transaction

The preceding scenario illustrates why CORBA needs a service that supports the enforcement of transactions across distributed objects.

A *transaction* is a unit of work that is *atomic*. In other words, it can't be broken down into smaller pieces. If, for some reason, the actions are interrupted (maybe the system fails or the user cancels the transaction), all effects of the transaction that have already occurred are rolled back.

For CORBA, a *transaction* means a set of requests and their results that works as a group.

A transaction is either *committed* or *undone*. When a transaction is committed, it is sent to a nice, quiet place where it can relax and enjoy peaceful days. Not exactly! Committing a transaction means making permanent all the changes made by the associated requests. As you may expect, when a transaction is undone, all changes made by the associated requests are undone. This undoing is often called *rolling back* a transaction.

Serving thousands every day

Elaborately detailing the Transaction Service isn't possible within the scope of this book. We asked ourselves what the next best thing was and decided that the answer was providing a tutor with each book. Our editor wouldn't go for that, though — something about the budget or some such nonsense. Anyway, we were left with a bulleted list of the service's characteristics and a few paragraphs that further support those bullet items. Don't look so sad. The list can be quite helpful in gaining an overall perspective of what the Transaction Service does and doesn't do.

So here's our list. The Transaction Service

- ✔ Provides support for the synchronization of transactions across a distributed client/server application.
- ✔ Doesn't require all requests within the scope of a transaction to have transactional behavior.
- ✔ Covertly works to increase the variety of low-fat and fat-free desserts.
- ✔ Provides operations to control the duration and scope of a transaction.
- ✔ Supports the association of changes in an object's internal state with a transaction.
- ✔ Supports the grouping of multiple objects into a single transaction.
- ✔ Works with applications that possess objects that do, and do not, support transactional behavior.
- ✔ Supports objects that use the service for some requests but not for others (this choice can be made by the client and the server of the requests).
- ✔ Supports transactions that include resources that are not object-oriented.
- ✔ Supports and upholds the virtues adopted by this great nation.
- ✔ Allows a client with an active transaction to make requests for the same transaction on multiple threads.
- ✔ Allows an object to support multiple transactions in parallel by using multiple threads.

A typical — or is that atypical? — transaction

In your average Transaction Service scenario, a client begins a transaction by issuing a request to an object that is defined by the Transaction Service. This request creates a transaction context that is associated with the client thread. Next, the client issues requests. These requests share the client's transaction context. When the client finishes its work, it terminates the transaction by issuing another request. Naturally! If no problems occur, the changes produced as a result of the requests are then either committed or rolled back.

The magic is in the *transaction context*. That's where the server objects that support transactions are supposed to store the changes, pending the committal of the entire transaction. Using the Transaction Service itself isn't enough — you still need to implement support for transaction-based processing in your server objects. You just use the nice interfaces defined in the Transaction Service to do it in an OMG-approved way.

The Transaction Service is, and will continue to be, implemented on a variety of differing hardware and software platforms. To meet these needs, the implementations themselves focus on communications, storage, and the kinds of transactions supported. When using your ORB, be sure to read its documentation carefully so that you know just what its Transaction Service does and doesn't do.

Implementing transactions

The Transaction Service defines a Control object that acts as the controller of a particular transaction. It also defines several objects representing the transaction context. You can use the Control object directly or indirectly use the operations it contains. You can either explicitly pass the context objects to every server operation you use in a transaction, or you can implement those operations implicitly, so that they get the context information themselves. Because you have two sets of two choices and $2 \times 2 = 4$, you have four different combinations in dealing with the control and context for a transaction. We describe those four choices in the next sections.

Direct context management with explicit propagation

Direct context management with explicit propagation is when the client application creates a Control object and accesses it to control the transaction. The client is also responsible for creating the necessary context objects and passing them into the operations of server objects participating in the transaction. This is the option for control freaks because you get to do everything!

Indirect context management with implicit propagation

Indirect context management with implicit propagation is when the client application creates a Control object and uses its operations to control the transaction. The client doesn't deal with transaction context objects at all.

This option is the simplest and easiest way to use the Transaction Service, but server objects participating in the transaction must be implemented in such a way that they retrieve the current context information before proceeding.

Indirect context management with explicit propagation

Indirect context management with explicit propagation is a middle-of-the-road approach in which the client application creates a Control object and uses its operations to control the transaction. It is still responsible for creating the necessary context objects and passing them into the operations of server objects participating in the transaction.

If server objects don't support implicit propagation, you have to use this approach or direct context management with explicit propagation.

Direct context management with implicit propagation

Direct context management with implicit propagation is the other hybrid approach, in which the client application creates a Control object and accesses it to control the transaction. The client can still use server objects that are implemented using implicit propagation, so long as they set up the Control object first.

If your server objects support implicit propagation, you have to use this approach or indirect context management with implicit propagation.

Checking Out the Concurrency Control Service

Just as a traffic cop is in control of making sure that cars don't ram into each other and make messes, the Concurrency Control Service is in charge of making sure that objects don't ram into each other's data and make messes.

Reading and writing . . . and writing and reading

Picture this scenario: Client A calls a reading operation in Server 1 at the same time that Client B calls a writing operation in Server 1.

Scenarios such as these easily and often occur. Obviously, something had to be done so that multiple clients could access resources without such scenarios bringing the system to its knees. The OMG developed the Concurrency Control Service in response.

The Concurrency Control Service is the CORBA traffic cop that coordinates access of shared resources by multiple clients so that resources remain in a consistent state. The service uses locks to lock out clients that could conflict and leave a resource's data in an inconsistent state.

A *lock* prevents access to a resource in a specific way.

How are conflicts prevented? A client must obtain an appropriate lock before accessing a shared resource.

Resources don't remain locked forever. A requester releases the lock when it no longer need the resource.

The Concurrency Control Service

✔ Is designed to be used with the Transaction Service to coordinate the activities of concurrent transactions.

✔ Supports both transactional and non-transactional modes of operation.

✔ Supports three kinds of modes: the multiple possession semantics, two-phase transactional locking, and nested transaction.

Lock granularity

Lock granularity is a description of the type of access a client wants. The Transaction service provides coarse-grained and fine-grained locks.

✔ **Coarse-grain lock:** You use a coarse-grain lock when you're locking something big — a database, an entire file, or the safe at Fort Knox, for example.

✔ **Fine-grain lock:** A much smaller lock on a portion of a resource is called a *fine-grain lock*. A record in a database, a specific field in a record, or the carry-on bag in your luggage can have fine-grain locks.

Locking modes

Several predefined locking modes are defined in the Concurrency Control Service. You may define other locks, but then you also need to define how these locks interact with each other.

✔ **Read (R)** is a fine-grain lock that's used when a client wants to read data with the assurance that no one else is writing to that data. A resource can have multiple R locks but no W locks on it at the same time.

✔ **Write (W)** is a fine-grain lock that's used when a client wants to update data with the assurance that no one else is reading or writing to it. A resource can have only one W lock and no other locks on it at a time

✔ **Upgrade (U)** is a fine-grain lock that's used when a client wants to read and then write a resource. A client obtains an upgrade mode lock first, reads the resource, then obtains a W lock, and then writes the resource. A resource can have only one U lock and no other locks on it at a time.

✔ **Intention Read (IR)** is a coarse-grain lock that's used on a resource's ancestor (for example, an entire database) before applying a fine-grain lock on a resource. A resource can have many IR and R locks but no W locks on it at the same time.

✔ **Intention Write (IW)** is a coarse-grain lock that's used on a resource's ancestor (for example, an entire database) before applying a fine-grain lock on a resource. A resource can have only one IW lock, but no IR or R locks on it.

Many locks for one client

The Concurrency Control Service allows a single client to hold multiple and even conflicting locks for the same resource. A lock is never upgraded. If you have a read lock and later get a write lock for the same resource, you still have the read lock as well. Heck, you can get as many read locks as you want for a single resource. The service just keeps a count of the number of locks a client has on a resource, and when all the locks are released by the client, the resource is actually unlocked. A client can get a conflicting lock for a resource as long as it is the only holder of the conflicting lock.

These restrictions lead to a natural pattern of locking in which a client gets a read lock, reads a resource, and determines that it needs to update that resource. The client then gets a write lock, updates the resource, releases the write lock, and then releases the read lock. In simpler terms, the Concurrency Control Service supports nested locks.

Locking with transactions

The Concurrency Control Service supports the two-phase commit approach to transactions. In the first phase, a transaction gathers locks on all the resources it needs to perform the action. In the second phase, it performs the action and then releases all the locks. Any resource locked in the first phase remains locked until the transaction is committed or rolled back.

Because you can always call the direct lock release operations in the Concurrency Control Service, even for locks associated with a transaction, you can design services so that they release some of the first phase locks before committing or rolling back a transaction.

Unless you're really sure about what you're doing, you're better off sticking with the full locking behavior defined for transactions.

Many locks for one transaction

Multiple transactions initiated by a client can also hold multiple locks. This capability enables you to create nested transactions for very complex updates. A nested transaction can get a lock for a resource that also happens to be locked by its enclosing transaction. When the inner transaction is committed, the lock that the enclosing transaction holds isn't released.

Chapter 21

You Can Be Very Persistent

In This Chapter

▶ Understanding the POS model

▶ Making data persistent with and without the POS

*W*hat would you do if every time you called your friend on the telephone, she asked for your name and some form of identification — again and again, no matter how many times you called her? You'd probably stop calling her pretty soon. Well, imagine a world in which server objects relinquish their data after they finish executing, never to remember it again. After a few of these amnesia episodes, the server objects wouldn't have any client application friends at all.

To fix this situation, the Object Management Group has specified a CORBAservice called the Persistent Object Service (POS). The POS provides operations for storing and managing the persistent state of objects.

A server object needs the POS if it has *state data*. When you use the POS with a server object, you select which of its internal data represents its *persistent state*.

> ✔ **State data:** The data that an object maintains within itself. For example, an employee object maintains data concerning a single employee's name, address, salary, and so on.
>
> ✔ **Persistent state:** Data that doesn't disappear when the object finishes executing. It is somehow stored for future use.

Like many of the other CORBAservices, the POS does things in a generic way so that you don't have to get involved in the down-and-dirty details. You can just use its operations and get things done.

Most ORBS don't include a POS. In fact, they can be pretty pricey add-ons, because they usually come with or work with databases or object stores. Having to use a do-it-yourself way to add persistence to your server objects isn't unusual.

Deciding What to Store

Not all of an object's data needs to be state data. Oh sure, objects that are part of a database need to have state data, but sometimes an object uses data and then cheerfully relinquishes that data at the end of its execution, having no need to store it.

Before applying the POS to an object's data, be sure that the data needs to be persistent.

Deciding How to Store

You must consider several situations when deciding if you need to use the POS:

- ✔ **The objects in an application have no state data:** You don't need the POS or any homemade version of storage because you don't have any data to save. Whew! That was a close one. Now you can save some time and skip this chapter. Go ahead and take a break. Get that donut and cup of coffee you've been thinking about.

- ✔ **The objects in an application have large amounts of state data:** For example, a human resources database would have a great deal of data that needs to stick around after queries are made. In this case, you definitely need ways to store the data. You can use the POS, you can create ways of your own, and you can use the mechanisms available from databases (relational, object-oriented, or flat file).

- ✔ **The objects in an application have several data items that are not too complicated:** You could probably make storage mechanisms of your own and use them. However, if the data items are complicated, you may be better off using the POS instead of something homemade. That's because the POS has characteristics that make it a good candidate for helping you easily store and retrieve this kind of data.

Things You Should Know about the POS

As with all the other CORBAservices, you have to spend some time getting familiar with the Persistent Object Service. What better way to get to know the POS than to talk about its qualities? Well, what better way besides dinner and a movie?

The open POS

Storing data for documents is quite different than storing data for accounting databases. So the POS is quite flexible in its ability to support a variety of different clients and implementations of the Persistent Object Service, so that they can work together. This capability is called *openness* by the OMG. Golly . . . yet another buzzword to add to your growing CORBA list!

Openness is a critical capability of persistent storage systems. You can't expect all data to be maintained in a particular kind of file or database system. The POS supports the ability to integrate existing storage services into the architecture. Essentially, openness is a requirement for plug-and-play components.

Not a jack of all trades

The Persistent Object Service is intended to be part of a collection of services. Therefore, it doesn't attempt to solve all the problems that may relate to storing data. Instead, it assumes that other services provide some solutions. For example, the POS doesn't do naming; it leaves that task to the Naming Service.

The POS Model

Being a typical CORBAservice, the POS has a model that describes how clients and servers interact with it. In this model are four participants:

- ✔ **The Persistent Identifier (PID)** is an object that identifies a persistent object. It's not a CORBA server object reference; it's like a database record key.

- ✔ **The Persistent Object (PO)** is that part of a CORBA server object that is persistent. As master PO often says, "Snatch the pebble from my hand. . . ."

- ✔ **The Persistent Data Service (PDS)** is the part of the POS that acts as the intermediary between a PO and the actual *datastore* used to save the persistent state. A datastore is the storage system used to hold the persistent data, and can be as simple as a disk file, or as complex as a relational or object database.

- ✔ **The Persistent Object Manager (POM)** is the part of the POS that acts as the intermediary between a PO and a PDS. The goal is to remove the knowledge of which PDS to use from the PO. The PO tells the POS to store its information and associate it with a PID. The POM figures out which PDS to use and tells the selected PDS to do the store.

These four things are represented by four IDL modules, which are defined in the Persistent Object Service specification:

- ✔ The `CosPersistencePID` module contains IDL interfaces that describe the attributes and operations supported for a PID.

- ✔ The `CosPersistencePO` module contains IDL interfaces that describe the attributes and operations supported for a PO.

- ✔ The `CosPersistencePDS` IDL interface describes the attributes and operations of the PDS. Many other interfaces describe several protocols that the PDS can use to talk with both the PO and datastores.

- ✔ The `CosPersistencePOM` module contains IDL interfaces that describe the attributes and operations supported for a POM.

Yikes! That's a lot of interfaces. Fortunately for you, all these interfaces come with a POS. If your goal is simply to use a POS to add persistence to your server objects, you deal most often with the PID, PO, and POM interfaces.

Working with the POS

What does using the POS in a server object actually look like, and how does it impact clients? We've been wondering that ourselves, so we're going to dig in and try it out.

Understanding the model

The first thing you need to understand about the POS is that it's a service. Unlike other CORBAservices, it may be implemented as a set of CORBA server objects or as a simple set of classes you use. If it's implemented as a set of servers, then who's the client, you ask? In the case of the POS, your server object is the client! That means that if you want your server to include persistent information, it may need to get a reference to the POS servers.

When you have a server object that you need to "get persistent," you do the following:

1. **In the constructor for the server, construct a PO object that actually holds the persistent information. Obtain a reference to a** `CosPersistencePID` **Factory server object.**

2. **Use the** `CosPersistencePID` **Factory server to construct a PID object based on information supplied to the constructor.**

   In other words, some uniquely identifying information must be supplied to the constructor so that the associated persistent data can be found.

3. **Obtain a reference to a** `CosPersistencePOM` **server object.**

4. **Call the POM's** `connect()` **method, passing in a reference to the PO created in Step 1 and the PID object created in Step 2.**

   This call returns a `CosPersistencePDS` server object reference.

5. **To restore the object to its last saved state, use the PDS's** `restore()` **method to retrieve persistent information. This operation invokes methods of the PO, created in Step 1.**

   Things vary here, based on the PDS protocol used.

6. **Whenever the persistent data changes in the server object, call the PDS's** `store()` **method to save the persistent information.**

If we sound wishy-washy here, it's because the POS offers so many options that figuring out exactly how it's supposed to work is often difficult. For example, according to the POS specification, you should be able to ignore the PDS object returned in Step 4 and deal exclusively with the POM server object. Then Steps 5 and 6 would have you call the `restore()` and `store()` methods of the POM, not the PDS as we describe. Even more perplexing, you may be able to ignore both the POM and the PDS, instead dealing directly with the PO when doing a `restore()` and `store()`.

 We suggest that you carefully read your ORB's documentation and decide exactly how you're going to deal with the POS before you implement anything. This way, all your code is consistent. We know that we sound like a broken record (or is that a broken CD?) when it comes to reading the documentation, but it really is the only way to cope with the many variations that the CORBA standard possesses.

Using databases and the POS

The POS is very flexible in that it supports any number of PDS implementations. If your POS supports the OMG standard Dynamic Data Object protocol, it may be mapped to a wide variety of relational databases. Similar mappings are possible for persistent object databases or even simple flat files.

You Can Count on Me

The POS looks daunting, doesn't it? Fortunately, you don't have to use the POS to get persistence. In this section, we show you a simpler do-it-yourself approach, where we just save the persistent data for an object to a file. We use Java in this example.

We've used the example of a Counter server elsewhere in this book. Here we extend it so that it maintains its current count persistently.

The IDL for the PersistentCounter example is in a file named Counter.idl on the CD-ROM at the back of this book, in the Examples\Chapter21\File directory.

```
module PersistentCounter{
    interface Counter {
        readonly attribute long Value;
        long GetNextValue(in long Increment);
        void Reset();
    };
};
```

This interface is the same as the one we present in Chapter 16. The server implementation is nearly the same. When we implement the server object, we add two private member functions, named _store() and _restore(), that maintain the persistent state of the Counter.

The complete source code for the Counter server object implementation is in a file named CounterImplementation.java. The server application is in a file named JavaServer.java. Both files are on the book's CD-ROM in the Examples\Chapter21\File directory.

A count that sticks around

Take a look at the parts of the server implementation that deal with persistence.

```
public final class CounterImplementation
    extends _CounterImplBase {
    public CounterImplementation(String key) {
        myKey = key;
        _restore();
    }
    public int Value() {
        return MyCounter;
    }
    public int GetNextValue(int Increment) {
        MyCounter += Increment;
        _store();
        return MyCounter;
    }
    public void Reset() {
        MyCounter = 0;
        _store();
    }
```

The constructor for the class accepts a String parameter. We use that string as the filename for the data file that holds the persistent information for the object. Next, we attempt to restore any previously saved value by calling _restore();

The method implementing the read-only attribute Value() just returns the current value, as it did for the non-persistent version. The GetNextValue() and Reset() methods call _store() to save the new value for the Counter.

```
private void _restore() {
    MyCounter = 0;
    java.io.ObjectInputStream myDataFile;
    try {
        myDataFile = new  ObjectInputStream(
            new FileInputStream(myKey));
        MyCounter = myDataFile.readInt();
    }
    catch(Exception e) {

    }
}
```

The _restore() method begins by setting the counter value in MyCounter to 0. Then it opens a Java ObjectInputStream, using the filename supplied in the constructor, and reads an integer from it. If it succeeds, it stores the value in MyCounter, thus restoring the persistent state of the Counter class.

```
private void _store() {
    java.io.ObjectOutputStream myDataFile;
    try {
        myDataFile = new ObjectOutputStream(
            new FileOutputStream(myKey));
        myDataFile.writeInt(MyCounter);
        myDataFile.flush();
    }
    catch(Exception e) {

    }
}
```

The _store() method does the same thing, in reverse. It uses an ObjectOutputStream to write the current value of MyCounter to a file.

Seeing persistence in action

Now we're ready to try out this example and see how it works. To do so, we compile the classes.

We've written a simple client application that lets you call the `Counter` server. We're not showing it here, but it's on the CD-ROM that accompanies this book. We've compiled all the classes for you, too, on the CD-ROM in the `Examples\Chapter21\File` directory. We've also included a Windows batch file named `vbmake.bat` that compiles all the classes with VisiBroker for Java. A batch file named `startserver.bat` that starts the `Counter` persistent server and a batch file named `client.bat` that runs the client are also on the CD.

To see persistence in action, follow these steps. Stuff that you need to enter is shown in bold:

1. **Run the server first in one window by using this command:**

   ```
   C:\PersistentCounter\> startserver
   ```

2. **Run a client in its own window, using this command:**

   ```
   C:\PersistentCounter\> client
   ```

3. **In the client, enter** n **and press Return to get the next counter value.**

   You see `Next counter value is :1`.

4. **Enter** x **and press Return to exit the client. Press Ctrl+C in the server window to exit the server.**

5. **Repeat Steps 1 through 3.**

   You see `Next counter value is :2`.

Notice how the `Counter` server retained its persistent state? Specifically, the count didn't start over at 1, even though you stopped and then restarted the server. Finally, a counter with a memory!

Saving an object's state this way works okay for simple stuff, but it doesn't really get you ready to use the POS. We show you the do-it-yourself approach for three reasons:

- ✔ You can make server objects with persistent state data without using the POS.
- ✔ You can decide for yourself if you need to go through all the trouble of buying and using a POS.
- ✔ You can see that there is always more than one way to skin a cat.

A Faux POS

We've written a very simple POS-like set of classes in Java, and we use it in this section to re-implement the `Counter` example one more time.

The POS classes we provide are no substitute for a real, $3,000 POM. Don't use them in mission-critical production code. They're very good at what they do — which is to illustrate what it feels like to use the POS — but they are not a substitute for the real thing.

We don't show the POS classes here, but they're on the book's CD-ROM in the `Examples\Chapter21\POS` directory, along with the re-implemented Counter example.

Counting on POS

The Counter server object's implementation is actually simpler than using the POS. First, we create a new class named `CounterPersistentState` that extends the `PO` class.

```
public final class CounterPersistentState extends PO {
    public CounterPersistentState(String key) {
        p(PIDFactory.create_PID_from_key(key));
        connect(p());
        restore(p());
    }
    public int GetCounter() { return counter; }
    public void SetCounter(int val) {
        counter = val;
        store(p());
    }
    public void _set(Object val) {
        counter = ((Integer)val).intValue();
    }
    public Object _get() {
        return new Integer(counter);
    }
    private int counter;
}
```

This class holds the persistent state information for the `Counter` server. Its constructor uses a supplied `key` (which in this case is just a filename) to create a `PID`. It then calls the base `PO` class `connect()` method and then the `restore()` method.

The base `PO` class takes care of contacting the `POM` and the `PDS`. Within the `PDS`, a call to the `restore()` method calls the `_set()` method of the `PO`, supplying a Java `Object` representing the restored state. Our subclass of `PO` overrides the `_set()` method to extract the integer value from this object.

To change the value of our counter, call the base `PO` class `store()` method. As before, the `PO` then calls the `POM`, which calls the `PDS`, which calls the _get() method of the PO to get a Java Object to save. The PO subclass overrides the _get() method to provide an Object holding the integer value of counter.

Because the protocol between the PO and the PDS is a Java Object, you can save and restore single values, just like we do. You can also use arrays or entire classes if they are subclassed from the Java serializable class.

POS servers can be simple

The CounterImplementation class is simpler when using the POS. Take a look:

```
public final class CounterImplementation
   extends _CounterImplBase {
   public CounterImplementation(String key) {
      MyCounter = new CounterPersistentState(key);
   }
   public int Value() {
      return MyCounter.GetCounter();
   }
   public int GetNextValue(int Increment) {
      int rc = MyCounter.GetCounter() + Increment;
      MyCounter.SetCounter(rc);
      return rc;
   }
   public void Reset() {
      MyCounter.SetCounter(0);
   }
   private CounterPersistentState MyCounter;
}
```

In the constructor, a new CounterPersistentState object passes in the key (which is the filename used to store the state). In the other methods, the GetCounter() and SetCounter() methods get and set the value of the counter. The server doesn't care that the counter value is persistent.

Running the steps

Compile the classes and run the same steps as the other Counter implementation. You'll see that this implementation works exactly the same.

With this implementation, we could change the PDS implementation to use some other datastore, and none of the server code would change.

Chapter 22
Those Other CORBAservices

The CORBA object services are intended to aid in the creation, maintenance, and use of applications. Their purpose in life seems pretty straightforward — no rocket science here. What is a bit more complicated, however, are the detailed descriptions of every service. We don't use the English muffin approach to explain the services — in other words, we don't explain every nook and cranny of why and how things are done. Instead, in this chapter we provide overviews of the following services, which are not described in other chapters:

Life Cycle Service	Relationship Service	Externalization Service
Query Service	Licensing Service	Property Service
Time Service	Security Service	Object Trader Service
Object Collections Service		

Every ORB vendor implements services in its own way because the services are provided as specifications and not as "this is the way it must be" implementations. Don't be surprised if you find that your ORB vendor doesn't provide all the services that we list here. The services aren't a required part of CORBA; only the interfaces to the services and their intended behavior are specified by the OMG, not their actual code.

Riding the Cycle of Life

CORBA objects undergo a certain life cycle for their creation and mainte-
nance. The Life Cycle Service defines conventions for the stages of an
object's life and for a group of related objects' lives. The Life Cycle Service

- ✔ Defines conventions for creating, copying, moving, and removing
  objects.

- ✔ Works on single objects as well as on *graphs* of related objects, like all
  the objects in a single document.

  When an object contains references to one or more other objects, the
  resulting group is often called a *graph*. That because you can draw the
  group as a set of points (one point per object) connected by lines (each
  line reflecting a reference to another object.)

- ✔ Supports conventions that are independent of any application domains.
  This fancy statement just means that you do the same things regardless
  of what kind of object you are dealing with. For example, you create a
  toaster object and a blender object the same way that you create a
  lawn mower object.

- ✔ Allows clients to perform life cycle operations on objects in different
  locations (a convention that's needed because CORBA applications are
  usually distributed).

- ✔ Deals with the target location for the object, its values, and any relationships — like containment or referential.

The Life Cycle Service talks quite a bit about Factory objects. These Facto-
ries are what the client uses to create new server objects in a remote
location. We use a Factory in the Portfolio example in Chapter 5. The
`PortfolioBroker` object is one form of a Factory.

The important thing to know about the Life Cycle Service is that the OMG
has created standardized ways of dealing with objects throughout the
various phases of their lives. You must read your ORB vendor documentation for more specific information about how to actually create, copy, move,
and remove objects.

Making Friends in the ER

No, we don't mean the hit TV series, but it got your attention, didn't it? ER
just sounds a bit more exciting than entities and their relationships, which
are what this section is about.

CORBA objects do not exist in isolation. They are related to other objects (also called *entities*). For example, a Portfolio object contains Stocks and Mutual Funds. The entities are the Stocks, Mutual Funds, and Portfolio objects. The relationship is *contains* (and, conversely, *contained in*). You need a way to represent these entities and their relationships.

The Relationship Service supports the representation of entities and relationships, as well as their associated attributes and operations. The service

- ✔ Represents relationships and roles as two new kinds of objects. A *role* is simply an object in a relationship.

- ✔ Allows the relationship and role interfaces to be extended to add relationship-specific and role-specific attributes and operations.

- ✔ Supports relationships between objects that don't even know the other object exists.

- ✔ Provides a standardized set of interfaces for containment and reference relationships.

- ✔ Supports the dynamic creation of relationships between objects without recompiling or changing the objects or their interfaces.

- ✔ Allows for the definition of relationships of arbitrary degree.

- ✔ Supports type checking, the checking of cardinality constraints, and exception handling.

    A *cardinality constraint* is a specification of the number of objects on each side of a relationship. For example, a husband object can be related to only one wife object but can be related to several offspring objects.

- ✔ Supports the traversal of graphs of related objects without their activation.

    That's a mouthful! All it means is that you can find each object in a group of related objects, by following their relationships. Because the relationships are kept separate from the objects themselves, you don't actually use the server objects in the group to get from one link to another.

- ✔ Categorizes relationships by a number of characteristics, including cardinality, degree, and type.

- ✔ Uses the IDL type system to represent relationship and role types.

In Chapter 5, we use a simple sequence of object references to relate Stock objects to a Customer object. The sequence is stored in the Customer object. This is the simple, non-Relationship Service way of doing things. The Relationship Service provides several advantages over object references:

✔ More than one-way relationships are supported, so the contained object can navigate to its container object.

✔ Relationships are available to third parties, so they can add, delete, or update relationships.

✔ Relationships can provide loving support in a time of crisis.

✔ Relationships are navigable as graphs, so they can be traversed without knowledge of or even accessing the related objects themselves.

✔ Relationships are extendible via attributes and behavior, so they can be easily categorized and can even contain relationship-specific operations.

The important thing to know about the Relationship Service is that you can create arbitrary relationships between objects without changing the implementation of these objects. This capability is valuable for modeling real-world entities in dynamic environments.

Externalizing Your Innermost Values

The Externalization service is really misnamed. It should be the Externalization/Internalization service because it works both ways. Which ways? Well, to externalize an object means to record the object's state in a stream of data. This data can exist on a disk file, in memory, or wherever. The data can then be transported across ORBs, across town, or just across networks and then input again into another object. The repeat inputting process is called internalization.

The Externalization Service

✔ Acts like an export/import mechanism for objects.

✔ Lets you copy and move objects.

✔ Lets you do something with the data inside an object before it is completely copied or moved. In other words, by breaking down a copy or move operation into steps, you can get at the intermediate result (the stream of data) and do something with it, if you want to.

✔ Supports the existence of the externalized object for arbitrary amounts of time.

✔ Supports the internalization of the object in a different, disconnected ORB.

✔ Is related to the Life Cycle service in defining externalization protocols for simple objects, for arbitrarily related objects, and for graphs of related objects.

The important thing to know about the Externalization Service is that it provides a way to copy and move an object's data while providing access to the data.

Ask Me No Questions, I'll Tell You No Lies

The Query Service allows users and objects to invoke queries on collections of other objects. The queries are *predicates* and can return collections of objects. In other words, you find objects whose attributes meet the search criteria you specify when using a query.

A *predicate* query is just a query which specifies an attribute, desired value, and comparison, or several such groups combined with Boolean tests.

The queries are specified using direct manipulation query languages, such as SQL. Such queries can invoke object services as well as services within the OMG environment, such as the Life Cycle Service.

The Query Service, which is based on existing standards for queries, includes the following:

- Queries that are general manipulation operations — deletion, insertion, selection, and update.
- The querying of any objects, with arbitrary attributes and operations.
- Queries on collections of objects. The objects in the returned collections can be chosen based on their satisfaction of a given predicate's evaluation.
- Performance-enhancing mechanisms, such as indexing.
- Various kinds of database systems. The Query Service maps well to these systems' internal mechanisms for using collections and indexing.

The Query Service also provides mechanisms for *nested* query evaluators. A *nested* query evaluator adds support for queries within queries. For example, "everyone in Montana with blue eyes who is also a dental floss tycoon" can be expressed as a nested query. First you query for everyone in Montana with blue eyes, then you feed the result of that query into another query, looking for dental floss tycoons.

If you know a standard query facility, then you pretty much have the idea of CORBA's Query Service. It builds on industry standards such as SQL, and uses the same terminology.

Getting Your CORBA License

Today's business world requires licenses to do just about anything. Unless you really like having litigation come your way, you probably want to find a way to create CORBA applications to support licensing.

Licensing focuses on controlling access to, and use of, your CORBA applications. The License Service allows developers of objects to control the use of their objects' services.

The License Service doesn't impose a specified business policy. Instead, it provides three attributes that you can use to limit service access. These attributes are time, value mapping, and consumer.

- The *time* attribute supports start, duration, and stop dates.
- The *value mapping* attribute supports licensing according to allocation or consumption units.
- The *consumer* attribute allows licensing for specific kinds of entities. For example, a developer can create selective user inclusion or exclusion lists for a particular type of license. So for example, the CEO doesn't need a license to access sensitive company information, but a line manager does.

The License Service

- Provides mechanisms for creating licensing without imposing specific business policies.
- Consists of three components: Producer Client, Producer Licensing Service, and Licensing Service Manager.
- Provides mechanisms for both synchronous and asynchronous messages so that a developer can decide which method is best for an application.

The important thing to remember about the License Service is that it supports software licensing without dictating any business policies.

Property Service

Properties are named values that are dynamically associated with an object. Properties are typed outside of the IDL system. You can think of properties as attributes that are dynamically associated with objects, or as real estate. Whatever you prefer.

The Property Service provides the ability to dynamically associate and manipulate properties. It

- ✔ Defines operations for creating and manipulating name/value pairs. The names are IDL strings. The values are the IDL `any` type.

- ✔ Defines operations for creating and manipulating name/value/mode tuples. A *mode* concerns the restrictions on read/modify access to a property. A *tuple* is just a fancy way to say a group of values with a name.

- ✔ Enumerates and checks for the existence of properties.

- ✔ Supports batch operations to deal with the needs of manipulating attributes in networked environments.

- ✔ Supports exceptions.

The Property Service defines operations for creating and manipulating properties. Think of properties as dynamic attributes.

Doing Time?

Applications need a source of time. Peering up at the sun each day and examining shadows just wasn't working out, so the OMG had to come up with a more accurate means of providing time. The OMG folks chose to use the Coordinated Universal Time (UTC) standard (formerly known as Greenwich Mean Time) for the Time Service.

The UTC keeps track of the time elapsed since October 15, 1582. Why this date? It's the day that monks invented clocks. No, not really. That date happens to be the beginning of the Gregorian calendar.

The Time Service provides the following operations and data:

- ✔ Operations for getting the current time, along with an error estimate.

- ✔ Operations for manipulating time values. These operations include adding an interval to a time to yield a new time and subtracting one time from another to yield an interval.

- ✔ Operations for managing time-triggered event handlers and the events that they handle.

- ✔ The current time, along with an estimation of accuracy.

- ✔ A time that is guaranteed to always be increasing.

The Time Service defines operations for maintaining a single notion of time across machines in a distributed environment. The Time Service also generates time-based events and participates in the computation of intervals between events.

Making the World Safe for Information Systems

Security is a real problem for today's information systems, particularly distributed ones. Because CORBA applications have parts all over the place, they possess more places that can be breached. The Security Service helps offset that risk. It

- ✔ Provides identification and authentication of users and objects.
- ✔ Provides authorization and access control of users and objects.
- ✔ Supports auditing to make users accountable for their actions.
- ✔ Deals with communication integrity and authentication.
- ✔ Provides evidence of actions.
- ✔ Supports security across an application that includes ORBs from different vendors who use the same security mechanism.
- ✔ Supports a trusted core set of security functionality, including the assurance that object invocations are protected; that access control and auditing are to be performed on object invocation; and that objects are prevented from interfering with each other or gaining unauthorized access to each other's state.
- ✔ Supports a security model that conforms to national government regulations.

The Security Service supports the authorization and access control of data by users and by objects in CORBA-compliant systems.

Making a Match

The Object Trader Service is fully specified as of this writing; however, it's not widely implemented by ORB vendors.

The Object Trader Service provides a way by which objects can locate other objects, specifically by the services these objects provide. The Object Trader Service provides dynamic discovery of, and late binding to, object services.

The Object Trader Service uses trader objects. A *trader object* is an object through which other objects advertise their capabilities and match their needs against advertised capabilities. The Trader Service supports the following operations and behaviors:

✔ **Advertising a capability or offering a service, both of which are called *exporting*.** During export, an object gives the trader a service offer. A service offer contains the service type name, a reference to the object that provides the service, and zero or more property values for the service.

✔ **Matching against needs or discovering services, both of which are called *importing*.** During import, an object asks the trader for a service having certain characteristics. The trader checks against the service descriptions it possesses and then responds to the importer with the location of the selected service's object. The importer can then interact with the service.

✔ **Federated traders.** This term means that a trader in one domain interacts with traders in other domains, thus increasing the area of negotiation for services. In other words, when a trader links to other traders, it makes the offers of those traders implicitly available to its own clients.

The Object Trader Service provides dynamic discovery of, and late binding to, services. Think of it as a matchmaking service, or the Naming Service on steroids.

Taking Up a Collection

An apt description of a collection of objects is the saying *the sum of the parts is greater than the elements themselves.* In other words, a collection of objects exhibits specific behaviors that are related to the nature of the collection rather than to the individual elements that they contain. Examples are sets, queues, stacks, and lists.

The Object Collections Service provides mechanisms for creating and manipulating the most common object collections in a generic fashion.

The Object Collections Service supports

- ✔ The grouping of objects into collections.
- ✔ Operations for the manipulation of the objects as a group.
- ✔ The use of iterators.
- ✔ Ordered collections, thereby supporting access to an element at a specific position.
- ✔ Collections with associative access to elements via a key.
- ✔ Testing for element equality.
- ✔ Testing for uniqueness of element.

The Object Collections Service supports the creation and manipulation of common object collections in a generic fashion.

Part V
The Part of Tens

The 5th Wave   By Rich Tennant

In this part . . .

Here we are at the Part of Tens. These chapters contain more than just some funny stuff we tossed onto the end of the book! You get good suggestions for things to consider before and after choosing CORBA. Then we give you some pointers on things better left undone. You also get plenty of great Web and Internet resources to all things CORBA.

Chapter 23

Ten Things to Consider Before Choosing CORBA

. . . .

In This Chapter

▶ Using diverse hardware and operating systems

▶ Distributing applications around a network

▶ Leveraging legacy systems

▶ An alternative to DCOM

▶ Acknowledging ORB overhead

▶ Affording CORBA

. . . .

*P*erhaps you've flipped to this chapter while standing in a bookstore deciding whether to buy this book. Perhaps you've already read all the chapters that come before this one. Either way, you may be looking for justification for spending a portion of your life reading the many pages you now hold in your hands. Knowing what you have to consider before using CORBA may help you decide whether you want to invest your time getting to know all the ins and outs of CORBA.

We think that CORBA is a really cool thing that's great to use in just about any situation you *can* use it in. To us, the decision to use CORBA is usually a no-brainer. But just in case you need the decision to appear to be a brainer, you can use the topics in this chapter in your why-we-should-use-CORBA memo to your boss.

Do I Have a Cross-Platform Kind of Environment?

Developing an application in a heterogeneous network is no small undertaking. You have to take care of all the nitty-gritty details of each kind of machine and each operating system on the network. The burdensome weight of the task is enough to send any decent developer running screaming from the building. It's quite a bummer, and all that screaming upsets the office environment.

Developers have few choices that enable them to avoid all the screaming, but one of those options is to join the growing number of firms who have decided to use CORBA. CORBA lets you develop an application across machines in a network without regard for the operating systems or the hardware of the machines themselves. So if you have such a situation, CORBA may be your answer.

Do I Have a Distributed Application?

If you don't need to use distributed objects in your application (lucky you!), you probably don't need CORBA.

If you *are* dealing with a distributed application, however, look at its patterns of communication. CORBA provides standard ways of communication that you can take advantage of, thereby saving you time and effort. A CORBA ORB, some CORBAservices, and this book can go a long way toward making distributed application development a breeze.

Do I Have Legacy Systems That I'd Like to Use Again?

Legacy systems usually take up space and are of only marginal benefit to your organization. But through the magic of CORBA, a legacy system can become an active resource. Wrapping a legacy system can make it CORBA-compliant and open the application to a new world of activity. Think of using CORBA as giving your legacy system some vitamins that make it strong and healthy again.

Do I Have a Choice Other Than DCOM?

CORBA, thankfully, is not DCOM, If you need a standard, CORBA is your choice. CORBA is supported by over 800 organizations, so it is much more standard than a single organization's solution — such as DCOM. DCOM is the Distributed Component Object Model from Microsoft, and it works primarily on Windows operating systems.

Can I Spare Any ORB Overhead?

Fully functional Object Request Brokers (ORBs) are usually not free. As a matter of fact, some can be quite costly. Luckily, some vendors provide medium-priced offerings. Even if you can find a low-cost or free ORB that suits your needs, just coming up to speed with its use and maintenance involves an inherent cost. If you can't afford an ORB and the cost of keeping up with its new versions, you probably shouldn't consider CORBA.

Can I Keep Up to Date with the OMG?

The standards coming from of the Object Management Group (OMG) are not going to stop any time soon. CORBA will continue to grow and change. Keeping up with these changes will use some of your organization's resources. If you can't afford to give those resources, you probably can't afford to use CORBA.

Can I Get Training in CORBA-Speak?

As usual, switching to CORBA means new terms, semantics, and syntax to master. This kind of knowledge doesn't just pop into someone's head, and if it does, you should seek immediate medical attention for that person. Remember that your personnel need to be trained in the art of CORBA. This book goes a long way toward supplying that knowledge.

Do I Have Reasonable Hardware?

An ORB doesn't run on a PC/XT. ORBs are state of the art software applications that require, at the very least, current or near-current machines. So you may need to buy hardware that is new enough and powerful enough to support an ORB.

Chapter 24

Ten Things to Consider After Choosing CORBA

In This Chapter

▶ Thinking about Object Request Brokers

▶ Thinking about CORBA

So you've decided to use CORBA. What do you do next? In this chapter, we present some ideas that you can start with.

Reflecting on Object Request Brokers (ORBs)

You're using an ORB, which is a finely crafted and sophisticated collection of software. Take the time to use it correctly.

Selecting an ORB

Now that you've decided to use CORBA, selecting an Object Request Broker (ORB) that will meet your current and future needs is imperative. Choosing an ORB is a task that takes some time and thought. Plenty of ORBs are available; the CD-ROM that comes with this book has quite a few. Chapter 26 lists URLs for Web sites where you can obtain even more ORBs. Selecting an ORB may be the single most important step you take, so give this decision your full attention.

Getting to know your ORB

ORBs come with a variety of options, such as multithreading, that can significantly enhance the performance of your application without substantially affecting the code. Take some time to review your ORB's documentation and try some options out.

Don't reinvent the toaster

ORBs come with services that are usually quite good, so don't spend a lot of time trying to re-create services on your own. Instead, spend some time researching the available services. Then select just the services you think you'll use most often and purchase them.

After you have some experience with selecting and using CORBAservices, you can look into buying some additional services. We suggest that you take a multistep approach to purchasing services — don't buy them all at once.

Feeling secure

Security is always an issue for an application. With a CORBA application, security is an even more important issue. If your application is in any way accessible to users or systems that could potentially pose a threat, you must protect it. Lucky for you, the Object Management Group (OMG) has specified a Security Service. If security is important to you, be sure to select an ORB that supports this service.

Pondering CORBA Itself

CORBA is much more than just the ORB and services. Use the power of CORBA to your advantage.

Mixing and matching those languages

Because CORBA supports multiple languages, you need to consider which languages your application will use. Our best suggestion is to use the benefits of each language to your advantage. For example, if your application has a Web piece to it, then Java is a good choice.

The entire application doesn't have to be written in one language; you can mix and match languages in one application.

Think DCOM, too

Keeping DCOM in the back of your mind isn't heresy; it's good business. Just because you've decided to use CORBA doesn't mean that you can't benefit from other technologies. In fact, maybe you can wrap a DCOM component and use it in your CORBA application. That way, no one will know that you're using DCOM, even though you are!

Brushing up and down

Brush up on your client/server skills. While brushing, consider this: CORBA is inherently concurrent and distributed. It makes sense, then, that you understand the concepts necessary to develop applications that exhibit these characteristics. In other words, when in Rome, do as the Romans do!

Designing with CORBA in mind

We spend all of Chapter 10 discussing the topic of designing with CORBA in mind. It's worth re-reading when you start to design your first CORBA application. You can do certain things to make your applications work more smoothly with CORBA, and Chapter 10 provides some solutions.

Mining your resources

CORBA isn't a trivial endeavor. If you're serious about gaining its full benefits, you need to read more than just this book. (AH! Our editor just passed out.) Consider how much time and money you have to dedicate toward finding out about CORBA, new OMG specifications, and client/server application development in general. Then find some good books and start reading. We don't think that more study is an optional step. We think it's mandatory.

World politics

Yes, you read that right — world politics. We think that if you've decided to use such an open system as CORBA, you must be an open-minded person. We all know that more open-minded people are needed in world politics. So would you consider changing professions and becoming an ambassador?

Chapter 25

Ten Stupid Object Tricks
with CORBA

In This Chapter

▶ Doing general CORBA stuff
▶ Doing specific server stuff

*T*his chapter contains ten things that you would probably be better off doing or not doing in CORBA-compliant applications.

Stupid Things to Do with CORBA

If you find yourself doing any of these things, stop!

Memorizing your ID

Clients use object references as the way to call upon a server. Don't hard-code (or memorize) these references in the client; starting and stopping objects causes new references to be issued anyway.

I take exception to that

Printing an error code and ending your application's execution when something unanticipated occurs isn't very helpful. You must be able to use the CORBA error-handling system, which involves throwing a fit, screaming like a banshee, and spitting printer paper all over the room.

Wait a minute. What we mean to say is that CORBA's way to handle errors is to throw an exception. You see, it was that throwing thing that got us confused.

Is anybody out there?

Please don't use the _non_existent() method when you're using the server-per-method activation policy. If you do, you'll see the server object activate and then exit. Although using this method can give anyone looking over your shoulder the impression that you're actually working, it just wastes time. When you use the server-per-method policy, the server activates when called and then exits upon completion of any method's execution. So calling the _non_existent() method just causes the server to activate, return FALSE, and then exit.

Starter fluid

Don't use the server-per-method activation policy on a server that takes ten minutes to start up. Instead, use the shared or persistent server policies. Your goal is to reduce the number of times that this kind of server potentially activates, because it takes such a long time to begin.

The in-your-face repository

Don't forget to put the IDL of your servers into the Interface Repository (IR) before you try to use them. Also, don't forget to update the IR if you have changed the IDL. It gets really nasty if you forget.

Time and time again

Don't make recursive method calls within a server object. It is generally unclear as to whether recursive method calls block or deadlock the server. Besides, recursive calling can create really wicked flashbacks for the server.

Waiting for an answer

Don't create server objects that wait for user input, such as from a console. For example, if a server prints a message to the system console such as "Client wants a Pizza, should I give it to them? (Y/N)" and then waits for someone to enter a Y or N, that server cannot respond to any other client requests until it gets its answer. The server could, theoretically, wait forever and create a big mess for all those clients that are blocked while waiting for it. Just think of the domino effect all this waiting could have. Then again, thinking about it could give you such a headache.

Avoiding Vendor-Specific Features

ORB vendors really are trying to make your life easier by adding non-standard features to their products. Avoiding these features as much as possible makes your code more portable.

Command-line switches

Vendors often create ORBs that respond to method calls. We suggest that you call these methods via command-line switches. These commands can be placed in a batch file that is executed as the application is about to be run. Put these commands in a batch file instead of placing the method calls inside the application itself in order to give your application all those lovely *ables* — portable, readable, maintainable, and Clark G-able.

Vendor-specific methods

Don't use vendor-specific methods such as `bind()`. Although they initially make your code easier to write because you don't have to deal with such things as the Naming Service, they also make your code less portable.

Don't forget to register

Register servers with the Implementation Repository if your ORB requires it. You can spend way too much time trying to figure out why things aren't working when the problem may be something as simple as this. We know from experience.

Part VI

Appendix

In this part . . .

*W*e assembled a terrific CD-ROM for your CD-ROMing pleasure. Lots of demonstrations, plenty of sample code, a bushel of software. Enjoy!

Appendix

About the CD

● ●

*H*ere's some of what you can find on the *CORBA For Dummies* CD-ROM:

- ✔ CORBAplus for C++
- ✔ Orbix 3.2
- ✔ Inprise Visibroker for Java and for C++

System Requirements

Make sure your computer meets the minimum system requirements listed below. If your computer doesn't match up to most of these requirements, you may have problems in using the contents of the CD.

- ✔ A PC with a 486 or faster processor.
- ✔ Microsoft Windows NT, Windows 98, or Windows 95.
- ✔ At least 16MB of total RAM installed on your computer. For best performance, we recommend at least 32MB of RAM installed.
- ✔ At least 200MB of hard drive space available to install all the software from this CD. (You'll need less space if you don't install every program.)
- ✔ A CD-ROM drive — double-speed (2x) or faster.
- ✔ A monitor capable of displaying at least 256 colors or grayscale.
- ✔ A modem with a speed of at least 14,400 bps.

If you need more information on the basics, check out *PCs For Dummies,* 6th Edition, by Dan Gookin or *Windows 98 For Dummies* by Andy Rathbone (both published by IDG Books Worldwide, Inc.).

How to Use the CD

1. **Insert the CD into your computer's CD-ROM drive.**

   Give your computer a moment to take a look at the CD.

2. **When the light on your CD-ROM drive goes out, double click on the My Computer icon. (It's probably in the top left corner of your desktop.)**

   This action opens the My Computer window, which shows you all the drives attached to your computer, the Control Panel, and a couple other handy things.

3. **Double click on the icon for your CD-ROM drive.**

   Another window opens, showing you all the folders and files on the CD.

Using the CD

1. **Double click the file called License.txt.**

   This file contains the end-user license that you agree to by using the CD. When you are done reading the license, close the program, most likely NotePad, that displayed the file.

2. **Double click the file called Readme.txt.**

   This file contains instructions about installing the software from this CD. It might be helpful to leave this text file open while you are using the CD.

3. **Double click the folder for the software you are interested in.**

   Be sure to read the descriptions of the programs in the next section of this appendix (much of this information also shows up in the Readme file). These descriptions will give you more precise information about the programs' folder names, and about finding and running the installer program.

4. **Find the file called Setup.exe, or Install.exe, or something similar, and double click on that file.**

   The program's installer will walk you through the process of setting up your new software.

What You'll Find

There are lots of useful tools and practice files on the *CORBA For Dummies* CD-ROM.

Sample files

All of the demonstration files and practice documents you need to follow this book's tutorials are organized by chapter number in the Examples folder. Additional examples can be found in the Motley folder.

If you have trouble accessing the Examples or Motley folders, or if you want a quick and easy way to copy the files to your computer, I have included the self-extracting archives Examples.exe and Motley.exe.

Acrobat Reader 3.01

Required tool for reading manual pages in Acrobat format.

CORBAplus for C++

CORBAplus for C++ is a leading CORBA 2.0-compliant Object Request Broker (ORB) for developing enterprise-class distributed object applications. This is a 60-day trial.

Inprise VisiBroker

VisiBroker provides a complete CORBA 2.0 ORB environment for building, deploying, and managing distributed applications. The CD includes 60-day evaluation versions of VisiBroker for C++ and Java.

Internet Explorer 4.0

Yes, it's everywhere you want to be.

Orbix 2.3

Orbix is a popular ORB that is fully compliant with CORBA 2. This is a trial version.

An Orbix evaluation license key is required to activate your Orbix 2.3 evaluation software — please do not begin the installation process without it. Keys can be obtained by registering at the following URL: `www.iona.com/dummies.OrbixEvents 1.0`

OrbixEvents implements the CORBA Event Service specification. This is a trial version.

An OrbixEvents evaluation license key is required to activate your OrbixEvents 1.0 evaluation software — please do not begin the installation process without it. Keys can be obtained by registering at the following URL: www.iona.com/dummies.

OrbixNames 1.1

OrbixNames tracks the many objects that may be created in a CORBA environment. This is a trial version.

An OrbixNames evaluation license key is required to activate your OrbixNames 1.1 evaluation software — please do not begin the installation process without it. Keys can be obtained by registering at the following URL: www.iona.com/dummies.

OrbixWeb 3.0

OrbixWeb references objects that are distributed across networks. This is a trial version.

An OrbixWeb evaluation license key is required to activate your OrbixWeb 3.0 evaluation software — please do not begin the installation process without it. Keys can be obtained by registering at the following URL: www.iona.com/dummies.

Important Note: Orbix Wonderwall is a powerful security firewall for Inter-ORB Protocol (IIOP) communication. Orbix did not have Wonderwall ready in time to be included on this CD, but they would love for you to take a look at it. Therefore, they are offering *CORBA For Dummies* readers a free trial version, which you can download from the same site where you get registration keys, www.iona.com/dummies.

OAK CORBA 2.0 ORB

Paragon Software's OAK is a popular CORBA-compliant ORB. This is a trial version.

Java Beans Development Kit

Beans are Java software components that can be managed and developed with visual programming tools. This is a beta version.

Sun JDK 1.1.6

The latest version of the Java Developer's Kit. You're welcome.

If You've Got Problems (Of the CD Kind)

We tried our best to compile programs that work on most computers with the minimum system requirements. Alas, your computer may differ, and some programs may not work properly for some reason.

The two likeliest problems are that you don't have enough memory (RAM) for the programs you want to use, or you have other programs running that are affecting installation or running of a program. If you get error messages like `Not enough memory` or `Setup cannot continue`, try one or more of these methods and then try using the software again:

- Turn off any anti-virus software that you have on your computer. Installers sometimes mimic virus activity and may make your computer incorrectly believe that it is being infected by a virus.

- Close all running programs. The more programs you're running, the less memory is available to other programs. Installers also typically update files and programs. So if you keep other programs running, installation may not work properly.

- Have your local computer store add more RAM to your computer. This is, admittedly, a drastic and somewhat expensive step. However, adding more memory can really help the speed of your computer and allow more programs to run at the same time. This may include closing the CD interface and running a product's installation program from Windows Explorer.

If you still have trouble with installing the items from the CD, please call the IDG Books Worldwide Customer Service phone number: 800-762-2974 (outside the U.S.: 317-596-5430).

Index

• P •

IDG Books Worldwide, Inc., End-User License Agreement

READ THIS. You should carefully read these terms and conditions before opening the software packet(s) included with this book ("Book"). This is a license agreement ("Agreement") between you and IDG Books Worldwide, Inc. ("IDGB"). By opening the accompanying software packet(s), you acknowledge that you have read and accept the following terms and conditions. If you do not agree and do not want to be bound by such terms and conditions, promptly return the Book and the unopened software packet(s) to the place you obtained them for a full refund.

1. **License Grant.** IDGB grants to you (either an individual or entity) a nonexclusive license to use one copy of the enclosed software program(s) (collectively, the "Software") solely for your own personal or business purposes on a single computer (whether a standard computer or a workstation component of a multiuser network). The Software is in use on a computer when it is loaded into temporary memory (RAM) or installed into permanent memory (hard disk, CD-ROM, or other storage device). IDGB reserves all rights not expressly granted herein.

2. **Ownership.** IDGB is the owner of all right, title, and interest, including copyright, in and to the compilation of the Software recorded on the disk(s) or CD-ROM ("Software Media"). Copyright to the individual programs recorded on the Software Media is owned by the author or other authorized copyright owner of each program. Ownership of the Software and all proprietary rights relating thereto remain with IDGB and its licensers.

3. **Restrictions on Use and Transfer.**

    (a) You may only (i) make one copy of the Software for backup or archival purposes, or (ii) transfer the Software to a single hard disk, provided that you keep the original for backup or archival purposes. You may not (i) rent or lease the Software, (ii) copy or reproduce the Software through a LAN or other network system or through any computer subscriber system or bulletin-board system, or (iii) modify, adapt, or create derivative works based on the Software.

    (b) You may not reverse engineer, decompile, or disassemble the Software. You may transfer the Software and user documentation on a permanent basis, provided that the transferee agrees to accept the terms and conditions of this Agreement and you retain no copies. If the Software is an update or has been updated, any transfer must include the most recent update and all prior versions.

4. **Restrictions on Use of Individual Programs.** You must follow the individual requirements and restrictions detailed for each individual program in the "About the CD" Appendix of this Book. These limitations are also contained in the individual license agreements recorded on the Software Media. These limitations may include a requirement that after using the program for a specified period of time, the user must pay a registration fee or discontinue use. By opening the Software packet(s), you will be agreeing to abide by the licenses and restrictions for these individual programs that are detailed in the "About the CD" Appendix and on the Software Media. None of the material on this Software Media or listed in this Book may ever be redistributed, in original or modified form, for commercial purposes.

5. **Limited Warranty.**

   (a) IDGB warrants that the Software and Software Media are free from defects in materials and workmanship under normal use for a period of sixty (60) days from the date of purchase of this Book. If IDGB receives notification within the warranty period of defects in materials or workmanship, IDGB will replace the defective Software Media.

   (b) **IDGB AND THE AUTHOR OF THE BOOK DISCLAIM ALL OTHER WARRANTIES, EXPRESS OR IMPLIED, INCLUDING WITHOUT LIMITATION IMPLIED WARRANTIES OF MER-CHANTABILITY AND FITNESS FOR A PARTICULAR PURPOSE, WITH RESPECT TO THE SOFTWARE, THE PROGRAMS, THE SOURCE CODE CONTAINED THEREIN, AND/OR THE TECHNIQUES DESCRIBED IN THIS BOOK. IDGB DOES NOT WARRANT THAT THE FUNCTIONS CONTAINED IN THE SOFTWARE WILL MEET YOUR REQUIREMENTS OR THAT THE OPERATION OF THE SOFTWARE WILL BE ERROR FREE.**

   (c) This limited warranty gives you specific legal rights, and you may have other rights that vary from jurisdiction to jurisdiction.

6. **Remedies.**

   (a) IDGB's entire liability and your exclusive remedy for defects in materials and workmanship shall be limited to replacement of the Software Media, which may be returned to IDGB with a copy of your receipt at the following address: Software Media Fulfillment Department, Attn.: *CORBA For Dummies,* IDG Books Worldwide, Inc., 7260 Shadeland Station, Ste. 100, Indianapolis, IN 46256, or call 800-762-2974. Please allow three to four weeks for delivery. This Limited Warranty is void if failure of the Software Media has resulted from accident, abuse, or misapplication. Any replacement Software Media will be warranted for the remainder of the original warranty period or thirty (30) days, whichever is longer.

   (b) In no event shall IDGB or the author be liable for any damages whatsoever (including without limitation damages for loss of business profits, business interruption, loss of business information, or any other pecuniary loss) arising from the use of or inability to use the Book or the Software, even if IDGB has been advised of the possibility of such damages.

   (c) Because some jurisdictions do not allow the exclusion or limitation of liability for conse-quential or incidental damages, the above limitation or exclusion may not apply to you.

7. **U.S. Government Restricted Rights.** Use, duplication, or disclosure of the Software by the U.S. Government is subject to restrictions stated in paragraph (c)(1)(ii) of the Rights in Technical Data and Computer Software clause of DFARS 252.227-7013, and in subparagraphs (a) through (d) of the Commercial Computer–Restricted Rights clause at FAR 52.227-19, and in similar clauses in the NASA FAR supplement, when applicable.

8. **General.** This Agreement constitutes the entire understanding of the parties and revokes and supersedes all prior agreements, oral or written, between them and may not be modified or amended except in a writing signed by both parties hereto that specifically refers to this Agreement. This Agreement shall take precedence over any other documents that may be in conflict herewith. If any one or more provisions contained in this Agreement are held by any court or tribunal to be invalid, illegal, or otherwise unenforceable, each and every other provision shall remain in full force and effect.

Installation Instructions

Make sure your computer meets the minimum system requirements listed below. If your computer doesn't match up to most of these requirements, you may have problems in using the contents of the CD.

- ✔ A PC with a 486 or faster processor.
- ✔ Microsoft Windows NT, Windows 98, or Windows 95.
- ✔ At least 16MB of total RAM installed on your computer. For best performance, we recommend at least 32MB of RAM installed.
- ✔ At least 200MB of hard drive space available to install all the software from this CD. (You'll need less space if you don't install every program.)
- ✔ A CD-ROM drive — double-speed (2x) or faster.
- ✔ A monitor capable of displaying at least 256 colors or grayscale.
- ✔ A modem with a speed of at least 14,400 bps.

Starting the CD

1. **Insert the CD into your computer's CD-ROM drive.**

   Give your computer a moment to take a look at the CD.

2. **When the light on your CD-ROM drive goes out, double click on the My Computer icon.**

   This action opens the My Computer window, which shows you all the drives attached to your computer, the Control Panel, and a couple other handy things.

3. **Double click on the icon for your CD-ROM drive.**

   Another window opens, showing you all the folders and files on the CD.

Installing software

There are lots of useful tools and practice files on the *CORBA For Dummies* CD-ROM. See the Appendix for details.

1. **Double click the file called License.txt.**

   This file contains the end-user license that you agree to by using the CD. When you are done reading the license, close the program that displayed the file.

2. **Double click the file called Readme.txt**

3. **Double click the folder for the software you are interested in.**

4. **Find the file called Setup.exe, or Install.exe, or something similar, and double click on that file.**

   The program's installer will walk you through the process of setting up your new software.

YOUR ONLINE RESOURCE

WWW.DUMMIES.COM

Discover Dummies Online!

The Dummies Web Site is your fun and friendly online resource for the latest information about ...*For Dummies*® books and your favorite topics. The Web site is the place to communicate with us, exchange ideas with other ...*For Dummies* readers, chat with authors, and have fun!

Ten Fun and Useful Things You Can Do at www.dummies.com

1. Win free ...*For Dummies* books and more!
2. Register your book and be entered in a prize drawing.
3. Meet your favorite authors through the IDG Books Author Chat Series.
4. Exchange helpful information with other ...*For Dummies* readers.
5. Discover other great ...*For Dummies* books you must have!
6. Purchase Dummieswear™ exclusively from our Web site.
7. Buy ...*For Dummies* books online.
8. Talk to us. Make comments, ask questions, get answers!
9. Download free software.
10. Find additional useful resources from authors.

Link directly to these ten fun and useful things at
http://www.dummies.com/10useful

WWW.DUMMIES.COM

For other technology titles from IDG Books Worldwide, go to
www.idgbooks.com

Not on the Web yet? It's easy to get started with *Dummies 101*®: *The Internet For Windows*® *98* or *The Internet For Dummies*®, 5th Edition, at local retailers everywhere.

IDG BOOKS WORLDWIDE

Find other ...*For Dummies* books on these topics:
Business • Career • Databases • Food & Beverage • Games • Gardening • Graphics • Hardware
Health & Fitness • Internet and the World Wide Web • Networking • Office Suites
Operating Systems • Personal Finance • Pets • Programming • Recreation • Sports
Spreadsheets • Teacher Resources • Test Prep • Word Processing

IDG BOOKS WORLDWIDE
BOOK REGISTRATION

Register This Book and Win!

We want to hear from you!

Visit **http://my2cents.dummies.com** to register this book and tell us how you liked it!

- ✔ Get entered in our monthly prize giveaway.

- ✔ Give us feedback about this book — tell us what you like best, what you like least, or maybe what you'd like to ask the author and us to change!

- ✔ Let us know any other ...*For Dummies*® topics that interest you.

Your feedback helps us determine what books to publish, tells us what coverage to add as we revise our books, and lets us know whether we're meeting your needs as a ...*For Dummies* reader. You're our most valuable resource, and what you have to say is important to us!

Not on the Web yet? It's easy to get started with *Dummies 101*®: *The Internet For Windows*® *98* or *The Internet For Dummies*®, 5th Edition, at local retailers everywhere.

Or let us know what you think by sending us a letter at the following address:

...*For Dummies* Book Registration
Dummies Press
7260 Shadeland Station, Suite 100
Indianapolis, IN 46256-3945
Fax 317-596-5498

BESTSELLING
BOOK SERIES
FROM IDG